1/25/01

For Peggy,
hoping you like it.
Best wishes,

Henry

JEWISH IMAGES
IN THE CHRISTIAN CHURCH

Left: The Church (Ecclesia) Right: The Synagogue (Sinagoga) West facade, Notre Dame de Paris

JEWISH IMAGES
IN THE CHRISTIAN CHURCH

■

Art as the Mirror
of the Jewish-Christian Conflict
200–1250 C.E.

HENRY N. CLAMAN

MERCER UNIVERSITY PRESS

2000

ISBN 0-86554-695-9
MUP/H514

© 2000
Mercer University Press
6316 Peake Road
Macon, Georgia 31210-3960

First Edition.

Book design by Mary Frances Burt

∞The paper used in this publication meets the
minimum requirements of American National Standard
for Information Sciences—Permanence of Paper for
Printed Library Materials, ANSI Z39.48-1984.

CIP data are available from the Library of Congress.

Picture Credits: Frontispiece: David Levy, Paris; Plates 1, 4, fig 3-5: Scala, Art Resource NY; Plate 2: Erich Lessing/Art Resource NY; Figs 2-1, 3-3: c. Princeton University Press; Figs 2-2 through 2-8: Foto Pontificia Comm. Arch. Sacra, Rome; Figs 2-9, 3-2, 4-1, 4-2, 5-3, 5-4: Bildarchiv Foto Marburg; 5-9, 6-1, 6-2; Figs 2-10, 2-11, 2-13, 2-14, 2-15: Yale University Art Gallery, Dura-Europos Collection; Fig 2-12: Yale University Art Gallery, Dura-Europos Archive; Plate 3: Nimatallah/Art Resource, NY; Figs 3-1, 3-4, 3-6: Alinari/Art Resource NY; Fig 4-3: Utrecht University Library; Plate 5: Foto Editions Gaud, France; Fig 5-1: National Museum, Copenhagen; Fig 5-2: Arch Phot. Paris, c. Caisse Nationale des Monuments Historiques et des Sites (CNMHS); Figs 5-5 to 5-8: Metropolitan Museum of Art, the Cloisters Collection, 1963, N.Y.; Fig 6-3: K. Utschinski, Denver; Plate 6: Israel Museum, Jerusalem; Plate 7: Stiftsmuseum, Klosterneuberg; Plate 8: The British Museum; Plate 9: J. Feuille, CNMHS; Plates 10, 13, 15, 16: c. Sonia Halliday and Laura Lushington; Plates 11, 12, 14: P. Lemaitre, CNMHS

Contents

For Janet, who asked the right question

Preface

This is a book for the general reader rather than for the specialist. It deals primarily with early Christian and medieval art. This is not a book about art alone, however, but about art in its social context; that is, what it reveals about both the people who produced it and the people who experienced it. This book looks at Christian art as it reflects Jewish-Christian relations during the period 200-1250 C.E.[1] The earliest art I bring into this discussion originated in Rome; later we will move to Western Europe, emphasizing France and Italy.

The idea for the book arose when my wife Janet and I were enjoying a brief side trip to Milan during our stay at the Rockefeller Conference Center in Belaggio on Lake Como. We visited the recently remodeled Museo del Duomo (museum of the Cathedral of Milan). We looked closely at many statues which had weathered badly during centuries spent on the roof and so had been taken down and replaced by copies. We wondered why so many figures and scenes from the Jewish Bible were on the roof of a Catholic Church. As we thought about it, we remembered many other churches and cathedrals we had visited also displayed a large number of Old Testament images.

Janet and I realized that not only was the image itself significant, but its size, its position inside or outside the building, and its relation to neighboring images all carried meaning. We became aware (as art historians have been for some time) that the Jewish images and stories depicted in churches convey specific messages about how these (presumably) Christian artists, or at least their Christian audience, thought about Jews. The messages so fascinated us that we began to revisit churches, armed with this new perspective. We looked at the art as a reflection of Jewish-Christian relations. This book is the outcome of that study.

---

[1] In accordance with current scholarly tendencies, I have not used B.C. or A.D. because of their pronounced Christian bias. I have used instead B.C.E. (Before the Common Era) and C.E. (Common Era).

Early Christian and medieval art as well as Jewish-Christian relations during the Middle Ages are both well researched topics. Rarely, however, have they been combined, as they are in this book. Each discipline is both broad and deep and, as I wished to make this a modest-sized book, I have been selective. I believe, too, that close study of a few outstanding examples is more informative than a wide-reaching but superficial survey. Finally, footnotes and references are also modest in scope. There is a vast and sometimes bewildering amount of literature on the subjects covered in this book; I have arranged the notes and references to best enhance the opportunity for further learning by the general reader.

Much of the source material for this book is available in scholarly translation. With the caution that "to translate is to interpret," I consulted an array of authorities on any given topic, who often offered strongly differing opinions. Dr. Samuel Johnson's apt description of the tribulations of literary research echoes daily in my heart. We both "saw that one inquiry only gave occasion to another, that book referred to book, that to search was not always to find, and to find was not always to be informed."[2] Although scholarly opinions may differ on matters of detail, there is general consensus about the history of Jewish-Christian relations and the art informed by it. Where important differences exist, I have tried to point them out; and where questions remain unanswered, to outline the possible reasons why. I have been thorough but, since neither history nor its study is static, opinions and interpretations will continue to change.

It is a challenge to veer from a lifelong career in medical teaching, research, and practice and (while still active in those areas) to write a book on medieval society, religion, and art. It is even more challenging to get it published!

I thank Timothy J. Standring for his enthusiasm and help from the start, and Michael J. Cook for his support and encouragement. Herbert Kessler gave me some suggestions early, and I thank Margaret Miles for her help. Rex Matthews of *The Scholars' Press* gave me good

---

[2] Samuel Johnson, *Dictionary of the English Language*, preface.

advice, and Natalia Lozofsky was very helpful in her critical review. Such support and endorsement was very valuable as it turned out to be harder than expected to break into print in a field so far removed from one's home turf. I thank Marc A. Jolley of Mercer University Press for skillfully guiding this book through the publication process.

I also wish to thank Kathryn Utschinski, my long-standing secretary and friend, for her help with the manuscript. I am grateful to Sara Higgins as well for her secretarial skills.

Above all, I thank my wife Janet M. Stewart, M.D. not only for encouragement during her lengthy term as a "book widow," but for giving me the idea for the book in the first place.

Introduction

The focus of this book is what might be called "public religious art," meaning art located in a place of worship and accessible to a large number of people. It includes painting, mosaic, sculpture, and stained glass, techniques seen primarily in places of worship such as churches and cathedrals. (The catacombs are included because they had quasi-public areas in them used for gatherings.) By contrast, this book does *not* emphasize illuminated manuscripts because they were usually only privately viewed, though they were often models for public images.

Excluding private art from this book is valid I believe for two reasons. First, illuminated manuscripts were expensive and therefore rare, commissioned by royalty and aristocracy or reserved for the clergy. Moreover, the majority of Western Europeans in the period covered by this book (200-1250 C.E.) could neither read nor write, so even if illuminations had been available to illustrate the text, that text itself would have been largely incomprehensible to the general populace. Hence, as Pope Gregory the Great reported in a letter from around 600 C.E., "Pictures are used in churches in order that those ignorant of letters may by merely looking at the walls read there what they are unable to read in books."[1]

The second reason is more subtle. Pictures in illuminated manuscripts such as Pentateuchs, Psalters, and Gospels usually illustrate text. This book, however, is mostly concerned with Christian symbols and their Judaic referents. Symbolic allusions, inferences, intimations, and other linking of Jewish and Christian themes are often better expressed by images not tied to any particular text. Freedom from the letter of the text allows the artist to juxtapose images with no direct scriptural ties whose pairing nonetheless brings to light a particularly

---

[1] James Snyder, *Medieval Art* (New York: Harry N. Abrams, 1989) 16.

telling point. For example, the frequent pairing of the story of Abraham and Isaac with the Crucifixion illustrates a father's ultimate sacrifice: his son. Just as Abraham was willing to give up his son Isaac, so did God permit the death of his Son Jesus Christ. Two images side by side vividly and instantly convey the same idea that I need many words to express.

Having just distinguished between two realms of religious art, I must qualify the distinction by indicating that the contrast between public (monumental) art and private (manuscript) art is not always sharp. Connections exist in that manuscript illustrations were sometimes models for or copies of public art. Loerke believes, for example, that the sixth-century illustrations in the Rossano Gospels are copies of lost wall frescoes or mosaics possibly from Jerusalem.[2] More substantial support for this idea comes much later in the form of the thirteenth-century mosaics of Genesis found in San Marco in Venice. There is general agreement that these were directly inspired by the Cotton Genesis manuscript written in the fifth or sixth century.[3] The relationship between manuscript illustrations and frescoed walls modeled after them will be discussed in greater detail as part of an analysis of the pictures in Dura Europos.

In any event, we need to remember that, although a given image may appear in a manuscript and also on a church wall and be almost identical pictorially, each is experienced in a unique context. The monk poring over images of *Ecclesia* ("Christian church") and *Sinagoga* ("Jewish synagogue") in a precious manuscript understands it quite differently than does a pilgrim who views similar images on a church wall on his way to Santiago da Compostela.

With regard to the social issues I will discuss, remember that Jewish-Christian relations in the period covered in this book emanat-

---

2 William C. Loerke, "The Monumental Miniature," *The Place of Book Illumination in Byzantine Art*, ed., K. Weitzmann et al. (Princeton: Princeton University Press, 1975) 61-89. Loerke's idea is mere conjecture, however, as the existence of these wall decorations is only inferred.

3 Kurt Weitzmann, *Late Antique and Early Christian Book Illustration* (New York: George Braziller, 1977) 15-16.

4 Brendan Cassidy, ed., *Iconography at the Crossroads* (Princeton: Princeton University Press, 1993) 8-9.

ed primarily from the perceived relationship between their two respective scriptures, the Old Testament and the New Testament. Each of the two religions believed its own Testament to be the word of God and so the ultimate authority. But right here at the beginning of our study, it is necessary to pause and consider how we are going to refer to the Two Testaments. The terms "Hebrew Scriptures" and "Jewish Bible" are reasonably unambiguous. However, as discussed later, most Christian authorities and clerics knew these pages not in Hebrew but in Greek translation. The term "Christian Bible," in turn, is ambiguous as it may be said to contain both Old and New Testaments. Therefore I shall generally use the separate terms "Old Testament" and "New Testament," as it is clear to what they refer.

As to the English translations, I have relied on the Hebrew Bible ("Tanakh"), Jewish Publication Society, 1985, the New Revised Standard Version, (the Harper Collins Study Bible), 1993, and the Revised Standard Version, 1952.

The images I will discuss are derived from these Testaments, as well as from secondary sources such as commentaries and elaborations. All of these played vital roles in Christian-Jewish relations.

But images cannot speak and those who interpret them do not always agree. As Brendan Cassidy notes, the relationship between text and image is not always straightforward. "Texts rarely inspire works of art directly…although they frequently provide art with its themes."[4] These themes are what concern us here. We begin with what seems a paradoxical question for an art history book: Why, for the first two centuries of its existence, was there no art in Christianity?

List of Illustrations

Frontispiece

Ecclesia and *Sinagoga*, west facade, Notre Dame de Paris (Nineteenth century adaptations)

Chapter 2

Chapter 3

Chapter 4

Chapter 5

Chapter 6

1 | Judaism and the First Two Centuries of Christianity

The development of early Christianity out of Judaism during the life and after the death of Christ is one of the most fascinating chapters in Western history. This complex story has been discussed at length by many others.[1] It is not my purpose here to cover it once again. Instead, the focus of this book is the examination of medieval Christian art and how themes and images reflect the ongoing dogmatic and societal tensions between Jews and Christians in Western Europe.

The frontispiece shows a classic illustration of this tension: female allegorical figures representing the "good" (Christian) Church contrasts with the "bad" (Jewish) Synagogue. The originals were made around the year 1200 and thus they appear rather late in our story. Therefore, the first chapters will discuss what led up to these rather distinctive and polemical figures. To begin, we should note that there is no distinctively Christian body of art before 200 C.E. (Speculations as to why this may be are at the end of this chapter.) Nevertheless, a brief account of relations between Judaism and early Christianity is necessary to understand what—including art—later came to pass.

Here I must express a caution. The study of Jewish-Christian relations in the ancient world raises special problems. As is still true today in religious debate, issues were weighty and emotions ran high. What we know about the relationship hundreds of years after the events is the result of "historical survivorship." As John G. Gager puts it, "Our sense of the past is created for us largely by history's winners. The

---

[1] See for example Marcel Simon, *Verus Israel*, 2d ed., rev., trans. H. McKeating (New York: Oxford University Press, 1986); Salo W. Baron, *Social and Political History of the Jews*, vol. 3, *Christian Era: The First Five Centuries*, 2d ed. (Philadelphia: Jewish Publication Society of America, 1952); Hershel Shanks, ed., *Christianity and Rabbinic Judaism* (Washington, DC: Biblical Archeological Review, 1992); Stephen G. Wilson, *Related Strangers: Jews and Christians, 70-170* C.E. (Minneapolis: Fortress Press, 1995); and Jacob Neusner, *Judaism and Christianity in the Age of Constantine* (Chicago: University of Chicago Press, 1987).

voices of the losers, when heard at all, are transmitted through a carefully tuned network of filters."[2] Only recently has scholarship turned from paying almost exclusive attention to the winner (in this case, Christianity) to exploring some historic strands in which voices have been muted, if not lost. These include important heretics such as Marcion, an early Christian bishop who believed Jews and Christians worshiped two distinctive gods. His works all disappeared; his position has been reconstructed out of the works of his victorious critics and detractors. The groups of "Jewish Christians," Jews who accepted Christ as the Messiah while retaining Jewish identification and practices, are similarly virtually invisible. Even within Judaism, what we call Rabbinic Judaism emerged from Pharisaism; all other voices dimmed after the fall of the Second Temple in 70 C.E. The Dead Sea Scrolls remind us there were many early Jewish groups on the scene. Thus the chorus of voices from the past is becoming gradually richer. For art that illuminates Jewish-Christian relations, the same is true. Much has been lost, and it is likely that a good part of what we see today also represents "historical survivorship" of what the winners wanted to see (and wanted us to see). Still, it is a rich harvest if tended carefully.

With regard to Jewish-Christian relations, we must remember that anti-Jewish attitudes on the part of Christians are very old. I do not wish to negotiate the minefields of scholarly opinions about how, when, and why such attitudes began.[3] It is useful, however, to make a distinction between "anti-Judaism" and "anti-Semitism." Though Langmuir believes that while this distinction is only one of degree, it

---

[2] John G. Gager, *The Origins of Anti-Semitism* (New York: Oxford University Press, 1983) 265.

[3] Gavin I. Langmuir, *History, Religion, and Antisemitism* (Berkeley CA: University of California Press, 1990) 39-40.

[4] The word *supersessionism* is derived from the Latin *supersedere,* meaning literally "to sit upon." According to the *Oxford English Dictionary, supersession* means "the setting aside, abrogation or annulment of a rule, law,

authority, conditions, etc." The first quote in the *OED,* taken from English theologian William Paley's *Horae Paulinae,* (1790) reads "Our Epistle...avows in direct terms the supersession of the Jewish law, as an instrument of salvation to the Jews themselves."

[5] There are exceptions. For instance, the Book of Daniel, a comparatively late section of the Jewish scriptures, was written partly in Hebrew and partly in Aramaic.

makes a valid point. "Anti-Judaism" is primarily a theological position objecting to Jewish tenets, laws, and beliefs, and generally based on interpretations of Jewish and Christian scriptures. "Anti-Semitism," on the other hand, is a broader social attitude not necessarily tied to Jewish theology. The earliest Christians seem mainly anti-Judaic rather than anti-Semitic. I will here anticipate history by introducing a term which, though unknown to early Christians and Jews, succinctly epitomizes the situation.

Supersessionism: The Christian Stance

From the earliest days of Christianity, a major religious quandary was the relationship of Christianity to Judaism, the new to the old. Others have discussed this problem with great authority (see footnote 1 for references). The basic view of the new religion was that the coming of the Messiah Jesus Christ rendered Judaism obsolete. This is the principle of *supersessionism*.[4] The tenets of this doctrine—not officially adopted but assumed by the Church—can be summarized as follows.

1. Christianity replaced Judaism as God's chosen revelation.
2. Judaism was a necessary prelude to Christianity.
3. The Hebrew Bible foretells the coming of Christ.

Supersessionist tendencies occur as early as in the writings of Paul when he says, referring to the Mosaic Law, that "we serve not under the old written code [Torah] but in the new life of the spirit" (Rom 7:6). The Gospels, of course, take this position further. Before proceeding, we should pause to discuss the formats and even the names of the two scriptures.

The Jewish scriptures were originally written in Hebrew, and thus can be called the Hebrew Bible.[5] This is the traditional or "Masoretic" text. Beginning in the third century B.C.E., however, it was translated into a Greek edition called the Septuagint or *LXX*.[6] The fact that Jewish scholars felt the need to translate their Bible into the *lingua franca* of the Hellenistic world testifies to the importance of that foreign culture among observant and literate Jews. Thus, even as early Christianity pulled away from Judaism, the Greek LXX was being used by early Church fathers, just as it was by Jews. Next, LXX was translated into the *Vetus Latina*, or "Old Latin" Bible. This, in turn, was replaced in about 400 C.E. by a newer Latin version translated by Jerome, mainly from the original Hebrew version. This Latin edition, known as the "Vulgate" because it was in the everyday, or vulgar, language of the late Roman Empire, became the standard. There are important differences between the Masoretic text, the LXX, and the *Vetus Latina*, as well as between these early rescensions and their descendants, such as the Greek Orthodox, Catholic, and Protestant Bibles.[7] They cannot be covered here, but I will point out specific instances where the differences are crucial.

Specifically Christian scriptures were being written and a canon was being defined during this period. This set of documents is called the New Testament (NT). I shall use this term, though some object that it implies that the Old Testament (OT) must be outmoded. I do not think the term "Old Testament" pejorative. In fact, the tenor of this book is that early Christians felt the Jewish Bible, that is, the OT, was the very foundation of the NT and the new religion it describes.[8]

With these stipulations in mind, we can inquire how the two scriptures were viewed. We must first remember that when Christianity was young and still developing its own Bible, many of the new faith had been brought up with the OT, and so for them it was authoritative. The NT is filled with quotations from and paraphrases

---

6 James Kugel, *The Bible as it Was* (Cambridge MA: Harvard University Press, 1997) 605, 614-15. Kugel writes, "A legend eventually sprang up about this translation to the effect that seventy, or seventy-two Jewish elders were commissioned to do the translation of the Pentateuch (Torah), each in an isolated cell; when the translations were compared, they all agreed in every detail, for the translators had been divinely guided. As a result, this translation became known as the *Septuaginta* ('seventy')."

7 These differences are clearly illustrated in A. Wayne Meeks, ed., *The Harper Collins Study Bible* (London: Harper Collins Publishers, 1993) xxxvii-xl.

8 I shall not use the term *Christian Bible*, however, since it includes both OT and NT and so is ambiguous.

9 Hans von Campenhausen, *The Formation of the Christian Bible* (Philadelphia: Fortress Press, 1972).

of the OT. Indeed, when a passage in the NT says that something is "according to scripture," it refers to the Jewish scripture (generally the LXX). Had the Christians not believed the Hebrew scriptures authoritative, they would have abandoned them entirely.

This scenario raises three questions. First, if Judaism were obsolete, why didn't the new faith reject Jewish scriptures? Second, if Christians did not consider Jewish scriptures obsolete, how did they regard them? Third, as Christians developed their own canon of holy texts, how did they foresee the relationship between the two Bibles? With regard to the first question, there was at least one attempt to completely abandon the Jewish Bible, particularly the Pentateuch. This approach was taken by Marcion, an early Christian bishop (c. 85-160 C.E.) who believed there was not one, but two Gods. One was the stern, judgmental Creator God of the Jews; the other, the merciful God of Christianity, incarnate in Christ. Marcion believed that this latter God had rejected the Jews, their Creator God, and the entire Hebrew scripture. The Church did not favor this view. Marcion was excommunicated in 144, at which time he founded his own church. Marcionism was powerful and popular for a time, but was later declared heresy. Marcion's sect, along with his writings, eventually disappeared.[9] Nevertheless, the Marcionite approach proved a distinct boon to Christianity. In advocating elimination of the Jewish scriptures, Marcion had insisted on replacing them with a new authority—a distinctly Christian Bible. He thus brought attention to the necessity of a Christian canon of divine revelation.

There were other reasons why Christians did not want to abandon the Hebrew scriptures. One was not primarily theological, but rather historical and practical. As a newly developing religious group, Christianity had no claim to legitimacy other than their Jewish heritage. Without that, they were just another upstart sect among the many coexisting in the Hellenic world. Because the powerful Romans had great respect for history and tradition, even a Jewish history, which was ancient if not always praiseworthy, gave early Christianity a ready-made measure of respectability.

Despite all, the Jewish Bible remained and the early Christians simply wrote their own, so now there existed two competing scriptures. The question of how they related to one another is vital to this book because the art described herein is the art of the two scriptures and a reflection of the ways in which early and medieval Christians interpreted *both*.

The Two Scriptures: Concord or Discord?

Most Christians looked at the relationship between the two scriptures (and indeed, between the two faiths) in one of two ways. The first attitude, *Concordia Veteris et Novi Testamenti* (Agreement of the Old and New Testaments), found perfect concordance between the Jewish Bible and the NT, as the "new" testament of the Christians was on a continuum with the "old" testament of the Jews. Accordingly, the new revelations of Christianity were, as Jesus said, "not to abolish the law [Torah] and the prophets but to fulfill them" (Mt 5:17). And, as previously noted, the NT quotes and paraphrases OT texts to provide examples and support for its new religion. An early example comes from Paul: "Christ died for our sins in accordance with the scriptures, that he was buried, that he was raised on the third day in accordance with the scriptures" (1 Cor 15:3). This seems almost casually spoken, for Paul does not back himself up with proof-texts. Since the "scriptures" he refers to can only be the Hebrew Bible, he leaves unanswered the obvious question: Where, exactly, does the Hebrew Bible state—or even imply—that Christ died for the sins of mankind?[10] Questions such as this mark a characteristic Christian attitude toward the Jewish Bible that will be explored as we continue.

Concurrent with *Concordia* literature of the first two centuries, there was another principle called *Adversus Judaeos* (Against Jews) after the titles of tracts which first appeared during these two centuries and continued through the Middle Ages. These tracts argued

---

[10] One OT passage often cited by Christians is Isaiah 53:3-12, which begins, "He was despised, shunned by men, a man of suffering, familiar with disease...."

[11] Rosemary Radford Ruether, *Faith and Fratricide* (New York: Seabury Press, 1974).

[12] A. Lukyn Williams, *Adversus Judaeos, A Bird's-eye View of Christian Apologiae Until The Renaissance* (Cambridge: Cambridge University Press, 1935). This is an excellent anthology of relevant sources, with commentary.

that the Jews' interpretation of their own Bible was false. The tracts went further to claim the Hebrew Bible, properly interpreted, not simply predicted but *proved* the validity of Christianity. How stupid the Jews of the time must have been not to realize this!

As Rosemary Radford Ruether (and many others) have pointed out, the *Adversus Judaeos* tradition was not something which began late in Christianity. It was, rather, "an attitude which was articulated as soon as it was clear that, whatever the Jews and the proto-Christians had in common, the Jews rejected the concept that the crucified Christ was the Messiah."[11] This attitude toward the Jews had begun with Paul and the Gospels, continues in Acts, and becomes most prominent in the *Adversus Judaeos* literature of the second through seventh centuries.[12]

These two opposing attitudes towards biblical interpretation, *Concordia* and *Adversus Judaeos*, naturally mirrored the ambiguous attitudes Christians themselves had towards Jews. On the one hand, (*Concordia*) Judaism was the necessary forerunner of Christianity. Indeed, the whole history of mankind as described in the NT is the same as that in the Jewish Bible, and the ancestors of Jesus and his disciples were all Jewish. The presence and persistence of the Jewish people had been necessary to the foundation of Christianity but, in the end, the Jews must convert before the Messiah reappears (Rom 9:27). On the other hand (*Adversus Judaeos*), Jews were evil because they had killed Christ. The loss of their Temple and the destruction of the Holy City of Jerusalem were signs that their own God had abandoned them. The Jews were blind not to see what their own Bible was telling them, namely that a new covenant had been made, superseding the old. The author of The Epistle to the Hebrews makes this point in a paraphrase of Jeremiah, saying a new covenant has made the old one obsolete (Heb 8:13).

Siker points out that Paul held either the *Adversus* or the *Concordia* position depending upon his audience.[13] In Galatians 3:23-25, he stresses the discontinuity between Christian faith and Mosaic Law: "Now before the faith came, we were confined under the Law…so that law was our custodian until Christ came that we might be justified by faith. But now that faith has come, we are no longer under a custodian." But in Romans 3:31, he emphasizes instead their *continuity*: "Do we then overcome the law by this faith? By no means! On the contrary, we uphold the law."

Today, the principle of *Concordia* is well recognized. But, as the tenets of *Adversus Judaeos* are less well known, I have included two specific examples to help explain them.

The Epistle of Barnabas. This letter, written in the late first or early second century, is one of the earliest Christian texts outside of the New Testament.[14] We are not certain by or for whom it was written, but the author does not seem to have been the Apostle Barnabas. It appears to have been written in Alexandria, addressed to Christians. This Barnabas was quite taken with the concept that it was not the letter of the Hebrew scriptures which counted as much as the spirit, or the hidden or allegorical meaning. In this, he went further than his predecessor Philo of Alexandria, a Jewish philosopher whom we shall meet later. While Philo believed the literal and the allegorical meanings of the Hebrew Bible were equally important, Barnabas thought many apparent meanings were not meant to be taken literally at all. This he felt was particularly true of Jewish rituals, which he opposed, saying, "External ritual is worthless as a means to this [the Godly life], whether it be sacrifices or fasts, for God never intended their literal observances."[15] He backs up his statement with quotes from Isaiah (1:11-14) and Jeremiah (7:22), thus taking a radical stance which goes far beyond similar passages in the NT to address directly the problems confronting Jews and Christians. In particular, he answers the questions Jews asked Christians: How can you hold the Pentateuch, the Psalms, and the Prophets—in fact the whole Jewish Bible—as the word of God when you do not observe (Saturday) Sabbath, circumcise your children, separate meat from

13 Jeffrey Siker, *Disinheriting the Jews: Abraham in Early Christian Controversy* (Louisville: Westminster/John Knox Press, 1991).

14 Williams, "The Epistle of Barnabas," *Adversus Judaeos*, 14-27 The complete text is in Alexander Roberts and James Donaldson, eds., *The Ante-Nicene Fathers*, vol. 1 (New York: Charles Scribner's Sons, 1905). It is also available on the Internet at {http://www.newadvent.org/cathen/}.

15 Williams, "Barnabas," 21.

16 Ibid., 19.

17 Ibid., 21.

milk, or abstain from pork? Barnabas outdoes Stephen, who had accused the Jews of disobeying their own laws (Acts 7:39, 51-3). He "accuses the Jews of misunderstanding them (the Lawgiver [Moses] and the Prophets) from beginning to end, and intimates that the ordinances of circumcision, of the Sabbath, of the distinctions of meats clean and unclean, were never intended to be literally observed, but had throughout a spiritual significance."[16] Barnabas claims the Jews could only understand literal, never true spiritual, meanings. Furthermore, Christians, "not unbelieving Jews, are the true heirs of salvation, as was understood by the Patriarchs...Moses, and the Prophets."[17] This may derive in part from Jesus' statement, "Truly, truly, I say to you, before Abraham was, I was" (Jn 8:58). While Barnabas uses scriptural references continually, he does not quote them as carefully as do some later authorities. Yet already he is expanding on the seeds of the ideas that the Jews were not the "true Israel" and that they misunderstood their own Bible.

Barnabas feels free to use allegory. In chapter 8 of his epistle, he likens Christ to the red heifer, the cow without blemish which is to be sacrificed (in an enigmatic passage in Numbers 19:2-10). Barnabas also makes much of the concept *the older shall serve the younger*. He mentions several OT examples including Jacob and Esau (Gen 25:23) and Ephraim and Manasseh (Gen 48:17), but he maintains in chapter 13 that the *true* meaning of the concept is that the younger covenant, Christianity, supersedes the elder, Judaism. This, of course, is the same point made by Paul (Rom 9:12), but neither Paul nor anyone else from the NT other than Jesus is mentioned by Barnabas. In sum, Barnabas claims the Christians have replaced the Jews as the beneficiaries of God's covenant.

The Dialogue with Trypho. Another form of polemic, the dialogue, also appears early in the *Adversus Judaeos* tradition. The dialogue had long been a popular framework for literary arguments in the Hellenic world, typified by the dialogues of Plato featuring the gadfly Socrates and his perplexed opponents. During the early years of the first millennium C.E., when Christianity was pulling away from Judaism, there must have been many arguments between Christians and Jews. (One would like to have overheard some of them!) At least one surviving manuscript seems to describe just such an argument. It was written in Greek by Justin Martyr around 155-161 C.E.; the usual English translation is *The Dialogue With Trypho*.[18] It purports to be a discussion between Justin and a Jew named Trypho who met in Ephesus and talked for several days. It is not possible that what we read today records an actual discussion. It is, in fact, not a dialogue so much as a harangue on the part of Justin, the Christian; his Jewish opponent Trypho has little chance to say his piece. Nonetheless, the scheme of the arguments and counter-arguments give us insight into very early Christian thought.

The Dialogue is a remarkable creation. More thorough and more sophisticated than *Barnabas*, in over 135 short chapters it lays out a variety of arguments designed to prove the legitimacy and superiority of Christianity over Judaism. The approaches are the same as those used in the NT and *Barnabas*, but the only source Justin quotes is the Hebrew Bible. Trypho says at one point in chapter 10 that he has read "the so-called Gospel" and does not see how Christians keep the precepts mentioned therein. And, since Christians do not observe Jewish Law, how can they be said to fear God?

Christian and Jew each try to establish his own religion is the one true faith. Each bolsters his argument by appeals to scripture. The methods of quotation and interpretation of scripture used are described in chapter 3 of this book. Here we are primarily concerned with the Christian's approach; Justin answers Trypho in several ways. First, in chapter 11 he says the OT itself predicts the Law (of Moses) shall be superseded, as in Jeremiah 31:31: "Behold, the days come saith the Lord, that I will make a new covenant with the House of Israel and the House of Judah." Justin claims this is a prophesy of Christianity, making himself and the other Christians "the true and

---

18 Williams, "Justin Martyr. The Dialogue with Trypho, " in *Adversus Judaeos* 32-42. The complete text can be found in Justin Martyr, *Dialogue of Justin, Philosopher and Martyr, with Trypho, A Jew* 194-270 and in Roberts and Donaldson, eds. *The Ante Nicene Fathers* (see note 14).

19 Williams, "Trypho," 36.

20 Pamela M. Eisenbaum, *The Jewish Heroes of Christian History: Hebrews 11 in Literary Context* (Atlanta: Scholars Press, 1997) 220.

spiritual Israel."[19] This is important. Justin emphasizes that what God promised to Abraham was not a Jewish nation, but Christianity! This is the concept of *Verus Israel*, covered in detail in the next chapter of this book. This theme may be traced to Paul (Rom 9:11) or to the author of Hebrews 11. As Pamela Eisenbaum finds, the latter "no longer sees scripture as the history of Israel; it is now the pre-Christ history of Christians. Abraham and Moses are not Israelites or Jews, they are *Christians*."[20]

Justin uses allegory to show that, despite certain episodes in the OT he believed prefigure Christianity, the Jews cannot understand the truth of Christianity because they "have understood all things in a carnal [literal] sense" (chapter 14). The Jewish Law thus becomes not a gift from God, but instead a mark for punishment. Specifically, God ordered circumcision to separate Jews from other nations so that they could be punished, for "[they] have slain the Just One" (chapter 16). Justin interprets the OT to predict the symbol of the Cross, as well as the coming of the Messiah. For instance, during the fight with the Amalekites (Ex 17:10-13), Moses kept his arms up and out-stretched with the help of Aaron and Hur so the Jews would prevail. According to Justin, this stance of Moses prefigures the Cross. The two goats in Leviticus 16:7-10 he claims refer to two aspects of Jesus. The scapegoat sent into the wilderness is the Jesus who suffers and dies; the goat designated as a sin offering to the Lord is Christ tri-umphant. Because of the many passages in the OT that Justin says prefigure Christ, he actually begins to think of it as a Christian docu-ment. This becomes obvious when, to the Jew Trypho, he refers to the OT as "your scriptures, or rather not yours but ours" (chapter 29).

Justin quotes several psalms, all of them in a Christological sense. In chapter 39 he points out the passage 1 Kings 19:14 where Elijah tells God that the Israelites have "put your prophets to the sword." This concept is constantly present in anti-Judaic polemic. To Jews, it means Jewish prophets, trying to keep their people obedient to the Law, were dishonored and disobeyed. To Christians, however, this pas-sage meant that the forerunners of Christ, who prophesied his coming and Christ himself, were killed by the Jews.

Trypho, on the other hand, apparently has little to say. When he does speak, it is to accuse Justin of selecting and quoting whatever he wishes from the prophetic writings.[21] Justin, in turn, accuses the Jews of removing certain passages from their own Bible because the text predicts Christ (chapter 72). Trypho points out to Justin in chapters 66-68 that there is a mistranslation in the LXX in Isaiah 7:14, where the Hebrew word for "young girl" is replaced by the Greek word meaning "virgin."[22] A great amount of space is devoted to this problem, but Justin does not provide an answer satisfactory to Trypho, who says the doctrine of the Virgin Birth comes from Greek mythology and Justin should be careful lest he "be convicted of talking foolishly like the Greeks" (chapter 67).

There is neither winner nor loser in *The Dialogue with Trypho*. Williams refers to the "kindly spirit of the disputants" who, in parting, wish each other well. He continues, "there is no dialogue as such which is conducted on quite so high a level of courteousness and fairness...until the end of the eleventh century."[23]

The *Epistle of Barnabas* and the *Dialogue with Trypho* are two of the earliest examples of *Adversus Judaeos* literature. We will refer to others later in this book. The approach for both Jewish and Christian debaters is to appeal to scriptural authority. It is not clear to whom such literature was addressed. Jews were not likely to read such material, and even if they did, it would be surprising if it swayed them. Christian theologians and apologists probably wrote them simply to solidify their thinking on Jewish-Christian scriptural relations and to communicate that thinking to others. They also may have used them to construct preaching texts. Interestingly, many of the specific interpretations we will see later in art are already present in these early written works.

---

[21] *Dialogue with Trypho*, chapter 27.

[22] Julio Trebolle Barrera, *The Jewish Bible and the Christian Bible* (Leiden: Koninklijke Brill, NV, 1998) 313.

[23] Williams, "Trypho," 42.

[24] Eisenbaum, *Jewish Heroes*, 191.

Reconciliation: Adversus Judaeos and Concordia

These two principles are not contradictory; rather, they are two sides of a single coin. Reconciliation of the two comes through a new interpretation of the Hebrew scriptures. *Concordia* is realized if the Hebrew scriptures are reinterpreted according to Christian supersessionist principles. When that is done, as we shall see, there is no difficulty in finding proof-texts to support Paul's contention (1 Cor 15:3) that the OT contains predictions which are realized in Christianity. As far as *Adversus* is concerned, the same is true: the Jews continue to take the literal approach to their heritage and, as long as they do so, they are blind to the real meaning of their own Bible.

Reinterpretation of the Hebrew Bible is, of course, key to supersessionism. It is impossible to tell exactly when this approach arose. Gradually, Christian writers and apologists appropriated the Jewish scriptures, viewing sacred history through a Christological lens. Pamela Eisenbaum, in her close reading of the eleventh chapter of the Epistle to the Hebrews, says it "marks a turning point in early Christian appropriation of biblical history."[24] The chapter contains a "hero list" of Jewish figures from Abel, Enoch, Noah, and Abraham to David, Samuel and the prophets. By their faith (Judaism), says the author of Hebrews, they achieved mighty deeds. But at the end of the passage comes a barb: "all these, though well attested by their faith, did not receive what was promised, since God had foreseen something better for us" (Heb 11: 39-40). Not a single one of these Jewish heroes gained redemption because their faith was in obsolete Judaism. In fact, Eisenbaum says, these heroes were subtly separated from Judaism and transvalued, in effect becoming Christians.[25] Although Eisenbaum's exegesis of this passage is itself very subtle, whether Hebrews 11 was perceived this way by early Christians can be argued. Nonetheless, the process of reinterpreting the OT was well under way, and its ramifications are fascinating. This is well stated by Van Campenhausen, who calls the *Epistle of Barnabas* "the most thoroughgoing attempt to wrest the Bible absolutely from the Jews and to stamp it from the very first word as exclusively a Christian book."[26]

Art and the Beginnings of the Jewish-Christian Conflict

This book does not actually begin its story of art as a reflection of Jewish-Christian relations until early in the third century, and it is appropriate at this point to explain why. After all, Jews and Christians certainly interacted during the first two centuries, and as we have seen in the *Adversus Judaeos* tradition, definite stances were taken. We will see that the groundwork for depicting Jewish-Christian relations in art has already been laid down in *Barnabas* and *Trypho*, including allegorical images and general themes. Nevertheless, there is no significant Christian art datable to before the third century. Certainly it is possible that the vicissitudes of time and the hostilities of mankind have obliterated a vital artistic legacy from the growing (but as yet illicit) religion. It is also possible that since very early Christianity was not secure in its self-identification, let alone the organization and localization of its places of worship, specifically Christian works of art may have been portable, occasional, and hence not likely to survive. There are also speculations that very early Christianity may have shunned visual art in deference to the Second Commandment.[27] These are "arguments from silence," suggesting that had there been a tradition of Christian art in the first two centuries, we would have some evidence for it. As will become apparent in the next chapter when we discuss the synagogue at Dura-Europos, this sort of argument is dangerous. Thus, all we can say at this moment is we are not certain whether early Christianity went through an aniconic (without images) phase. Indeed, the question of how thoroughly Jews themselves obeyed the Second Commandment is a subject of controversy we will discuss in the next chapter.

In any event, the first substantial body of surviving Christian religious art is found in the catacombs, and it is to these burial sites we will turn after setting the stage.

---

[25] Eisenbaum, 220-21.

[26] von Campenhausen, *Formation*, 70.

[27] Andre Grabar, *Early Christian Art* (New York: Odyssey Press, 1968) chapter 1.

2 | Emergent Christianity and Redefined Judaism (200-313 C.E.)

Judaism After the Destruction of the Second Temple

During the period of 200-313 C.E., Judaism regrouped after two major losses: the loss of its religious center in the destruction of the Second Temple and the loss of two disastrous wars to the Romans. Judaism changed in several ways. The Patriarchs and the Rabbis, inheritors of the tradition of the Pharisees, bore responsibility for interpreting and teaching Jewish law. Jews had migrated to many different parts of the Roman Empire, from Palestine (as the Romans renamed conquered Judea) to large cities such as Alexandria, Antioch, and Rome itself. It is estimated that, at that time, five times as many Jews lived in the Diaspora as in Palestine. These Jews spoke Greek and their grasp of Hellenic culture was greater perhaps than their understanding of their own heritage. The foremost Jewish philosopher and Biblical scholar of the time, Philo of Alexandria (c. 20 B.C.E.-50 C.E.), knew little, if any, Hebrew.[1]

Without the high priest in the Temple, to say nothing of the disappearance of the Essenes and the Sadducees, uncertainties arose concerning Jewish Law and its interpretation in the post-Temple period. Something needed to be done to stabilize matters. One important step the Rabbis took was to define and close the Jewish Biblical canon during the second century C.E. Their second major accomplishment was to compile and write down the *Mishna*, the core of the massive code of Jewish law eventually called the *Talmud* (comprising both the Mishna and its commentaries, the *Gemara*). Writing the Mishna was a long process involving the identification and codification of oral laws going back hundreds of years. It was organized by a number of gifted rabbis, including Rabbi Akiva and Rabbi Meir. The patriarch

---

[1] Samuel Sandmel, *Judaism and Christian Beginnings* (New York: Oxford University Press, 1978) 281.

Judah-ha-Nasi (Judah the Prince) is credited for its final redaction around 200 C.E.

Judaism flourished in Galilee, particularly as Jerusalem had been obliterated and Jews were not permitted inside its successor, the Roman city Aelia Capitolina. The future of Judaism did not lie in Judea, anyway, but rather in the Diaspora lands including the Western and Eastern parts of the Roman Empire. One could argue that, paradoxically, the loss of Jerusalem and its Temple actually *strengthened* the position of Diaspora Judaism, which never depended much on either one.

By the third century it was clear that Jews and believers in Jesus Christ were discrete groups. There had been a bridge group called by historians Judeo-Christians—Jews who practiced their religion as of old yet believed the young Jew, Jesus of Nazareth, was indeed the promised Messiah.[2] This group still practiced circumcision, obeyed the dietary laws, and kept the Jewish Sabbath. They, too, like the Essenes and the Sadducees among other sects, eventually disappeared, having had to decide between Judaism and nascent Christianity. At the same time that Judaism lost much of its concern with Messianism and Apocalypticism, Christianity emphasized these very aspects of religion.[3] Rabbinic Judaism, the product of all these changes in the Jewish world, turned increasingly inward as it concentrated on the definition and observance of the Law; simultaneously it turned increasingly away from the Hellenistic way of life. An indication of this trend was the appearance of a new version of the Torah known as the *Targum*, which translated the Torah into Aramaic, the Jewish vernacular.

---

[2] For more description, see Jean Danielou, *The Theology of Jewish Christianity* (London: Darton, Longman & Todd, 1964); also Simon, *Verus Israel.*

[3] James H. Charlesworth, "Christians and Jews in the First Six Centuries," chap. 9 in *Christianity and Rabbinic Judaism*, Hershel Shanks, ed. (Washington, DC: Biblical Archaeological Society, 1992) 305-325.

[4] John Beckwith, *Early Christian and Byzantine Art* (Harmondsworth/ Middlesex: Penguin Books, Ltd., 1970).

[5] There is some evidence that during the brief reign (361-363 C.E.) of Emperor Julian ("The Apostate"), who turned back to paganism from Christianity, Jews were hostile to Christians. See James Parkes, *The Conflict of the Church and the Synagogue* (New York: Soncino, 1934/New York: Atheneum, 1974).

[6] Baron, *Political History*, 2:165.

Nascent Christianity

Christianity, meanwhile, continued to gain strength both in Palestine and in the Diaspora. It was clear by now that its evangelistic program would best be served by converting Gentiles (pagans), rather than the smaller population of Jews. The latter still were proving to be "stiff-necked," as the Lord described them in their own scriptures (e.g., Ex 32:9, Deut 9:6). Christianity did not, however, become a *religio licita* (accepted faith) of the empire until 261 C.E., although Judaism retained that status.[4] Further, Christians suffered sporadic eras of persecution depending upon the proclivities of the sitting emperor. The most severe of these periods occurred under Nero (54-68), Domitian (81-96), Decius (249-251), Valerian (353-360), and Diocletian (284-305). The persecution ended definitively only with the ascension of Constantine in 312.[5]

At the same time the growing religion was countering pressure from without, there was considerable turmoil within. The disputes concerned a wide variety of theological and liturgical issues, that is, over the tenets, as well as the practice, of the new religion. The Church soon organized itself around the Bishop of Rome. Later titled "pope," this leader was a spiritual descendent of Peter, who was entrusted by Christ to establish the Church. The increasingly widespread popularity of Christianity throughout the empire required the additional establishment of a hierarchical network of archbishops, bishops, deacons, and local clergy. By the end of the third century about ten percent of the empire's population was Christian.[6]

During this period, Judaism and Christianity existed as minorities in a sea of pagan Roman beliefs, as well as other Eastern religions such as Mithraism and Zoroastrianism. Judaism and Christianity had their own internal concerns. Exactly what they thought of each other is often difficult to discern. Popes and emperors may issue encyclicals and decrees, but official pronouncements by civic or religious leaders may or may not represent the attitudes of the proverbial "man in the street," Christian or Jew.

One aspect of their relationship, at least, seems relatively straightforward: Judaism took little notice of the growing Christian religion.[7] The latter is barely mentioned in the entire voluminous

Talmud. Judaism was tending to its own issues; external matters were mainly in relation to their Roman rulers, rather than to what Jews most likely regarded as an upstart sect. Christianity, on the other hand, had a great deal to say about Jews and Judaism. This came partly from the need to differentiate their new path from Judaism. The two faiths had so much in common that it was difficult to assert a Christian tenet without saying or implying how it was similar to (or different from) some point in Judaism. Christianity consistently rubbed up against Judaism, whether the latter acknowledged it or not. The greatest point of contact was, of course, their shared cornerstone of the Bible (Hebrew Bible or OT). Both religions were based scripturally, and both looked back to this common scriptural root.

In this context, the *Adversus Judaeos* tradition continued. Tertullian (c. 160-230) was born in Carthage and converted to Christianity when he was about forty years old. He was a vigorous Christian apologist and theologian. In his *Adversus Judaeos* tract titled *In Answer to the Jews*, he makes a vital distinction between the Laws of Moses and the "True Law."[8] This Law Tertullian said arose with the very creation of the world. Sometimes called "Natural Law," it operated in the Garden of Eden and was later obeyed by Noah and again by Abraham. It was *this* law, and not Judaism, that the priest Melchizedek served in Genesis 14:18. The major rituals and commandments that define Judaism—circumcision (Gen 17:9-14), dietary rules (Lev 11), the Saturday Sabbath (Ex 16:23, 20:8, 31:14, and so forth)—appeared *after* Natural Law. Similarly, all the laws given to Moses at Mount Sinai were, according to Tertullian, an aberration, a blind alley that finally had been corrected by the *reappearance* of the true law in the Christian Revelation. This was the "new covenant" prophesied by Jeremiah (Jer 31:31).

---

[7] In addition to Neusner's previously cited book, see Stephen G. Wilson, *Related Strangers; Jews and Christians, 70-170 C.E.* (Minneapolis MN: Fortress Press, 1995). Wilson notes, "there are, even on the most optimistic count, very few allusions to Christianity or its founder in rabbinic literature and most of these are uncertain and obscure" (168-69).

[8] Williams, *Adversus Judaeos*, 43-52.

[9] Simon, *Verus Israel*,

[10] Andrew McCall, *The Medieval Underworld* (London: Hamish Hamilton, 1979) 260.

Thus Tertullian divided world history into three epochs. The first epoch, beginning with God's dispensation to Adam and Eve and their offspring, is the "True Israel" (*Verus Israel*), which operated under Natural Law. According to this interpretation of history, the people described in the Bible, from Adam to Noah to Abraham, are the original Hebrews. The second epoch witnessed the aberration of Judaism under Mosaic Law; this disenfranchised all Jews from that time onward from *Verus Israel*. The climactic third epoch began with the birth of Christ, which spiritually united Christianity with *Verus Israel*. This was an impressive argument, not at all in accordance with the *Concordia* tradition. It told the Jews they once again had misunderstood the meaning of their own Bible, and indeed the very meaning of human history!

In his book *Verus Israel*, Marcel Simon tells us that Eusebius of Caesarea (c. 260-340) made particularly clear the distinction between the Jews and the Hebrews.[9] The Hebrews, the original people, took their name from Eber, ancestor of Abraham (Gen 10:21). Before the Law of Moses (*Ante Legem*), the Hebrews lived in accordance with Natural Law—there was no need for written commandments. These people were the ancestors of the Christians. The Jews, on the other hand, took their name from their ancestor Judah. The "Jewish Period" that began under the Law of Moses (*Sub Lege*) was a deviation ended by Christ's coming, at which time Grace (*Sub Gratia*) supervened. Finally, Christianity, derived from the original Hebrews, prevailed. Shaky as Eusebius' etymologies are for "Hebrew" and "Jew," this was a powerful thesis in the supersessionist armamentarium.

So why did Jews persist in their Judaism after the coming of Jesus? Paul said that they would be redeemed at the end of time (Rom 11:5, 9:27). Augustine elaborated on this idea by emphasizing the necessity of having the Jews continue "this testimony, which, in spite of themselves, they supply for our benefit by their possession of these [Old Testament] books,"[10] an idea he bolstered by referencing the Jewish Bible, "Do not kill them lest my people be unmindful" (Psalms 59:11). Augustine also provided a vivid metaphor to describe the relationship between Jew and Christian and their respective scriptures. Though it seems a perfect supersessionist image, I know of no visual translation of it: "The Jew carries the book from which the Christian takes his faith. They have become our librarians, like slaves who carry books behind their masters; the slaves gain no profit by their carrying, but the masters profit from their reading."[11]

Early Christian Art

As mentioned in the previous chapter, no known significant Christian art is datable to before 200 C.E. As noted there, many explanations have been put forward for this lack. It is likely that early Christians, because of their aniconic Jewish heritage, were uncomfortable with religious art, but we are not certain of this. For whatever reason, these two minority faiths, Judaism and Christianity, existed in the midst of a pagan society rich in sculpture, bas-relief, painting, and mosaic. Still, they chose not to use art as a means of worship until about 200, by which time Tertullian said idols were commonplace in Christianity.[12] This change in attitude toward religious pictures and sculpture is a watershed event. Ernst Kitzinger sums it as follows: "In the entire history of European art it is difficult to name any one fact more momentous than the admission of the graven image by the Christian Church. Had Christianity persisted in the categorical rejection of images and, indeed, of all art, which it proclaimed during the first two centuries of its existence, the main stream of the Graeco-Roman tradition would have been blocked."[13]

Christian art had finally appeared. The best, earliest examples are underground in Rome.

---

[11] Margaret Miles, "Santa Maria Maggiore's Fifth-Century Mosaics: Triumphal Christianity and the Jews," *Harvard Theological Review* (1993): 155-75.

[12] Caecilia Davis-Weyer, *Early Medieval Art, 300-1150, Sources and Documents* (Englewood Cliffs, NJ: Prentice Hall, 1971) 3-6.

[13] Ernst Kitzinger, *The Art of Byzantium and the Medieval West: Selected Studies* (Bloomington IN: Indiana University Press, 1976) 91.

[14] "The Latin expression *ad catacumbas* conceals the original Greek *kata cumbas*, which means something like 'at the hollows,' perhaps referring to the site of the underground burial places." As defined in James Stevenson, *The Catacombs: Life and Death in Early Christianity* (Nashville: Thomas Nelson, Inc. 1985/Thames and Hudson, 1978) 7. See also Paul C. Finney, *The Invisible God: The Earliest Christians on Art* (New York: Oxford University Press, 1994). Finney dates the catacombs of Callistus to c. 200 C.E., thus making them the earliest known considerable body of Christian art.

FIG 2-1. Arcosolium. Jewish Catacomb of Villa Torlonia, Rome. A fresco at the back of a burial chamber. In the center is a representation of the Ark of the Covenant with the doors open and a Torah scroll leaning on its side. Flanking the Ark are twin menorahs with small oil lamps at the top of each branch. (Goodenough, vol. 3, figure 817)

The Catacombs of Rome

The largest body of early Christian art decorates the walls of the burial sites known as "catacombs."[14] Decorated catacombs exist in middle and southern Italy, Malta, and Tunisia. The largest and most studied group is just outside the walls of Rome, and it is on these I will concentrate. Catacombs were used for burials from approximately the second to the fifth centuries, much less so after the sack of Rome in 410 C.E. Their precarious survival from antiquity and rediscovery in the seventeenth century are two aspects of the catacomb story almost as fascinating as the sites themselves.[15]

Our knowledge of the builders, users, and occupants of the catacombs is fragmentary. We do not know whether a large proportion or just a few of the dead were buried there; probably the latter. We do know that gatherings—of the families of the deceased or other faithful—took place in some of the larger rooms. But since, of course, we are limited to those catacombs that have been found, whether or not we even have a representative sample to study is impossible to know. The astonishing discovery of the extensively decorated Via Latina catacombs in 1955 makes one wonder what other unsuspected underground treasures await us.

The catacombs were once believed to be secret burial and worship havens of clandestine Christians. It is recognized now that Christian dead were interred in the catacombs primarily for practical economic reasons in times Christians were persecuted and in times they were not, and even after Christianity became a tolerated religion. Furthermore, there were Jewish and even pagan catacombs, meaning

FIG 2-2. Fresco from Via Latina Catacomb, Rome. At the left are Adam and Eve, dressed in animal skins. To Adam's left is the serpent. On the right are Abel, holding a lamb and Cain holding some grain. (Gen 4)

these burial sites were not particular to Christianity. Catacombs were built at the city's periphery because, by Roman law, the dead had to be buried outside city walls for reasons of public health. Since property was expensive, it made sense to dig burial sites many levels deep underground, thereby maximizing usable surface acreage.

We experience the catacombs today far differently than did the Jews, Christians, and pagans of the third and fourth century. Only a few of the many Roman catacombs are open to visitors, and when we do see one of them, we benefit from modern lighting. When they were originally used, illumination came from the occasional air shaft or the uncertain flickering of oil lamps and flambeaux. And for those who cannot visit them, the catacombs remain isolated pictures in books, brightly lit through the magic of electricity. These brilliant photographs do not convey the feel of the tombs. It is instructive to read a reminiscence of St. Jerome (347-420?):

"When I was a boy at Rome and was being educated in liberal studies, I was accustomed, with others of like age and mind, to visit on Sundays the sepulchers of the apostles and martyrs. And often did I enter the crypts, deep dug in the earth, with their walls on either side lined with the bodies of the dead, where everything is so dark that it almost seems as if the psalmist's words were fulfilled: 'Let them go down alive into hell.' [Ps 55:15] Here and there, the light, not entering through windows, but filtering down from above through shafts, relieves the horror of the darkness. But again, as one cautiously moves forward, the black night closes round, and there comes to the mind the lines of Virgil: 'Surrounding horrors all my soul affright/And more, the dreadful silence to the night.'"[16]

15 Stevenson, "Rediscovery of the Catacombs," chapter 3 in *Life and Death*. I have surveyed the entire scope of Roman catacombs in *this* chapter, although they were constructed and used until the fifth century. I feel this is valid because typological thinking did not change much over these two centuries and most changes that did occur were ones of style. For a good recounting of the catacomb story, see William Tronzo, *The Via Latina Catacomb. Imitation and Discontinuity in Fourth-Century Roman Painting* (University Park PA: Pennsylvania State University Press, 1986).

16 Antonio Ferrua, *Catacombe Sconosciute (The Unknown Catacomb)* (New Lanark, Scotland: Geddes and Grosset, 1991) 9. This magnificent volume, superbly illustrated, concerns itself solely with the Via Latina tombs.

The physical burial arrangements are basically the same in Jewish, pagan, and Christian catacombs. The cemeteries themselves were cut into soft *tufa* stone and consisted of series of passages, rooms, and chapel-like areas. Some catacombs are small and on a single level, while others occupy several levels in a three-dimensional network. The most common type of resting-place was the *loculus*, a shallow horizontal niche in the wall, dug out alongside a passageway. The linen-wrapped body was placed inside the tomb, which was then sealed with rock, clay, or tile. Some niches, called *kokim*, were placed endwise, perpendicular to the passage. There were also large chambers called *cubicula*, where a family might be buried together. A *cubiculum* owned by a wealthy family might feature elaborate arched niches called *arcosolia*. It is in and around the cubicula and arcosolia that the wall decorations are found. Additionally, some cubicula contained stone sarcophagi. There are a few larger rooms for the gathering of the faithful and some of these are likewise decorated.

One final point is that, for us, the catacombs exist more or less by themselves. That is, we have virtually no written records of the circumstances of their building, burial rites, financial arrangements, or any rituals or services that may have occurred in them after interment. What is known comes from the archaeologists, art historians, and others who enter the catacombs to investigate, record, and later—in the research laboratory, library and scholarly office—piece together facts and inferences into a coherent picture of what the catacombs mean. It is a daunting challenge; that the experts do not always agree is hardly surprising. In these differences of opinion, however, lie some of the many reasons art history is so fascinating.

Jewish catacombs. There were at least six Roman catacombs that were either entirely or predominantly Jewish. Of these, only two containing significant art have survived. The Vigna Randanini catacomb on the Via Appia was discovered in 1857. It is to the southeast of Rome, amidst at least a dozen other (mainly Christian) catacombs. The largest Jewish catacomb was discovered in 1920 under the Villa Torlonia, along the Via Nomentana just outside the Aurelian walls to the northeast.

FIG 2-3. Fresco, The Binding of Isaac. Via Latina Catacomb, Rome. At the top, Abraham raises his arm to slay the bound kneeling Isaac. To the left of the wood burning on the altar is a ram. Below is one of Abraham's servants, waiting at the bottom of the mountain with the donkey. (Gen 22)

In Jewish catacombs the main illustrations are of the *menorah* or of the *lulab* (palm branch) and *etrog* (citron), both symbols of the harvest festival *Sukkot*. There also appears the *shofar*, the ram's horn blown in the synagogue on the High Holy Days of Rosh Hashanah and Yom Kippur, and also the Ark of the Covenant. These are the same symbols used on Jewish sarcophagi and gold-leaf drinking glasses. They are clearly illustrated in a fresco on the back wall of an arcosolium tomb in the Via Torlonia catacomb (figure 2-1). In the center is a Torah shrine, opened to show six scrolls. Above the shrine is a star with a sun and a moon on either side. Flanking the shrine are two large menorahs with flaming branches. In addition there are illustrations of what might be called the portable paraphernalia of Jewish ritual: shofar, pomegranate, lulab, etrog, flask, and knife. Certainly not every fresco was as elaborate or as well executed as this one.

FIG 2-4. Fresco, Moses and the Crossing of the Red Sea. Via Latina Catacomb, Rome. A young, beardless Moses points his staff at the drowning Egyptians on the left, while the Israelites walk safely on dry land. (Ex 14)

Human figures are very rare in Jewish catacombs, which is understandable considering the Second Commandment. There are a few exceptions, however: a ceiling in the Vigna Randanini bears a winged figure crowning a young man with a wreath. Another ceiling shows the goddess Fortuna, cornucopia in one hand, libation cup in the other. But by no means can these be considered Jewish; they are typical Roman pagan designs. It is not known whether these rooms were built for pagans before or after Jews occupied the site, nor whether the existence of these images indicates that the rooms served as burial places for pagans or for those of syncretic (mixed) faith.

In this respect, it is important to emphasize that in none of the Jewish catacombs do we find the Jewish Biblical scenes so typical of Christian catacombs. The symbols represented just may escape the strictures of the Second Commandment's proscribing "graven images," but only if the latter are considered to comprise only human representations. The meanings of the symbols are, of course, open to interpretation. Some have said they are logos of identification marking the burials as Jewish. At the other extreme is Erwin Goodenough, who believed the decorations have a mystical connotation. He thought of the seven-branched menorah, for instance, as a surrogate image for God (creator of light) and a symbol of our seven-planet universe.[17] Most other interpretations fall somewhere between these two.

While most scholars seem not to go as far as Goodenough in attributing extensive mysticism to the images, certainly the decorations shown in figure 2-1 are more than mere logos of Jewish identification; for that, a single menorah would suffice. Here, however, the careful elaboration on the design indicates a significant celebration of Judaism, its rituals, and, by implication, its way of life.

Christian catacombs. The growing Christian community built and occupied a large number of catacombs surrounding the walls of

---

17 Erwin R. Goodenough, *Jewish Symbols in the Greco-Roman Period* (New York: Bollingen Foundation/Pantheon Books, 1953). This scholarly masterpiece traces the evolution of Jewish symbols into Christian ones and simultaneously reveals much about both religions. It comprises thirteen volumes, but is very readable.

Rome; at least thirty-five have been identified.[18] As in the Jewish catacombs, the images are primarily on the walls of the arcosolia and the cubicula. Many of the images, in fact, still are taken from the Jewish Bible. As this was a scripture held in common by Christians and Jews, this is not totally unexpected. A partial listing of common imagery includes Adam and Eve with the serpent, together with Abel and Cain (figure 2-2), Abraham about to sacrifice Isaac (figure 2-3), and the appearance of three "men" (angels) to Abraham. Moses also is seen in several episodes, including those of the Burning Bush, crossing the Red Sea (figure 2-4), and striking the rock for water (figure 2-5). Jonah, Job, Daniel, Susanna and Tobit from the Apocrypha, Balaam, and Elijah appear in many scenes. The discovery of the catacombs of the Via Latina brought to light a number of additional images taken from the Pentateuch: the drunkenness of Noah, Isaac's blessing Jacob, the dreams of Joseph, etc. For some reason, David—a figure popular in later Christian art—does not appear often in the Christian catacombs. Of particular iconographic interest is the fresco showing Jacob on his bed crossing his arms to bless Ephraim and Menasseh (Gen 48:13-20). We will return to this image in chapter 3.

The concept of a narrative cycle of biblical scenes had not yet developed, so there seems to be little rationale behind locating a picture in one place or another. (Later, as medieval iconography progressed in sophistication, the placement of images became very important.) In general, therefore, the catacomb pictures exist independently, in what Mathews calls a "staccato" style.[19] For instance, one cubiculum has a picture of Jesus and the 5,000 loaves in one arcosolium; facing it is the scene of the three Hebrews in the furnace. Apart from the fact that each represents a miracle, it is difficult to discern a narrative theme.

---

[18] Stevenson, *The Catacombs*, 8.

[19] Thomas F. Mathews, *The Clash of Gods: A Reinterpretation of Early Christian Art* (Princeton NJ: Princeton University Press, 1993). Margaret R. Miles, *Image As Insight* (Boston: Beacon Press, 1985), points out the peaceful character of catacomb images, far removed from the vigorous apologetic texts of the Church Fathers.

When considering the extraordinary frescoes in the Via Latina catacomb, one may wonder how decisions were made about which picture went where. Perhaps they were chosen by the deceased while alive, or by the surviving family. Unfortunately, this catacomb is closed to the public; however, the excellent photographs in Antonio Ferrua's previously cited book (footnote 16) demonstrate that the cubicula are like extensively frescoed galleries in which not only are the walls lined with pictures, but the spaces between the pictures and

FIG 2-5.
Fresco, Moses Strikes the Rock to Provide Water. (Ex 17, Num 20)

even the ceiling are completely decorated! In spite of the lack of an overall iconographic message, one discerns a pattern in terms of image selection. Scholars believe most of the stories depict the theme of deliverance in two related ways: deliverance from sin and deliverance from death. Thus we see many famous instances of deliverance: Isaac from the knife of Abraham, Daniel from the lions, and, in a superbly impressionistic picture, Jonah from the great fish (figure 2-6). Also depicted are Susanna's deliverance from the lecherous old men, the salvation of the Israelites from the Egyptians, and so forth. Since the images are in cemeteries, they likely convey thoughts and feelings about life after death, a subject of intense concern to early Christians. An interesting liturgical connection has been suggested by Charles Morey; he notes there may be a precedent for certain themes based on their inclusion in the ancient *Commendatio Animae* or prayer for the dying still in use, in which God is implored to 'free the soul as Thou didst free Noah from the Flood, Isaac from the hand of his

FIG 2-6. Fresco, Jonah Spewed Out by the Great Fish. Via Latina Catacomb, Rome.

father, Daniel from the den of lions, the three youths from the furnace of burning fire.'[20]

The New Testament also suggests which scenes from the Jewish Bible might be appropriate. For instance, the patience of Job is quoted (Jas 5:10-11) to support the anguish of Christians awaiting redemption and deliverance. The message is that as Job was rewarded, so the Christian believer will find redemption, no matter how bleak the situation. A more famous passage occurs in Matthew 12:40; Jesus says that as Jonah was in the belly of the great fish for three days and three nights (Jon 1:17), so he will be in the heart of the earth for the same period following the Crucifixion. In this case, the popular image of Jonah can be read in two ways. Jonah's story can be seen simply as an example of God's redemption of the faithful from sin and disobedience. Alternately, it may be seen as an allusion to Christ's redemption (as well as the Christian deceased's) from everlasting death. Or it can refer to both; the ambiguity of symbols is one of their sources of power. In this early instance, however, it seems more likely that the Jonah picture is indeed a simple illustration of God's deliverance independent of a possible reference to Christ. The second interpretation, however, will become more prominent in successive centuries.[21]

Not all catacomb pictures have origins that may be assigned so easily. Certainly the story of Susanna is one of deliverance from evil personified in the lustful Elders. Yet, in fact, although this story is in the book of Daniel, it is not included in the Hebrew Bible because it is part of an addition to Daniel which is *not* part of the Jewish canon. The addition did get into the LXX, became part of the Deuterocanonical Catholic scriptures, and, finally became the Protestant Apocrypha.

The Christian catacombs also contain many images derived directly from the NT. From the life of Jesus, there are Annunciation

[20] Charles R. Morey, *Medieval Art* (New York: W.W. Norton, 1942) 42. For a similar idea, see Emile Male, *The Gothic Image, Religious Art in France of the Thirteenth Century* (New York: Harper and Row, 1958) and James Hall, A *History of Ideas and Images in Italian Art* (New York: Harper & Row, 1983) 69.

[21] Samuel Terrien, *The Iconography of Job Through the Centuries* (University Park PA: Pennsylvania State University Press, 1996).

scenes and Nativity scenes including several images of the three Magi, as well as a probable Virgin and Child in Cimiterium Majus. Also, there are illustrations of Jesus' baptism by John, the meeting of the Samaritan woman with Jesus at the well (figure 2-7), and the Sermon on the Mount. Most common are illustrations of the miracles performed by Jesus, such as the wedding at Cana and the healing of the paralytic, shown carrying his bed. Finally, it is not surprising that in a burial place the most frequently portrayed miracle is the raising of Lazarus (figure 2-8 on the right side).[22]

Another common image is that of the Good Shepherd, used in the catacomb of St. Callixtus (figure 2-9) and in the catacomb of Praetextatus. The Good Shepherd is not an exclusively Christian image; it far predates Christianity. The concept that the Lord cares for his faithful as a shepherd cares for his flock is found in several psalms (for example, 23, 78, 80, 100), as well as in the Prophets. The Romans, too, knew of the icon; the Shepherd is portrayed on a number of pagan sarcophagi. In Christian scriptures Matthew and Luke both speak of a shepherd and his sheep. However, it is in John (chapter 10) that the concept is given its most poignant rendering: Jesus says repeatedly that he is the good shepherd who gives up his life for his sheep. Thus, the symbol represents not just Christ, but the atonement for sin he offers believers via his death and resurrection.

As mentioned previously, there are few references this early to the Passion of Christ and no images of the Crucifixion. Kitzinger points out that the images in the Christian catacombs seem to have been chosen and then designed in "a studied attempt to avoid any suspicion or encouragement of idolatric practices."[23]

At this point, we take an unexpected journey 2,000 miles east to look at the excavation of a small town on the Euphrates, in what is now Syria. The sensational findings there shook up the usually staid world of early religious art.

Revelations at Dura-Europos

Dura-Europos was a small Roman garrison town of no particular distinction located at the eastern end of the empire. It was besieged

---

[22] Stevenson, *The Catacombs*, 92-93.   [23] Kitzinger, *Art of Byzantium*, 95.

FIG 2-7. Fresco, Jesus and the Woman of Samaria at the Well. Via Latina Catacomb, Rome. (Jn 4)

and taken by the Sassanians in 256 C.E. but later abandoned. Slowly buried by the sand, it disappeared from history to become just another *tel* in the Syrian desert, undisturbed for over 1,600 years until its rediscovery in the early 1930s. Now it is internationally famous; a small library of books has been written about it and still a lot of unanswered questions remain.

We do know it was a typical Roman town. Surrounded by a defensive wall, it had the usual orderly grid of streets, many private houses, and, of course, an amphitheater and baths.[24] It also had an amazing number of temples, even when one considers the plethora of gods in the Roman pantheon; certainly the number was stunning for a small town of several thousand people at most. We find three temples dedicated to various personifications of Zeus, as well as temples to Adonis, Aphiad, Artemis, Atargatis, and others. Since Eastern religions were influential in the Roman Empire of the early third century,

FIG 2-8. Fresco, Jesus Raises Lazarus. Catacomb of Peter and Marcellinus, Rome. (Jn 11)

it is not surprising that we find a Mithraeum (temple devoted to the sun god Mithra) and a temple dedicated to the gods of Palmyra.

The Illustrated Synagogue. Excavations had been ongoing for several years when, in 1932-1933, the stakes rose precipitously. It was one of those strokes of luck archaeologists and art historians dream about, a once-in-a-lifetime miracle of serendipity. Forty-five years later, director of the expedition Clark Hopkins described the excitement of the event: "The back wall was undercut and fell away, exposing the most amazing succession of paintings! Whole scenes, figures and objects burst into view, brilliant in the sunshine…[The crew experienced] sudden shock, astonishment, disbelief, it could not be."[25] They did not even know yet what the pictures meant or what the building was, but the sight was apparently unforgettable. One of the archaeologists found a Greek inscription beneath the figure of a man. Hopkins recalled, "Du Mesnil [from the French Academy] slowly read it. 'Moses, when he went out from Egypt and cleft the sea.'"[26] A picture of Moses on a wall! The archaeologists encountered an illustration of Aaron (also given an inscription), and then a picture of a menorah. They could only have discovered a synagogue, and one entirely walled with frescoes—a situation without parallel or precedent.

The building's demise and preservation have been explained by historians as follows. As the Sassanians prepared to attack the town, the Romans took defensive steps. Believing the walls were insufficiently strong, they pulled down the upper stories of the buildings just inside the walls and filled up the ground floors with the debris, rocks, and sand to make a sturdy rampart. (The same fate befell a place of worship just down the street—the "Christian House"—as we shall see next). The city was lost by the defenders in any event, but as it was never occupied, the filled-in buildings remained untouched until archaeologists uncovered them. The frescoes on the walls therefore were preserved from sand, wind, and rain—almost from time itself.

As the room was cleared, it seemed obvious that it was in fact a synagogue. This was clinched by the existence of an arched niche located centrally in the long wall of the room, an architectural feature typical of contemporaneous synagogues found in Judea. The concept of a decorated synagogue was shocking to everyone because the Second Commandment prohibited Jews from making "graven images" as a defense against idolatry. So how could there be pictures of Moses in a Jewish house of worship? As we have seen, this injunction held in the Jewish catacombs of Rome (contemporary with Dura); human figures pictured there are not believed to be Jewish.

24 Karl Kraeling, "The Christian Building," *The Excavations at Dura-Europos* (New Haven: Dura-Europos Publications, 1967) Final Report, VIII, Part 2.

25 Clark Hopkins, *The Discovery of Dura-Europos* (New Haven: Yale University Press, 1979) 130-31.
26 Ibid., 131.

It is beyond the scope of this chapter to describe in detail the frescoes of the synagogue of Dura-Europos. The interested reader should consult Erwin R. Goodenough's masterpiece *Jewish Symbols in the Greco-Roman Period*. This magnificent work comprises thirteen folio-size volumes, three of which are devoted wholly to Dura. Goodenough was a splendid scholar: his work is detailed, but very readable and well illustrated. If the whole of his major thesis is not quite accepted (see below), his book is thoughtful, full of fascinating data and intriguing questions.[27]

Most of the surviving fresco panels can be identified, and their range and complexity are impressive. There is no discernible pattern to their arrangement, however, so they cannot be considered a set of narrative cycles. There are scenes from the Pentateuch's books of Genesis, Exodus, and Numbers, including Jacob's dream at Beth-El, Jacob's blessing Ephraim and Menasseh, Moses at the Burning Bush, and Moses' crossing the Red Sea. From the books of the Prophets we see Samuel anoint David, David fight Goliath, Solomon with the Queen of Sheba, and Elijah revive the widow's son. There are also portrayals of Isaiah, Jeremiah, and Ezekiel in the Valley of the Dry Bones. From the writings we see the triumph of Mordechai (the Book of Esther). We do not, however, see any figures identifiable as Job, Jonah, or Daniel, all so conspicuous in the catacombs. We do not know whether they were truly not portrayed at Dura or resided on the upper walls and were lost when the Romans pulled down these sections.

Several scenes in the Dura synagogue require special attention. The first is a small sequence from the story of Ezekiel in the Valley of the Dry Bones (Ezek 37:1-10 [figure 2-10]). To the left, we see Ezekiel (in Mesopotamian garb, as are most of the figures) in the presence of

---

[27] Jacob Neusner, himself a leading scholar of early Judaism, has performed an outstanding service by making a one-volume edited abridgment of Goodenough's magnum opus *Jewish Symbols*, etc. This abridged edition, edited and with a foreword by Jacob Neusner, is published by Princeton University Press, 1988. It covers the most important concepts of Goodenough's work regarding the appearance of pagan and Jewish symbols in early Christianity. It also provides a great deal of information about Dura-Europos.

FIG 2-9.
Fresco, The
Good Shepherd.
Catacomb of
Callixtus, Rome.

dismembered bodies rather than bones. Moving to the right, Ezekiel appears four more times while the bodies reassemble as a result of his prophecies. Above each Ezekiel figure is the hand of God; indeed, the passage begins, "The hand of the Lord was upon me." This series is as close as we get in this early era of representation to a narrative cycle of images. In effect, this scene unfolds from left to right as if we were reading a scroll.

The picture of Moses at the well of Be'er is also unusual (figure 2-11). The Biblical reference is brief (Num 21:16-18), only indicating that Moses gave the Children of Israel water in the desert during their forty years of wandering. (The episode also is conflated with that in Exodus 15:27.) The need for an adequate water supply is mentioned frequently in the Bible and was a determining factor in population growth and movement in the Middle East. There does not seem to be anything peculiar about this small episode, which is mentioned almost in passing. Nonetheless, it is illustrated magnificently with a very large

Moses figure putting his staff (not actually mentioned in this story) into the well so water flows to the twelve tribes. Each tribe is represented by a person in the *orans* (praying) position before a little house. In the center are a large menorah and two candlesticks that must symbolize the Law (Torah). Because the orans position indicates prayer, one concludes that this is also a deliverance story. Protected by the Deity (represented by the menorah), the people thirsting in the desert prayed for water, which was supplied through the agent Moses.

Finally let us examine the picture over the central niche in which the Torah stood. During its brief life, the synagogue was apparently remodeled. It is generally agreed that this painting above the niche was made first.[28] Thus, it had priority both in production and in location (figure 2-12). The painting is a collection of symbols rather than a narrative illustration. To the left is a large menorah; in the center, a building façade with two pairs of columns and a closed door between them; and to the right, three humans and one animal. Between the menorah and the facade are an etrog and a lulab. The menorah needs no comment—it is the preeminent symbol of Judaism. Goodenough

FIG 2-10. Fresco, Ezekiel in the Valley of the Dry Bones. Synagogue, Dura-Europos. (Ezek 37) A series of images, to be read from the left. Ezekiel, aided by the hand of God, assembles the pieces of the dead. This occurs in several stages according to the several prophecies made in Ezekiel 37. (The winged creatures at the right are not mentioned in the Bible.)

believes the central building represents the Torah, though in the sense of neither the Ark of the Covenant (which had long since disappeared) nor the Temple in Jerusalem. Rather, he thinks it is a portable Torah shrine that housed the scrolls. Thus the wall's central scene reflects the function of the niche physically carved below it. Both the real and the painted shrine are similarly designed, featuring a centrally placed scallop shell.

The scene on the right of figure 2-12 is enigmatic in several ways. It is easily recognized as representing the *akedah*, or binding, of Isaac. Abraham holds the knife, and below him is the sacrificial ram. On the altar to Abraham's left lies a curious figure whom Goodenough takes to be Isaac. He is bent over the wood, his head to the right, and presumably bound. If this is Isaac, then who is the small figure in the distance at the upper right? Goodenough says it is Sarah. If that is so, her depiction could only be symbolic since she was not present when the akedah took place. And why do only these figures turn from us, while all the others confront us? Why did this scene need to be depicted differently? Goodenough says these three figures face the hand of God in the distance. This is possible, but it seems an unsatisfactory answer because he does not say why the Ezekiel figures (or any others) do *not* face the hand of God. The unexpectedly arranged figures of Abraham, Isaac, and (maybe) Sarah, seen from behind, at the center point of the synagogue imagery, are unprecedented and disquieting.[29] Perhaps they were meant to be simply that. The findings in the synagogue were extraordinary enough, but Dura held another significant surprise: the "Christian House."

The Christian House. Perhaps because of the profusion of the synagogue's decorative frescoes and the mass of iconologic questions they spawned, excavation of the synagogue at Dura has overshadowed another archaeological first—the uncovering of the Christian House in 1930-1932. This building, however, represents a milestone in our understanding of early Christianity. The house was only three blocks down the street from the synagogue, close to the perimeter

---

28 Goodenough, 9:19.

FIG 2-11. Fresco, Moses at the Well of Be'er with the Menorah and the Twelve Tribes. Synagogue, Dura-Europos. (Num 21 and Ex 15)

wall. It was considerably smaller than the synagogue, suggesting that the Jewish community was larger than the Christian.[30]

The Christian House was originally a private home of the atrium type; that is, it had a central patio that opened to rooms from all sides. Not many years previous, it, like the synagogue, had been remodeled into a house of worship. All the rooms, including the largest (apparently the assembly room), were plain, except for one small one with a pool at one end. This was apparently a baptistery. The wall decorations there are of considerable interest.

Before I describe them, I should point out that the Christian building is as unique in its own way as the Synagogue. While discussing early Christian art in Rome, I mentioned that virtually all the structures accessible today that had been used for Christian worship before Christianity became an officially tolerated religion (e.g., those built prior to 313 C.E.) were underground. It is certain, however, that Rome and other large cities had, in addition to catacombs, small Christian houses of worship above ground. Such a structure, called a *titulus* or a *domus ecclesiae* (house of assembly), was usually a converted private house used for meetings or rituals. There may have been at one time more that twenty in Rome alone, but not a single one has survived. Every one of them has fallen prey to the passage of time, urban renewal, or deliberate destruction. We should not immediately conclude that the Dura Christian house replicates early Roman *tituli*. Kraeling, a careful scholar, says that rather, the Dura structure is just one possible prototype; in this case, a titulus modified from a private house.[31] However, it should also be acknowledged that, pending other astounding archaeological discoveries like Dura, we are unlikely to get a much better idea of the kind of building early Roman Christians actually did use for worship.

As mentioned, the baptistery decorations bear close scrutiny. There are scenes from both Old and New Testaments. These include the Good Shepherd and his sheep, together with a small inset showing Adam and Eve with the serpent (figure 2-13), two men walking on water in front of a boat full of disciples, and a woman at a well, and David (named) about to kill Goliath (also named). The woman at the well is probably the Samaritan described in John 4:5-42, but the scene also resonates strongly with the story of Rebecca and the servant of Isaac (Gen 24:10-21). There is also a scene from the healing of the paralytic in Mark 2:1-12 (figure 2-14). It is fascinating not only

---

29 This small figure's heading into the distance remains enigmatic. The particularly intriguing idea that it is Ishmael, dismissed into the desert, is found in Kurt Weitzmann and Herbert Kessler, *The Frescoes of the Dura Synagogue and Christian Art* (Washington, DC: Dumbarton Oaks, 1990) 157 n.14. Note: The Dura paintings may more properly be called "secco" (painted on dry wall) than "fresco" (painted on wet plaster), but because of its familiarity, the term "fresco" is generally used, as in the title of the Weitzmann and Kessler book.

30 Kraeling, "Christian Building," 127-41. This source contains a treasure trove of information about the House, including a wonderful map of the site.

31 Ibid., 139-41.

because it shows a dramatic sequence (the sick man on his pallet; the same man, healed, carrying it away) but also because it shows Christ—infrequently portrayed at this time—pointing with his right hand at the bedridden man.

These images, like those in the catacombs, are primarily, though not exclusively, ones of deliverance. There is another sequence that has occasioned a great deal of comment. It shows several women (five on each side) next to a large sarcophagus with a star at either end (figure 2-15). This may represent the women at the Jesus' tomb whom the Gospels describe as first to find it empty (Mt 28:6; Mk 16:2; Lk 24:2; Jn 20:1), and thus it may be an allusion to the Resurrection. If so, this is a complicated reference since the Resurrection is implied but never actually described, even in the Gospels.

The Place of the Dura Frescoes in History

Other temple walls at Dura, such as at the Temple of the Palmyrene Gods and the Mithraeum, have paintings. I will limit my discussion, however, to the frescoes in the Synagogue and the Christian House. Stylistically, both are roughly similar, although the painterly technique of those in the synagogue is more sophisticated. Two major questions immediately arise about the synagogue frescoes. First, how could adherents of a religion devoted to the Second Commandment build what can only be described as an illustrated synagogue? Second, given their obvious abandonment of aniconism,

---

[32] To be entirely accurate, we must note that human figures are portrayed in at least five other synagogues, all in Judea: Hammat Tiberias, Bet Alfa, Horvat Susiya, Na'aran, and Sepphoris. See Lee I. Levine, ed. *Ancient Synagogues Revealed* (Jerusalem: The Israel Exploration Society, 1981). Each synagogue apparently was built in the fourth to sixth century and had the same pictorial construct of two menorahs' flanking a facade as that seen in the Villa Torlonia catacombs (figure 2-1). Next to each of these complex motifs on the synagogue floor (but not in the catacomb) is a square containing a large and elaborate wheel of the twelve zodiacal signs. Some of the designs are animal in nature; others are human. At the center of the wheel is either the head of the sun god Helios or a chariot symbolic of him. Additionally, the symbols of the four seasons located at the corners of the square have human faces. It is clear the human figures in Jewish art (aside from Dura-Europos) occur almost exclusively in the context of stereotypic astrological symbols. Biblical or sacred representations are very rare, for idolatry was too great a concern.

FIG 2-12. Fresco over the Torah niche. Synagogue, Dura Europos. In the center is the Temple of Jerusalem (now destroyed), also symbolizing the Ark of the Covenant. To the left is a seven-branched menorah with oil lamps at the top of each branch. Between the menorah and the Temple is the *etrog* (citrus) and the *lulab* (palm branch), symbols of *Sukkot*. To the right is the scene of the binding of Isaac (see text).

we demand to know what the pictures mean.[32] Tackling these two questions puts us into the thick of many academic arguments that will only be outlined here. As usual, though, the interested reader will find a wealth of books in which to pursue farther these issues.[33] I should tip my hand right now by saying we do not have definitive answers to either question. This is not surprising: there is so little information, other than the synagogue itself, that people are bound to disagree.

It is possible that in the third or fourth centuries (influenced by Christian iconography?), the prohibition against human images in synagogues was relaxed. Geza Vermes says that in the Palestinian Talmud about 300 C.E. there was some indication that figurative decoration of religious buildings was allowed as long as the teaching in Leviticus 26:1 was adhered to, that is, that such images were not to be bowed down to (worshipped).[34] The existence of other decorated sanctuaries from the same period might help confirm this, but of the many contemporaneous synagogues in Palestine and Syria, all that is left are stone walls, some columns, and foundations; any wall decoration was lost centuries ago. Synagogue mosaics have fared better, and some reveal human figures from the Bible, including the akedah on the floor at Bet Alfa in Israel and the David-Orpheus in the Gaza synagogue. These and similar images date to hundreds of years later, however—from approximately the sixth century—and so are not exactly analogous.

The Lost Illustrated Bible

Since the question of whether other illustrated synagogues existed in the third century C.E. and earlier cannot be answered, we turn to more a practical question about the origin of the images at Dura. It seems beyond doubt that the painters of both the Christian House and the Synagogue pictures must have worked from portable images

FIG 2-13.
Fresco, Adam, Eve, and the Good Shepherd. Christian House, Dura-Europos. To the lower left are Adam and Eve beneath the fruiting tree; the serpent is below their feet.

such as sketches or drawings. Artists do not usually carry such complex compositions entirely in their heads. At Dura, an outpost on the edge of the empire, an artist could not have gone quickly to a nearby building to find inspiration—or even something to copy. And it was the rule in this sort of art to maintain faithfulness to previous images. It seems, therefore, that there may well have been pattern books, small panel paintings, or cartoons to serve as models.[35]

Indeed, there may have been much more third-century Jewish art than what remains. Clearly the discovery of the Dura frescoes made obsolete the assumption that there could be no Jewish religious art. Jewish religious art did exist. Now we can ask how widespread it was. Karl Schubert goes to great lengths to show "the existence of a widespread Jewish pictorial art, the oldest attestations for which came from the third century C.E., but the beginnings of which can be dated with probability in the second century."[36] All these considerations support an idea extant in the art history world for at least a century, namely that there is a lost version of the Septuagint that was illustrated and served as a source for Bible illustrations. This fascinating concept of "the lost picture-Bible" is too complicated and controversial to be examined in detail in this book, though a few comments are warranted.[37] What might the book have looked like? Weitzmann argues that since there were over 300 miniatures in the original manuscript of the Cotton Genesis (a single Pentateuch book), if the lost LXX were as densely illustrated, size alone would mandate that it could not have been a complete Bible. Perhaps it was a Pentateuch or an Octateuch, although known illustrated Pentateuchs and Octateuchs appear only in later centuries. While they themselves might be derived from earlier lost originals, we cannot be sure when those originals were made. Kessler favors the prior existence of illus-

---

[33] For yet other outstanding discussions of the synagogue at Dura-Europos, see Joseph Gutmann, *The Dura-Europos Synagogue. A Reevaluation (1932-1992)* (Atlanta: Scholars Press, 1992).

[34] Geza Vermes, "Bible and Midrash—Early Old Testament Exegesis," *The Cambridge History of the Bible*, Peter R. Ackroyd and C.F. Evans, eds. (Cambridge: Cambridge University Press, 2: 199-231.

[35] Mary Lee Thompson, "Hypothetical Models for the Dura Paintings," in Gutmann, *Dura-Europos*, 31-52.

trated single books, such as Genesis or Psalms. If an illustrated LXX (or segments of it) did exist, it could have been used as a source of images by both the Christian painters of the catacombs and the Christian House, as well as by the Jewish artists of the Dura synagogue. It is impossible to know whether it may have been written by Jews or Christians. Ah, but there always remains the tantalizing hope that a copy of the lost illustrated LXX will be discovered!

Back to the Dura frescoes: what could be their purpose or their meaning? Because the pictures are historically based (on the Jewish Bible) but do not form a clear narrative cycle, interpretations abound. Gutmann puts it well: "Each scholar finds a different meaning in the cycle depending on the conceptual framework he [or she] brings to his [or her] interpretation."[38] Goodenough was one of the first interpreters. He believed the aggregate of the scenes in the synagogue must be viewed as mystical, precisely because of the lack of a clear pictorial narrative. In the spirit of Philo, he favored an allegorical interpretation. He thought the images represented the existence of a kind of Judaism not otherwise familiar, a brand of Judaism more esoterically inclined than Pharisaical or Rabbinic Judaism, which stressed the practical Law. Furthermore, he believed this school of Jewish thought had been suppressed by mainstream Rabbinic Judaism (which certainly would have been extremely hostile to their violating the Second Commandment). Goodenough's thesis is provocative, but not accepted by all scholars.[39]

[36] Heinz Schreckenberg and Karl Schubert, *Jewish Historiography and Iconography in Early and Medieval Christianity* (Minneapolis: Fortress Press, 1992) 189-90.

[37] For more information on the lost LXX, see Morey, *Medieval Art*; Gutmann, "Prolegomenon" to *No Graven Images: Studies in Art and the Hebrew Bible* (New York: KTAV Publishing House, 1981); Weitzmann and Kessler, *Frescoes*; and Stanley S. Ferber, "Disputatio," in Paul E. Szarmach, ed. *Aspects of Jewish Culture in the Middle Ages* (Albany: State University of New York Press, 1979)

188-95. The fascinating, complex and controversial questions about the place of the Dura frescoes in Jewish traditions, and the possible Jewish sources—pictorial or textual, Rabbinic or non-Rabbinic—in Early Christian OT iconography are well-discussed in an article which appeared while this book was in press. See Karin Kogman-Appel, "Bible Illustration and the Jewish Tradition," in John Williams, ed., *Imaging the Early Medieval Bible* (University Park PA: Pennsylvania State University Press, 1999) 61-69.

FIG 2-14. Fresco, The Healing of the Paralytic. A dual scene. Christian House, Dura-Europos. To the right, Jesus points his right hand at the paralyzed man lying on his bed. To the left, the healed man carries his bed. (Mt 9)

Gutmann has his own interesting views. He calls the frescoes an "apparently discontinuous series of pictures...organized around a set of ceremonies, liturgical prayers and midrashic ideas...These paintings must be understood as theological advertisements or religious propaganda perhaps intended to win converts."[40] Later, he notes that the Torah was probably carried around the sanctuary during services (the ritual known as *hakafah*), most likely during chanting. He then postulates that scenes on the wall mirrored the substance of the chant that, in turn, recounted scenes from the history of the wanderings of the Tabernacle and the Torah shrine. An original concept!

Art and Jewish-Christian Relations

At this early stage in our story, it appears difficult still to uncover evidence that the Jewish-Christian conflict was reflected in public art. We have seen that Christians mined both the Old and the New Testaments for images, at both Rome and Dura, while Jews referred only to their own scripture, and even that only at Dura. Although both *Concordia* and *Adversus Judaeos* principles were influential in Christian writings, the images seem to be isolated from the literature.

Perhaps there was simply little contact, artistic or otherwise, between Jews and Christians. We know, however, the two groups did interact, although we do not know what type or to what extent contact existed between these two minority religions in the Western Roman Empire. Leonard Rutgers has carefully investigated the meager information we have about Jews and Christians in Rome to conclude there were common artistic concerns among them and, therefore, common societal traditions as well. Jews and Christians patronized common workshops where artisans painted, made gold leaf glass decorated with figures, and cut stone sarcophagi. Rutgers' interpretations are based on stylistic similarities in the artifacts produced

---

38 Gutmann, *Dura-Europos*, 139.

39 Neusner in his foreword (see footnote 28) discusses some scholarly responses to Goodenough's work. See also Michael Avi-Yonah, "Goodenough's Evaluation of the Dura Paintings: A Critique," Gutmann, *Dura-Europos*, 117-35.

40 Gutmann, *Dura-Europos*, xix-xx.

41 Leonard V. Rutgers, *The Jews in Ancient Rome* (Leiden/New York: E. J. Brill, 1995).

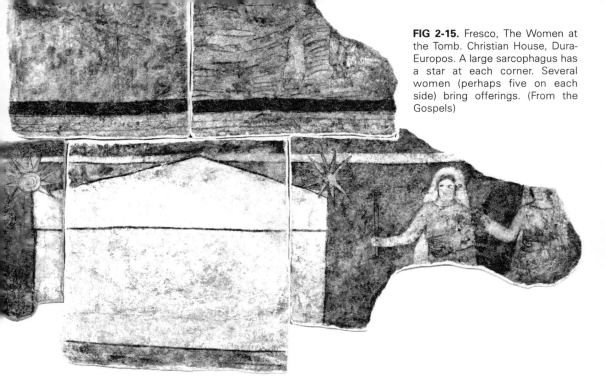

FIG 2-15. Fresco, The Women at the Tomb. Christian House, Dura-Europos. A large sarcophagus has a star at each corner. Several women (perhaps five on each side) bring offerings. (From the Gospels)

and used by both Christians and Jews. Thus, while he believes that the Jewish and Christian communities were separate in terms of burial places and customs, they were not separate in society and they knowingly placed orders for works of art at the same workshops.[41] But there is more. If the Dura synagogue is slow to reveal its secrets, scholars continue to probe the possible meanings of the images in relation to Judaism of the time. Herbert Kessler has added a particularly fascinating interpretation especially relevant to this book.

Kessler notes that the Dura synagogue was remodeled and repainted (perhaps more than once) before being buried in 256 C.E. He carefully records a sequence of paintings in the crucial locale above the Torah niche. The pictures have deteriorated, but we can see the themes in drawings done by Kessler after Goodenough.[42] First, we see a large tree-vine, significantly barren of grapes, flanked by an empty throne. Later, a single male and a lion were set in the vine and two smaller scenes crowded in below the branches. One of these shows Jacob blessing all his sons; the other shows him blessing his grandsons Ephraim and Menasseh (Gen 48:14). Above this scene rests a man on a throne with his attendants nearby, identified as

"David, King Over All Israel." Kessler points out that a vine *without* fruit symbolizes the future coming of the Messiah (at which time the vine will bear fruit); the empty throne also symbolizes Him, as he must be a descendant of Jesse and David (Is 11:1). In sum, Kessler believes these additions formed a response to Christianity. In particular, the later overpainting responded to the two main supersessionist claims of the new Church: first, that the heritage of Israel would be voided by the coming of the Messiah and the resultant New Covenant and, second, that Jesus of Nazareth *was* the Messiah predicted by the Jews. The new Dura pictures counter these assertions by showing the legacy of Israel still intact (represented by Jacob and his sons and grandsons) and the Messiah of the house of David yet to come (the empty throne in the still-fruitless vine).

Thus interpreted, the pictures in the Dura synagogue may be considered visual counters to *Adversus Judaeos* arguments. Or one could call them the first salvo in the "art war," fired by the Jews of Dura at the growing army of Christians theologians. However, as Dura has no known artistic offspring of any magnitude, and as the iconic phase of Judaism failed to flourish, the rest of the salvos were fired by Christians. The war, one-sided as it became, heated up until it reached its climax in the thirteenth century. At this point—wishing we had more information on these topics—we move on to one of the most momentous incidents in the history of Christianity.

---

42 Weitzmann and Kessler, *Frescoes*, 157-64, along with figures 195, 196, reproduced from Goodenough, *Jewish Symbols*, vol 3.

3 | The Maturation of Christianity and the Position of Judaism, 313-800 C.E.

The Rise of Christianity

The Conversion of Constantine. This event in 312 C.E. provoked a major transformation of the Roman Empire. The Emperor's conversion should be considered not as a sudden stroke of history but as the culmination of a centuries-long series of events, including the political and moral decay of the position of emperor, extraordinary instability of the empire, and the beginning of an economic downslide. During the third century, the growing number of Christians, who by now comprised about ten percent of the population,[1] were intermittently attacked by pagans. To quote Will Durant: "Pagan civilization was founded upon the state, Christian civilization upon religion. To a Roman his religion was part of the structure and ceremony of government, and his morality culminated in patriotism; to a Christian his religion was something apart from and superior to political society; his highest allegiance belonged not to Caesar but to Christ."[2]

Just after the third century, the rulers of the empire provided their harshest attack yet. They decreed "the destruction of all Christian churches, the burning of Christian books, the dissolution of Christian congregations, the confiscation of their property, the exclusion of Christians from public office, and the punishment of death for Christians detected in religious assembly."[3] These decrees fortunately were not always enforced, though Christians did lose life and property. Their persecution ended when the dying Galerius issued an edict recognizing Christianity as a legal religion in 311.

---

[1] Baron, *History of the Jews*, 2:165.

[2] Will Durant, *The Story of Civilization*, vol. 3, *Caesar and Christ* (New York: Simon and Schuster, 1944) 647. It is fashionable in scholarly circles to look down the long academic nose onto the Durant volumes. This is a mistake, at least for the general reader. This multivolume history represents succinct generalization and apt comparison; and for warm, yet skeptical, analysis, it has no equal.

3 Ibid., 651.

The next year, co-emperor Constantine defeated his rival Maxentius at the battle of the Milvian Bridge north of Rome. According to tradition, on the day before the battle Constantine saw a flaming omen in the sky—probably a cross—and the words *en toutoi nika*, Greek for "in this sign conquer."[4] That night he dreamed he was to fix a symbol to the soldiers' standards: an "X" dissected by a vertical line with its top curled over, making the monogram *Chi-Rho*, the first two letters of the Greek *Christos*. Constantine's action indicated his approval of—usually considered his conversion to—Christianity. Whether this was truly a crisis of belief or a strategic recognition and encouragement of the many Christians in his army cannot be known. At any rate, the troops fought well and prevailed over Maxentius, and Constantine became a strong advocate of Christianity. The next year Constantine and remaining co-emperor Licinus issued the Edict of Milan from one of their many capitals, extending toleration to all religions including Christianity, and restoring confiscated property to rightful owners. Constantine himself became a Christian, though common custom dictated he not be baptized until near death.

Christianity became the leading religion of the empire and Constantine encouraged conversion. He began a vigorous program of building churches throughout the empire, particularly in Rome and in what could now be called—because of the ascendance of Christianity—the Holy Land. This building program was carried out irrespective of Constantine's decision in 325 to move the capital of the empire from Rome to the city of Byzantium, which he renamed Constantinople, on the Bosphorus.

The Organization of the Christian Church and the Maturation of Ritual

Constantine promptly tended to the structure, teachings, and rituals of his newly chosen faith. Christianity had a number of problems in need of attention, the most pressing being its very definition, as there were many variations in doctrine and ritual throughout the empire. The conflict between the doctrines of Arius and Athanasius, in particular, Constantine had to settle. He promptly organized the

Council of Nicaea, which met for several months and made great strides in clarifying Christian doctrines in what became known as the Nicene Creed. This creed, still solemnly recited at every Catholic Mass, was "the first dogmatic definition of the Christian Church."[5]

While the Nicene Creed pertained solely to the Christian faithful, there were actions taken that concerned and reflected Jewish-Christian relations. During most of the fourth century, although Christianity thrived in its favored status, pagan religions were still tolerated and their temples stayed open—but their days were numbered. In 380-81 Theodosius I (379-95) proclaimed Christianity the sole legal religion; by 395 paganism was abolished. Judaism was tolerated, but not much more. In 416 Judaism was called *superstitio* rather than *religio*—definitely not a good omen.[6]

The Observance of the Sabbath and Easter

Decisions about the proper day of rest and for the observance of Christ's Resurrection (Easter) revolved partly around doctrinal issues, but were undoubtedly also a means of separating Christians from Jews. Christians had from early times rested on Sunday, as opposed to Saturday, the Jewish Sabbath. In 321 Constantine made Sunday a legal holiday, although the fact that a church council later in the century found it necessary to tell Christians not just *to* rest on Sunday but *not* to rest on Saturday strongly suggests some Christians were celebrating both.[7]

Determining the date for the observance of Easter was more of a problem. Some churches tied Easter to Passover. But Passover, based on the lunar calendar, might fall on any day of the week, while Christians decided, according to Eusebius, to celebrate Easter only on Sunday.[8] For a while, Easter Sunday still was tied temporally to

4 Ibid., 654.

5 *New Catholic Encyclopedia* (New York: McGraw-Hill, 1967) 10:433.

6 Neusner, *Age of Constantine*; also Fergus Millar, "The Jews of the Graeco-Roman Diaspora Between Paganism and Christianity, A.D. 312-438," in Judith Lieu, John North and Tessa Rajak, *The Jew Among Pagans and Christians* (London: Routledge, 1992) 97-123.

7 Jacob Rader Marcus, *The Jew in the Medieval World* (New York: Athanaeum, 1972) 104.

Passover, but Eusebius quotes Constantine as saying the Council of Nicaea explicitly wanted to break that tie. This was accomplished by establishing Easter as the first Sunday after the first full moon following March 21.

Roman Law and the Position of the Jews

As for the social situation of the Jews, particularly by comparison with the dominant Christian community, Parkes has wise words. He says, "In the medieval period there is only one certain rule, and that is that there are no certain rules by which any aspect of the status or the conditions of the medieval Jewries may be safely decided on the basis of the situation elsewhere."[9] This generalization holds just as true as regards Jews in the early Christian period, information about which is even scarcer.

When considering laws affecting Jews, we need to remember the distinction between Roman (civil) law and Church (canon) law. Under Roman law, which was maintained to a great extent even after the collapse of the Empire, Jews were Roman citizens. This was no small matter. "The most precious privilege of a Roman citizen was the safeguarding of his person, property, and rights by the law, and by his immunity from torture or violence in the trying of his case. It was the glory of the law that it protected the individual against the state."[10] Over time, however, the laws regarding the Jews were changed, so their rights and privileges as Roman citizens became abridged simply because of their Jewishness. In addition to civil law, there was Church law, from papal encyclicals to local regulations, concerning religious beliefs and practices. Many of the religious authorities who wrote the

---

[8] Marcus, *The Jew*, 103-104. The complicated subject of the dating of Easter and its relation to Passover is discussed by Faith Wallis in the introduction to her *Bede: The Reckoning of Time* (Liverpool University Press, 1999) xv-ci.
[9] James Parkes, *The Jew in the Medieval Community* (London: Soncino Press, 1938)

preface. For the Jews under both Roman and Church laws, see Mark R. Cohen, *Under Crescent and Cross* (Princeton: Princeton University Press, 1994) 30-51
[10] Durant, *Story of Civilization*, 395.
[11] Marcus, *Medieval World*, 3-4.
[12] Parkes, *Conflict*.

laws looked at the Jews with suspicion at best and active dislike, if not hatred, at worst.

The two main objectives of the Church were to prevent Jews from religiously influencing Christians and to enforce Christians' social superiority. A long view of those laws which specifically identified Jews (and other non-Christians including "Heaven-Worshippers" and Samaritans) reveals that their concerns consistently fall into certain areas—though they covered all aspects of Jewish-Christian interaction. One law prohibited Jews from actively proselytizing (315 C.E.); another prevented Jewish men from marrying certain Christian women (339), followed soon after by an outright prohibition of any intermarriage between Christians and Jews (388).[11] Beginning in 383, any Christians who converted to paganism, Manichaeism, or Judaism had their property confiscated.[12] In 439 Theodosius II closed leading government offices to Jews, and in 531 Justinian forbade Jews from testifying in court against Christians. All these laws limited the civil role of Jews, but it is obvious that they were beginning to constrict Jews' religious freedom, as well. A number of these laws were reenacted later, a fact which scholars have taken to indicate they were not frequently enforced and so needed reintroduction.

Repugnant as slavery seems to us, we must recognize the custom was an integral part of society transferred from pagans to Christians. Slaves frequently came from Slavic countries and Jews, given their linguistic and commercial ties to the Balkans and Middle East, were prominent traders. Elaborate concerns over Jewish ownership of slaves, pagan or Christian, are evident in many laws. The main fear was that Jews might convert Christian or pagan slaves to their own abominable religion. This fear of Jewish proselytism eventually extended to a ban on Jews holding office or serving in the military, situations in which they might influence or even coerce those under them.

The laws of Constantine and his successors were gathered together in the *Codex Theodosianus* around 450 C.E. The laws about Jews included those mentioned above, as well as one designating it a crime to convert *to* Judaism, the punishment for which was the forfeiture of property. Some Emperors were harsh toward Jews and heretics, while others were more lenient, but always there remained some measure of protection for Jews, even in the Theodosian Code. In 493 Theodoric the Ostrogoth said, "As for the Jews, let the [religious] privileges they enjoy be preserved and let them preserve their own judges [of the ancient Jewish courts, the *bet din*]."[13] He went on to allow that if a synagogue were damaged, restitution was to be paid.

The question of which methods were acceptable for converting Jews to Christianity remained a hot one. However desirable this conversion, there was general agreement that Jews were not to be converted by force for at least two reasons. First, conversion under duress was deemed insincere and thus theologically invalid. Second, the Church believed at least some Jews must persevere, both as witnesses to the triumph of Christianity and as a source of the non-believers who must convert just before the Second Coming of the Messiah.

The Church and the Jews

Adversus Judaeos thinking remained active during these centuries, with hostility towards the Jews that at times seems overwrought. John Chrysostom (Golden-Mouthed) of Antioch (c. 347-407) was acutely aware of "Judaizing Christians," that is, Christians who frequented the synagogue and sympathized with (or even performed) Jewish rituals. In an effort to point out the error of this, he called the Jews (among other things) "gluttonous...drunkards,...no better than senseless beasts."[14] Indeed, Chrysostom was, ironically, the master of anti-Jewish invective.

Augustine (354-430 C.E.), the bishop of Hippo in North Africa, was a passionate advocate of Christianity and one of the most influential churchmen of the West. A prolific writer, he continually emphasized the stain of original sin on all of humankind and the need for baptism and divine grace to overcome it. He also enunciated the

13 Parkes, *Conflict*, 207.

14 Quoted in Simon, *Verus Israel*, 217.

15 Williams, *Adversus Judaeos*, 312-18.

16 Ibid.

17 Karl F. Morrison, *Tradition and Authority in the Western Church, 300-1140* (Princeton: Princeton University Press, 1969) 87-89.

18 Williams, *Adversus Judaeos*, 306-311.

supremacy of the Church over the State, later a source of enormous controversy between pope and emperor. Augustine put forth his attitude toward the Jews (at least in part) in his sermon A *Discourse in Answer to the Jews* (*Tractatus Adversus Judaeos*).[15] In it he quoted the passages in Romans 11:17-24, in which the true faith is likened to an olive tree with its roots going back to the Patriarchs. The Jews are represented by broken-off branches. At the break, a "wild olive shoot" (Christianity as *Verus Israel*) is grafted on. (This section of Romans is important because it mentions the remnant [Rom 11:5 and 9:27], the possibility of the errant branches being grafted back on via conversion [11:23], and the final conversion of the Jews [11:26].)

Augustine responded to Jews who criticized the Christians by asking how they (the Christians) could adhere to the Old Testament, but fail to observe the prescribed Jewish rituals. Augustine's answer to the Jews, reminiscent of the approach in the Epistle of Barnabas centuries earlier, was that Christ's appearance meant the old laws were to be kept in spiritual significance only; literal adherence was no longer necessary. It should be noted that this sermon, presumably directed to a Christian congregation to tell them how to defend their faith to Jews, maintains a rather unique reasonability.[16] Not all sermons of this period were so mild. Pope Leo I (440-461), described as "a man of spacious and receptive intellect" and of "a rare conciliatory spirit," had this to say to the Jews: "On you, on you, false Jews and princes of the people of sacrilege, weighs the whole weight of this crime [killing Christ]…worthy of the hatred of the human race."[17]

A century later another bishop of Hippo, Maximinus, wrote *An Arian Treatise Against the Jews* (*Contra Judaeos*).[18] As with Augustine's and some other earlier approaches, the tone here is mild. Maximinus says it is the duty of Christians to win the Jews over to Jesus Christ, but without force, for he insists on "our warfare being only spiritual." He uses two allegorical themes that later will be elaborated upon in art. One is the story of Cain and Abel, which is used to prefigure Christianity. Cain, rejected by God, represents the Jews; he kills Abel, the one chosen by God, who represents Christianity (and Christ).

Maximinus concentrates on the theme of the older serving the younger mentioned earlier by Paul, Barnabas, and Augustine, among others. Maximinus points out that in the Bible, younger sons frequently gain ascendancy over elder sons. This certainly is true in the case of Jacob, who, although the younger, receives Isaac's blessing (Gen 27:18-29). Jacob, in turn, gives his blessing to his younger grandson Ephraim over the older Menasseh (Gen 48:8-20). In another Bible story, Joseph, the (next-to) youngest, becomes favored over his elder brothers. And Rachel, second wife of Jacob, takes first place in his affection over his first wife Leah. All these instances are mentioned as proof that the OT clearly prophesied that the new covenant (Christianity) was destined from the earliest time to replace the older dispensation (Judaism). These same examples were later used extensively in art, as we will discuss later in this chapter.

Maximinus also applies the displacement of the elder by the younger to Moses' two visits to the top of Mt. Sinai. On the first ascent he received one set of tablets containing the Law (Ex 31:18), which he later broke in anger over the Jews' sinful idolatry in worshipping the golden calf (Ex 32:19). This set of tablets represents Judaism. The stone tablets Moses received on his second ascent (Ex 34:28-9) were preserved; these are considered to represent Christianity. Cyril of Alexandria (d. 444) said about the Law of Moses, "For the Law is a type and a shadow" in comparison to the Christian revelation.[19]

The positions of the Church and the empire regarding the Jews are further exemplified by Gregory the Great (c. 540-604), although he is not consistent. On civil grounds Gregory believed in protecting some Jewish rights. He wanted Jews to live on papal estates at reduced rent and, while he forbade the building of new synagogues, he protected existing ones. Some of his letters, however, show him to have been hostile to Jews on theological grounds. His inconsistency—typical of the establishment's attitude towards Jewry in the seventh century—is exemplified by an excerpt from an intriguing letter Gregory wrote to the Bishop of Naples. It is an interesting missive for

[19] As quoted in Robert L. Wilken, *Judaism and the Early Christian Mind* (New Haven: Yale University Press, 1971) 81.

[20] Edward A. Synan, *The Popes and the Jews in the Middle Ages* (New York: Macmillan Company, 1965) 217.

several reasons, among them the fact that it seems the Jews of Naples somehow reached the pope with a complaint about their Christian neighbors' interfering with the celebration of Jewish festivals. After first saying he thinks Jewish observances are "empty," Gregory goes on to say that Christians should act so that:

> "...showing them [the Jews] *what we say out of their own Books* we might be able to convert them, with the help of God, to the bosom of the mother Church. And thus Your Fraternity [probably referring to a local Neopolitan clergyman] using admonitions, to be sure, as far as he can, may be afire for conversion with the help of God, but may not permit these men to be disquieted with respect to their solemnities. Rather let them enjoy their lawful liberty to observe and to celebrate all their festivities, as they have enjoyed this up until now, they and their forefathers as well, worshipping through long ages past [emphasis mine]."[20]

This is a clear restatement of an earlier idea from the Epistle of Barnabas that if the Jews understood their Bible correctly (as the Christians did), they would convert. Christian images were thought to help in that process. It is appropriate at this point to consider exactly how the Christians *did* interpret the Jewish Bible.

Principles of Biblical Interpretation

Much of the material in this book concerns visual and textual interpretations of the Jewish and Christian scriptures and interpretations of the relationship between the two. Biblical interpretation is as old as the Bible itself; the Jews interpreted their own scriptures even *within* their own scriptures. The book of Daniel (9:2, 24) interprets earlier prophecies of Jeremiah describing "the end of the desolations of Jerusalem." In a more subtle way, any retelling of a story or redescription of a law or ritual, as occurs in large sections of Deuteronomy, can be considered as interpretation. In this sense, the prophets are interpreters of their own messages and visions. Later in

Jewish history, just before the appearance of Christianity, sages or wise men appeared in "wisdom literature," including such books as the *Wisdom of Ben Sira* (or *Sirach*) and the *Wisdom of Solomon*.

The development and use of various methods of biblical interpretation is a continually unfolding story of great fascination. In his recent book *The Bible As It Was*, Kugel lists four assumptions about the Hebrew Bible to which Jews and Jewish Bible interpreters adhered:

1. "The Bible is a fundamentally cryptic document." This is immediately evident to any serious reader. For example, there must be some hidden meaning behind the two versions of Creation in Genesis that apparently do not agree with each other—at least not on the surface.

2. "Scripture constitutes one great Book of Instruction, and as such is a fundamentally *relevant* text."

3. "Scripture is perfect and perfectly harmonious." This concept relates to the first in that apparent mistakes or discrepancies disappear if the Bible is properly interpreted.

4. "Scripture is somehow divinely sanctioned, of divine provenance, or divinely inspired." This too is related to assumptions one and three. God does not make mistakes.[21]

But Bibles are not interpreted without method—there are precedents, rules, and procedures. This is true for Jewish interpretations of the Hebrew Bible and for Christian interpretations of both Old and New Testaments. Biblical interpretation is often called *exegesis*, from the Greek meaning to "lead out" or "guide." There are important parallels between the Jewish and Christian policies of exegesis. The basic approach is the use of the "proof-text." This is the appeal to authority; in this context, it is an appeal to scripture. A statement is made and then supported by citing a biblical passage on the same subject. Simply put, murder is wrong because the Sixth Commandment in Exodus 20:13 says, "Thou shalt not kill." This principle is the backbone of Christian exegesis and also of the Talmud. Biblical exegesis also uses a more indirect method of proof, the allegory. This is hardly a new method of interpretation; rather, it was used by the Greeks and Romans, particularly when dealing with myths from other cultures in the writings of Homer and Virgil.

The authors of the NT used allegory freely. Paul, for example, begins an important passage with, "This is an allegory" (Gal 4:22-6). He then goes on to say that Ishmael, child of the slave Hagar, stands for the Jews; Isaac, child of the free woman Sarah, stands for Christianity. (That this allegorical interpretation would not be acceptable to Jews underscores the many problems that arise when scripture is handled in this way.) Then, in 1 Corinthians 9:9, Paul quotes Deuteronomy 25:4: Moses says, "You shall not muzzle an ox when it treads out the grain" and Paul comments that Moses implied the ox is entitled to gain some benefit from its work on the harvest by eating a little of it. Paul continues, "Is it for oxen that God is concerned? Does he not speak entirely for our sake?" Thus Paul indicates that God, in this case speaking through Moses, also uses allegory.

But Paul does not use allegory systematically. For this we turn to Philo of Alexandria (c. 20 B.C.E.-50 C.E.), a Hellenized Jew with both Jewish and Christian intellectual offspring. Philo was attracted greatly to non-literal interpretations of the Hebrew scriptures, at least partially because he found it impossible to understand some of the laws (for instance, "an eye for an eye") in a literal sense. Some of his methodology probably derived from his admitted hero Plato, in that he presented a three-fold set of interpretations—the literal, the moral, and the spiritual—corresponding to the Platonic categories of body, soul, and spirit.[22] Philo's methods also included close attention to numerology and etymology.[23] Numbers were of great symbolic importance to Philo and other Greek philosophers such as

---

[21] Kugel, *Bible As It Was*, 17-23. It will become clear as we proceed that Christian interpreters agreed implicitly and explicitly with these assumptions.

[22] "Philo" in *New Catholic Encyclopedia*, 11:287-91.

[23] Beryl Smalley, *The Study of the Bible in the Middle Ages* (Notre Dame IN: University of Notre Dame Press, 1964) 5.

Pythagoras, who believed numbers underlay the structure of the universe. Thus, Philo says the world was created in six days because six is the perfect number, being both the sum and the product of its first three units (one, two, and three).[24]

The Fathers of the Church carried this allegorical tradition forward. As mentioned previously, the OT was considered prophecy by many of the chief authorities of the early Church such as Origen, Novatian, Lactantius, Athanasius, and Eusebius. But this same Old Testament they considered to be holy because it prophesied Christ included many passages they did not think pertained to Christians. What was to be done with them? One popular reasoning was that the *moral* demands in the Jewish Bible applied to Christians ("the New Israel"), but the Jewish *rituals* were to be interpreted allegorically.

Philo's technique was introduced into the mainstream of Christian exegesis by Origen and his mentor, Clement of Alexandria.[25] Origen (c. 185-254) was a great scholar and a prodigious writer from Alexandria who attempted to reconcile Greek philosophy with Christianity. He knew some Hebrew, although he undoubtedly mainly consulted the Septuagint and Jewish authorities. Since he preached frequently, he found the allegorical approach convenient not only for interpreting the liturgy, but for polemic purposes as well.

---

[24] Jewish mystical and Kabbalistic thinking also uses numerical symbolism, whereby each letter in the Hebrew alphabet is assigned a numerical value. The study of numbers, letters, and words in this context is called *gematria*.

[25] R. P. C. Hanson, "Biblical Exegesis in the Early Church," in *Cambridge History of the Bible*, eds. Peter R. Ackroyd and C. F. Evans, vol. 1 (Cambridge: Cambridge University Press, 1970) 412-53.

[26] Smalley, *Study of the Bible*, 27-28.

[27] Jaroslav Pelikan, *The Christian Tradition*, vol. 3 of *The Growth of Medieval Theology (600-1300)* (Chicago: University of Chicago Press, 1978) 40.

[28] Michael Fishbane, "Jewish Biblical Exegesis: Presuppositions and Principles," in Frederick E. Greenspahn, ed. *Scripture in the Jewish and Christian Traditions*, (Denver: University of Denver, 1982) 92-110. See also Edward L. Greenstein, "Medieval Bible Commentaries," chap. 4 in Barry W. Holtz, ed. *Back to the Sources*, (New York, Summit Books, 1984). Geza Vermes, *Cambridge History*, 220, mentions that the four pathways described above were derived using various sets of "rules" of interpretation (*middot*). Hillel had seven rules. By the early second century, Rabbi Ishmael had expanded them to 13, and later they were enlarged to 32.

[29] Smalley, *Study of the Bible*, 28.

Four Meanings of Christian Scripture. Whether Origen or St. John Cassian or someone else is responsible for expanding the three-fold matrix into a four-fold one is not important.[26] By the time of Augustine and Gregory the Great, exegesis was partitioned into the one literal and three spiritual meanings for most texts. The three spiritual meanings are the theological (or allegorical), the moral (or tropological), and the anagogic (or eschatological, which deals with "last things," such as death, judgment, and immortality). In time, the three spiritual senses came to be compared with faith, charity, and hope. Thus the four principles of Christian exegesis can be outlined as follows:

- Literal meaning
- Spiritual meanings
  1. Theological (allegorical) meaning = faith
  2. Moral (tropological) meaning = charity
  3. Anagogic (eschatological) meaning = hope[27]

Four Meanings of the Torah. It is of considerable interest that Jews had developed a similar method for interpreting the Torah. The origin of this four-fold system, too, is hidden in the distant past, but the path is as follows:

Peshat—the literal meaning of the text, "as determined within the parameters of historical, literal, and linguistic content."
Remez—the allusive meanings; what the text hints at; its similarities to or connections with other texts
Derash—the moral lessons
Sod—the "secret" meaning or mystical interpretation[28]

Having outlined the principles of Christian and Jewish biblical exegesis, it is time to list examples. Smalley quotes, and I here paraphrase, St. John Cassian on the four-fold meaning of "Jerusalem." On the literal level, Jerusalem is the city of the Jews. Allegorically, it is the Church of Christ. On the moral or tropological level, it is the soul of man. Anagogically, or eschatologically, it is the Heavenly City of

God.[29] The Jewish method can be shown by interpreting the scene in which Abraham meets the three men by the tree of Mamre (Gen 18:2-8). It was hot; Abraham greeted them and offered them a place to rest and wash, saying, "And let me fetch a morsel of bread that you may refresh yourselves." He asked Sarah to prepare a whole meal, "and he waited on them under the tree as they ate." This passage, with the section following in which the birth of Isaac is promised, has been interpreted by Chaim Pearl using the four-fold method. According to Pearl, the literal meaning (*peshat*) is the text as it stands, but even that raises questions such as these: How did the men just appear?; Why didn't Abraham see them approach? The allusion in the text (*remez*) concerns a host's proper behavior, meaning that Abraham probably said a blessing over the food. The moral meaning (*derash*) might be that while Abraham said he would give them a *morsel* of bread, he provided an entire meal. It is good to do more than you promise. The secret or mystical meaning (*sod*) might suggest the morsel of bread is the Torah, the staff of Jewish life.[30]

The Christians were very partial to this text as well. We will see a mosaic depicting it later in this chapter. They, of course, interpret the story quite differently aside from its literal sense. Theological interpretations include the idea that the three men were actually angels who mysteriously appeared and prophesied that Abraham and Sarah would have a child, or that the morsel of bread prefigures the Last Supper. A Christian moral interpretation might be that it was by divine intent that Abraham and Sarah gave birth to Isaac, and hence to the succession of ancestors leading up to the Messiah. The eschatological meaning is that the three men indicate the Trinity and so the scene implies redemption through Christianity.

---

30 Chaim Pearl, *Rashi* (New York: Grove Press, 1988) 26.

31 A number of books deal with typology, including James Hall, *Dictionary of Subjects and Symbols in Art* (New York: Harper and Row, 1932); Gertrude Schiller, *Iconography of Christian Art*, vol. 2, *The Passion of Jesus Christ* (London: Lund Humphries Ltd., 1971); Gaston Duchet-Suchaux and Michel Pastoreau, *The Bible and the Saints* (Paris: Flammarion, 1994); and Marc Thoumieu, *Dictionnaire d'Iconographie Romane* (Zodiaque, 1996).

The beauty of these very flexible methods of biblical exegesis is that there is a world of rich allusions and meanings hidden in text that might otherwise be considered dry, prosaic, even arcane. Whether these methods reflect the real intent of the Bible's authors and editors cannot be answered, and interpretations by these same methods can become rather far-fetched. What may be one person's nugget of hidden meaning can be the next person's extravagant fantasy.

Typology. The use of types, or symbols, should be considered as a form of exegesis used extensively in Christian art. This approach antedates Christianity but came into its full flowering in the Christian interpretations of the Old and New Testaments. (In the context of typology, the terms "Old" and "New" in reference to the scriptures are extremely apt.) Typology involves allusive thinking whereby a person in the Hebrew scriptures (the "type") is matched with a person in the New Testament (the "anti-type"). This mode of thinking was used by Paul when he referred to "Adam, who was a type of the one who was to come," meaning Jesus (Rom 5:14). Another common example casts Noah as type and Jesus as his anti-type. Noah and Jesus each play a central role in a cataclysm in human history involving divine intervention: Noah in the deluge, Jesus in the Christian Revelation. The typological approach exemplifies the essence of supersessionism.[31]

Typological analogies are not, however, limited to persons; they cover scenes, stories, rituals, even abstract concepts. One example is the story of the binding of Isaac. As Isaac carried the wood—the means of his impending sacrifice—up Mount Moriah (Gen 22:6), so did Jesus carry the wooden cross. Thus one frequently finds a depiction of Abraham and Isaac (type) in proximity or opposition to Jesus carrying the Cross (anti-type). (There are additional correspondences between these two scenes. One of the fascinations of early and medieval art for me is the challenge of uncovering these allegorical meanings.) Other examples abound: Moses crossing the Red Sea prefigures Christian baptism, while the meeting of Melchizedek and Abraham alludes to the Eucharist. Typology and allegory can easily be confused, as they are both non-literal methods of scripture interpretation. So, to clarify, allegory refers to hidden meanings in language, often in biblical discourse dealing with the fulfillment of predictions. Typology, on the other hand, concerns correspondences between persons and events, or to recurrent patterns in history.

Typology was a major approach used by Christian writers to show the correspondences between the two Scriptures. In fact, it was used so extensively that one can see why the Rabbis, upon learning the fantastical Christian interpretations of the Hebrew Bible, might be inclined to concentrate instead on the *peshat*—the literal meaning of scripture. Jews became disenchanted with the LXX translation of their own scriptures because of extensive Christian interpretation of it using allegory and typology. Gradually, Jewish commentators abandoned Philo's approach and adhered strictly to the text. Origen said the Jews were the masters of the literal interpretation of their own scriptures, but he did not mean this as a compliment. "If anyone wants to hear and understand these things strictly literally, he ought to address himself to the Jews rather than to the Christians, but if he wants to be a Christian and a disciple of Paul, let him hear him saying 'for the law is spiritual.'"[32]

---

[32] G. R. Evans, *The Language and Logic of the Bible: The Earlier Middle Ages* (Cambridge: Cambridge University Press, 1984) 115. For more about Origen, see Joseph W. Trigg, *Origen, the Bible and Philosophy in the Third-century Church* (Atlanta: John Knox Press, 1983) 125.

[33] Trying to find the origins of images said to come from the *Glossa Ordinaria* is frustrating. Of course there is no single standard edition, since it was a series of commentaries and comments upon commentaries and I have not found a good edited rendition. See also M. Gibson, "Carolingian Glossed Psalters," in Richard Gameson, ed., *The Early Medieval Bible: Its Production, Decoration and Use* (Cambridge: Cambridge University Press, 1994) 78-100.

[34] I have not seen it analyzed in detail, but there is an interesting similarity between the GO and the Talmud. In each, the text commented upon appears in the center in larger type, with commentaries grouped around it. See Adam Steinzaltz, *The Talmud, A Reference Guide* (New York: Random House, 1989); and Christopher DeHamel, *A History of Illuminated Manuscripts* (Boston: David R. Godine, 1986).

[35] See G. R. Evans, *Language and Logic* and B. Smalley, *Study of the Bible* and Margaret T. Gibson, "The Twelfth Century Glossed Bible." In *Studia Patristica*, vol 23 (Leeuven: Peeters Press, 1989) 232-44.

[36] E. Male, *The Gothic Image, Religious Art in France of the Thirteenth Century* (New York: Harper, 1958/1910) 141.

The Glossa Ordinaria. One of the richest sources of typological thinking is the Biblical *Glossa Ordinaria* (GO). This does not refer to a particular book, but rather to a large number of Biblical commentaries developed in Europe throughout the Middle Ages.[33] The comments, or glosses, were made either in the margins of the Bibles or interlinearly.[34] The GO gathered popularity in the eleventh and twelfth centuries and perhaps the first authoritative compilation was made under Anselm of Laon (d. 1119) and his pupil Gilbert the Universal, or perhaps by Hugh of St. Victor.[35] Because of the aggregate nature of the GO, it is generally impossible to determine when (over a span of perhaps 600 years) or by whom a certain typological analogy was made. The scholar Emile Mâle refers to the GO for a number of typologies, such as the binding of Isaac (Gen 22). Abraham represents God the Father; Isaac, God the Son. The two servants represent the divisions of Jews (Israel and Judah); the ass, the Synagogue.[36] Many of the typological analogies in the GO found their way into the visual arts.

By the third, fourth, and fifth centuries, non-verbal and non-literal interpretations of the OT were common. The use of allegory and typology was widespread and served the supersessionist agenda of finding Jewish prophecies for Christian happenings. The visual translation of typological and allegorical thinking is beautifully shown in the characteristic public and quasi-public art of the early Christian period, sarcophagi and mosaics.

Roman, Christian, and Jewish Sarcophagi

Among the most magnificent examples of early Christian art are the carved marble sarcophagi of the third to sixth centuries. The styles and techniques used on sarcophagi are the heritage of the outstanding tradition of Greek and Roman sculpture. A superb example of free-standing Roman-Christian sculpture is, once again, the Good Shepherd (plate 1). By contrast, sarcophagi were sculpted in bas-relief or high relief. Thanks to the lasting nature of stone, as well as to the locations of the burials, a relatively large number of these have survived in good to outstanding condition. Used only by the wealthy, some sarcophagi were deposited in catacombs, others came to lie in churches and cathedrals, and still others were eventually dismantled to provide large decorated marble slabs for church walls. An astonishing trove of sarcophagi was found piled up in the necropolis of the Alyscamps at Arles, but they also have been found throughout the Western Empire. The largest collections are in the Vatican Museum in Rome and in the Archaeological Museum in Arles.

Burying the dead in stone coffins was, of course, not a Christian innovation. There had long existed a rich Mediterranean tradition of decorated sarcophagi and ossuaries (although, of course, some were covered only with abstract designs and many others were absolutely plain). These illustrated sarcophagi provide beautiful illustrations of the transition from pagan to Christian artwork and iconography. (We even have a small number of similar Jewish sarcophagi for compari-

FIG 3-1. The Dogmatic Sarcophagus, marble. Fourth century. Pio Christian Museum, Rome. (See text for a description of the scenes.)

son; see below.) Marble sarcophagi were used by the Greeks and Romans. Favorite themes were the hunt, military battles, scenes of the pagan gods—particularly Dionysus and the Four Seasons. Portraits of the deceased were often placed centrally on the front. Christians adapted these conventions to their own purposes. It is fascinating to see the metamorphosis of a cupid, busy harvesting the grapes for the wine god Bacchus, into a Christian cherub. Similarly, it is difficult to distinguish the Christian Good Shepherd, his sheep over his shoulder (figure 2-9), from the Roman (perhaps also Christian?) Good Shepherd (plate 1). There is, too, a rich legacy of Jewish and Christian Biblical stories, almost as if scenes from the catacombs had been transferred to marble.

Biblical Scenes on Christian Sarcophagi. The scenes depicted on sarcophagi cover a range of OT and NT images, the choice of which is not always obvious. Prominent images are Christ enthroned or entering Jerusalem, the three Magi, the raising of Lazarus, the kiss of Judas, and the arrest of Paul. Sometimes they seem to lead the viewer to read theological motifs into the entire sarcophagus. One magnificent specimen in the Vatican, "The Dogmatic Sarcophagus" (figure 3-1), seems to do just that. In the upper register, reading from the left, we see the Creation of Man with a tiny supine Adam and an equally small standing Eve. What is unusual here is that the Creator appears to be *three* male figures (the Trinity), making this a uniquely Christian interpretation of an OT story. The Deity appears between another Adam and Eve pair, this one life-size, showing them to be sources of sustenance (grain and a lamb, which also symbolize Cain and Abel). Meanwhile the serpent, entwined around a tree, looks on. In the clipeus (central medallion) is an unfinished portrait of the deceased. To the right of the medallion is Christ with loaves and fish and, on the far right, the resurrection of Lazarus.

The bottom register shows the Holy Family—Joseph behind Mary and the infant Jesus—with the three Magi in their Phrygian caps. Next to that, Jesus heals the man blind from birth. The scene of Daniel in the lions' den is central; to the right Jesus prophesies to a doubtful Peter (whose hand strokes his beard) that Peter will deny Him three times. Further to the right is the arrest of Paul or Peter, and at the right edge, Moses strikes the rock for water. Thus we have OT and NT scenes side by side: scenes of deliverance, images of the Passion, miracles, and stories of the Creation, all laid out before us.

Some sarcophagi also depict scenes from the Jewish scriptures, such as that of Adam and Eve, the binding of Isaac, Moses crossing the Red Sea, Moses receiving the Law, Jonah and the great fish, Elijah in his chariot, the three Hebrews with the statue of Nebuchadnezzar, and Susannah and the Elders. As in the catacombs, many are either deliverance stories or allusions to Jewish versus Christian dispensations. Some images are more difficult to decipher, and at least one recurring image remains ambiguous (to us, but perhaps not to early Christians). This mysterious scene shows a man striking a rock to get water, seemingly an obvious reference to Moses (Ex 17:6; Num 20:10). There was, however, also a story about Peter's miraculously obtaining water for his jailers, a story apparently lost. Further, Peter might be alluded to in this image because his name means "rock." Jesus said, "You are Peter, and on this rock I will build my church" (Mt 16:18). This episode, which designates Peter as first head and pope of

FIG 3-2. The Two Brothers Sarcophagus, marble. Fourth century. Vatican. The scenes on the top, beginning from the left, depict the following scenes: the raising of Lazarus, Peter's denial, Moses receives the Law from the hand of God, the two deceased men (in the *clipeus*), Abraham is stayed by the hand of God from sacrificing Isaac, Pilate washes his hands. On the lower level we see Moses-Peter strike the rock for water, the arrest of Peter, Daniel in the lions' den, Peter's receiving the Law, the healing of the blind, and the miracle of the loaves and fishes.

the Church, also alludes to some interesting linguistic twists. Peter's given name was Simon. In John 1:42, Jesus calls Simon *Cephas*, "rock" in Aramaic. In Greek, the language of the Gospels, "rock" is *petra*; it becomes *petrus* in Latin. As is the case here, it is often not clear whether Peter or Moses is the man striking the rock for water, so the image is often called "Peter-Moses" to cover both possibilities. This very ambiguity highlights the intimate relations between the two scriptures. Another parallel between Moses and Peter will be seen in the Two Brothers Sarcophagus, described later in this chapter.

The forms and styles of sarcophagus decoration are most properly the subject of a more in-depth tome of art history, but there are some general design characteristics which bear mentioning. The scenes are always spread horizontally along the front, though some sarcophagi have scenes on the ends and lids, as well. On some sarcophagi the images exist in two registers, one above the other; on others, all the scenes occupy only one register. Some sarcophagi have a large central medallion, often shaped like a shell and usually containing a portrait of the deceased person or couple. Occasionally the shell contains an image not of the deceased, but of Christ or the Chi-Rho monogram that represents Him, or, in the case of a Jewish sarcophagus, a menorah (see below).

Close scrutiny of the scenes portrayed on disparate sarcophagi often reveals recurring themes. For instance, the sarcophagus of the Two Brothers (figure 3-2), now at the Vatican, which takes its name from the very touching medallion portrait of two men, and the sarcophagus of Adelphia, now in Siracusa, Sicily, show the same two scenes flanking the central medallion. On the left Moses reaches up to receive the Law from the hand of God; on the right the hand of God reaches out to stay Abraham as he is about to sacrifice Isaac. There are at least two possibilities to explain the similarities in the two sarcophagi. One is that the sarcophagus makers followed a well-known pattern that indicated which image belonged in which place, perhaps based upon pedagogy or iconography. Another possibility (not opposed to the first) is that large workshops pre-made standard models of tombs with the medallion left blank, ready to be carved. When the eventual occupant was (or occupants were) identified, the medallion was custom carved to represent him or her (or them). Perhaps supporting this idea is the observation that the two sarcophagi's medallion fluting is precisely the same. Nevertheless, many of the scenes are not the same and there are subtle dissimilarities between the styles of carving seen in the figures.

The Two Brothers Sarcophagus shows, in addition, two scenes which certainly exemplify *Concordia*. On the upper register, left of the central roundel, Moses reaches up to receive the Law from the hand of God. Below the central picture is a scene called "traditio legis," in which Jesus symbolically confers upon Peter the leadership of the Church by handing him a scroll. Thus we have another image, like that of the rock, in which Moses and Peter occupy analogous positions as the recipients of the OT and NT traditions, respectively. Moses is the type and Peter is the anti-type

Jewish Sarcophagi. Jewish ossuaries are not uncommon in the Holy Land.[37] Most frequently they are plain or have rosettes carved

FIG 3-3. Jewish sarcophagus, marble. Catacomb Vigna Randanini, Rome. Depicts a menorah in the clipeus medallion, surrounded by the seasons.

on the sides; occasionally they bear incised inscriptions. One ossuary from the Via Torlonia catacomb is mostly plain, with a handsome seven-branched menorah in relief.[38] More informative for us is a sarcophagus from the Vigna Randanini catacomb (figure 3-3), obviously a ready-made object with pagan scenes. The central medallion was left blank while the winged figures holding it, as well as other figures symbolizing the seasons, were carved. Three putti tread grapes under the medallion, in whose center one finds a menorah, instead of a bust of the deceased, as one might expect to find on a Christian or pagan sarcophagus.

The Sarcophagus of Junius Bassus. The best preserved, best studied, and, possibly, most magnificent early Christian sarcophagus held the mortal remains of one Junius Bassus, prefect (mayor) of Rome who died in 359 C.E. His elaborate sarcophagus (figure 3-4; plate 2), now in the Vatican Museum, has ten major scenes arranged in two tiers on the front. A recent book by Elizabeth S. Malbon, *The Iconography of the Sarcophagus of Junius Bassus* (Princeton UP, 1990), contains an exhaustive analysis of this superb artifact. There are four scenes from the OT and six from either the NT or from stories of the apostles. Reading left to right on the upper register we see Abraham and Isaac, the arrest of Peter, Christ enthroned (central), the arrest of Christ, and his judgment by Pilate. On the lower register we see the unhappy Job with two friends, Adam and Eve with the serpent, Christ's entering Jerusalem (center), Daniel in the lions' den, and the arrest of Paul. So a diagram of these scenes' arrangement would look thus.

Abraham and Isaac	Arrest of Peter	Christ Enthroned	Arrest of Christ	Pilate's Judgment
Job & Friends	Adam and Eve	Christ Enters Jerusalem	Daniel in the Lions' Den	Arrest of Paul

[37] Jews in antiquity buried their dead in two phases. First, the body was wrapped and left to decay. After one year during which the flesh decomposed, the bones were collected for the secondary burial, often in stone caskets called *ossuaries*. See Hershel Shanks, *Jerusalem, An Archaeological Biography* (New York: Random House, 1995) 115-16, 169-70.
[38] Goodenough, *Jewish Symbols*, 3: figure 8-18.

FIG 3-4. Sarcophagus of Junius Bassus, marble, 359 C.E. Vatican. (See text for a description of the scenes.)

Typologists and iconographers have had a typological feast with this tomb and its ten scenes (plus other little scenes of lambs in the spandrels above the columns of the lower tier), but even the amateur can appreciate the two central images of Christ. On the upper register, He sits on the throne (of both Roman Empire and Heavenly Kingdom); below and center, He enters Jerusalem triumphant. These two correspond vertically. On either side of Christ enthroned, we see two arrests: that of Jesus on the right, mirrored by the arrest of his chief disciple Peter on the left. On the lower register, flanking Jesus on his donkey, are parallel deliverance scenes: the Garden of Eden (Christ delivers Christians from Original Sin) on the left, and Daniel on the right.

All these pairs are examples of balancing images within one or another scripture. When an OT scene or figure is the type of a NT anti-type, the correspondences may not be quite as clear to us, though we must remember that would not necessarily have been the case for early Christians or Jews. On the upper tier, the binding of Isaac (left) is paired with the judgment by Pilate (right). In later centuries the binding of Isaac will be paired instead with the Crucifixion, but at this stage, the Crucifixion had not yet been incorporated into Christian iconography. The binding of Isaac balances the judgment by Pilate since the latter can be interpreted to represent the imminent Passion of Christ and subsequent Crucifixion, which were the consequences of Pilate's decision.[39]

Early Italian Churches and Mosaics

A number of very early churches (often much restored) still stand in Italy. A large part of their iconographic interest derives from mosaics, the use of which is a direct legacy of the great Roman mosaic tradition. Magnificent mosaics—many of them are still remarkably fresh—adorned both public and private buildings throughout the Empire.[40]

Santa Sabina. For more than one and one-half millennia, the Church of Santa Sabina has watched over the river Tiber from its place on the edge of the Aventine Hill. Today the Aventino, one of the famed seven hills of Rome, is a quiet residential neighborhood. Just down the hill are the ruins of the Circus Maximus, racetrack of the caesars. When Santa Sabina was consecrated in 432 C.E., church and circus (recently restored by Constantine) competed for the attention, if not the very soul, of the Romans. The Church won—at least for a while. Santa Sabina is a large basilica, meaning that instead of the usual cross shape, it is laid out as a long hall with an aisle down

---

[39] For more ingenious pairings and interpretations of the remaining scenes, see Malbon. Such efforts are beyond my scope, but they demonstrate the intricacies and fascination of typological exegesis.

[40] Many books illustrate Roman mosaics. Particularly interesting and beautiful are early Christian mosaics from Jordan, which adapted Roman styles. See Michele Piccirillo, *The Mosaics of Jordan* (Amman, Jordan: American Center of Oriental Research, 1993).

either side and a central, rounded apse. It has been beautifully restored and it holds two sets of images of great interest.

The first images of note are found when you enter through a set of large wooden doors on the west facade. They contain a number of bas relief panels that have been well preserved by a porch overhanging the doors. The panels show two sets of scenes, one from the OT and one from the NT. The doors are famous because one panel (now located at the upper left) shows what is believed to be the oldest image of the Crucifixion (figure 3-5). The panel depicts Christ with one thief on each side.[41] In this early depiction, though Christ is shown with arms outstretched as if he were on a cross, the cross itself is not shown. The rest of the door is also of interest because of its scriptural scenes. Those from the Hebrew scriptures include many featuring Moses: receiving the Law from the hand of God, the miracle of the quail and the manna, striking the rock to get water, the Burning Bush, crossing the Red Sea, and so forth. In addition, there is a small scene from the Apocryphal portion of Daniel in which an angel carries Habakkuk by his hair to enable him to feed Daniel in the lions' den.

Most of the images, however, are from the life of Jesus, including several miracles, His denial by Peter, His appearances before Caiphas and Pilate, the Crucifixion, and the Ascension. The panels have been moved around so we cannot be certain of their original order or, consequently, whether there were deliberate "Old" and "New" pairings. The best example of such parallel imagery may be two longitudinal panels now located side by side. One shows two miracles of Christ, the multiplication of the loaves (in Matthew, Mark, and Luke) and the turning of water into wine (John 2:1-11). The adjacent panel shows

---

41 The image of Christ on the Cross and the veneration of the fragments of the True Cross became prominent in the fourth century. The growing influence of these may be traced to the expedition of Constantine's devout mother Helena to the Holy Land, where she believed she found the True Cross of the Crucifixion.

42 Richard Krautheimer, *Rome: Portrait of a City, 313-1308* (Princeton: Princeton University Press, 1980) 45, figure 39.

Moses receiving the Law and the miracles of the quail, manna, and water from the rock.

Inside the church, on the inner wall of the west facade, are two mosaic female figures. One is titled *Ecclesia ex Gentibus*; the other is *Ecclesia ex Circumcisione*. Now many people think that *ecclesia* is Latin for "church," but actually it is Greek for "assembly." Over the years it was assumed into Latin and came to mean church. These female figures, "Church among the Gentiles" and "Church among the Jews," portray the new Christianity, book in hand, teaching the main religion of the empire to two groups, the pagans and the Jews. [42] There seems to be no animosity. Both images appear again across Rome in the apse

FIG 3-5. Detail, door of church of S. Sabina, Rome. Fifth century. Christ is crucified between the two thieves, believed to be the earliest depiction of the Crucifixion. (It is interesting that the crosses are not shown.)

of the church of Santa Pudenziana, where each woman is placing a halo-shaped wreath on the head of an apostle.

Santa Maria Maggiore. Immediately after the Council of Ephesus declared Mary the Mother of God, Pope Sixtus II (432-440) remodeled and redecorated this church and dedicated it to her as Santa Maria Maggiore. Therefore it is a close contemporary of both Santa Sabina and of nearby Santa Pudenziana. It has been redone many times since then and so represents an architectural palimpsest with its neoclassical exterior, nave featuring a parade of granite columns recycled from old Roman temples, twelfth-century Cosmatic floor, and Renaissance-style coffered ceiling.

We are here to look at a series of small mosaics high up on the sides of the nave. Originally there were forty-two, of which twenty-seven remain, all much restored. These comprise four cycles of scenes from the lives of Abraham, Jacob, Moses, and Joshua. Many of them show two scenes in one frame (they are two-tiered). The upper and lower scenes are related, exemplifying the "simultaneous" method of presentation.[43] The Abraham and Jacob series is on one side of the nave, comprising chronological, but not complete, life stories of the protagonists. On the other side are scenes from the life of Moses, with those of Joshua's following directly. These mosaics in the nave,

---

[43] The "simultaneous" method of presentation is discussed in Kurt Weitzmann, *Illustrations in Roll and Codex* (Princeton: Princeton University Press, 1947).

[44] Processions as part of religious services are an ancient practice, but little is written about them. Certainly, though, they are important in the Church today, so there is no reason to doubt that they were during the Middle Ages. While we have virtually no descriptions of processions, we have elaborate processional crosses which were carried through churches.

[45] An *octateuch* is a section of the OT containing the Five Books of Moses (the Pentateuch), plus the books of Joshua, Judges, and Ruth. Octateuchs were often profusely illustrated, having over 300 pictures. Although the extant octateuchs are Byzantine and date no earlier than the tenth century, still their existence reflects the mystery of the lost illustrated Bible discussed in chap. 2. See J. Lowden, *The Octateuchs—A Study in Byzantine Manuscript Illustration* (University Park PA: Pennsylvania State University Press, 1992) 95-104.

[46] Jean Paul Richter and A. Cameron Taylor, *The Golden Age of Classic Christian Art* (London: Duckworth & Co., 1904).

[47] Morey, *Medieval Art*, 149.

[48] Andre Grabar, *Christian Iconography. A Study of Its Origins* (Princeton: Princeton University Press, 1968) 46.

together with those on the arch and in the apse, rate three stars (highest recommendation) in the Italian edition of the *Michelin Guide* ("worth a journey"), a well-deserved award.

Before discussing the iconologic significance of two outstanding panels, a word about the general layout is in order. These OT mosaics are arranged along the sides of the nave so that, as the worshipper or celebrant of the mass walks down the nave towards the altar, he or she literally moves through the OT into the NT, illustrated in the very place where Mass—the central mystery of the Christian faith—is celebrated. Correspondingly, the mosaics on the arch and in the apse, near the main altar, deal not with OT prophecies, but with NT concerns: the life of Christ and the glorification of Mary, to whom the church is dedicated. We should also not forget the church was the scene of frequent processions that began at the entrance of the church—or perhaps elsewhere in the city, but that always marched into the church.[44] Their progress from the Old to the New dispensation would not have been lost on the moving ensemble.

The Santa Maria Maggiore mosaics have received a great deal of attention from art historians, and deservedly so. That the experts do not agree on all points is to be expected. Morey believes an illustrated OT must have been a model for the mosaics. Richter and Taylor, on the other hand, who in their 1904 classic devote over 400 pages to this church alone, doubt the images are derived from an illustrated Bible—whether one of the Octateuchs[45] or a complete LXX.[46] Morey calls Richter's and Taylor's dating of the mosaics "an unfortunate attempt,"[47] but commends their diligent analyses of the imagery—up to a point. That point does not include their interpretation of the series as an allegory of Church versus Synagogue (an interpretation I believe is correct.)

As Early Christian and medieval art matured, pictures came to be regarded as either descriptive (literal) or symbolic (allegorical). Let us examine two celebrated mosaics on the right wall of the nave, asking in part whether they are strictly descriptive or typologically symbolic. Grabar puts them into the descriptive category but, as we will see, the distinction between descriptive and symbolic is not always clear.[48]

One mosaic (plate 3) shows the meeting of Melchizedek and Abraham, an encounter very briefly described in the Bible (Gen 14:18-20). Abraham and his men have just returned from rescuing Lot and his family from capture. Abraham is met by Melchizedek, a priest of Salem whose name in Hebrew means "The Righteous King." Melchizedek blesses Abraham and gives him bread and wine. Abraham, in turn, gives the priest "a tenth of everything," that is, a tithe.[49] Abraham and his men are dressed Roman-style, an artistic convention widely used in European art until the Renaissance.[50]

A number of things need to be said about the significance of this episode. Melchizedek is not a Jew, as there were no Jewish priests at that time, so he must be a Gentile. Indeed, he is often called the orig-

---

[49] Who gave what to whom? Hebrew is a very compact language that, for this very reason, sometimes is ambiguous. In this case, the Hebrew actually translates as "he gave him a tenth." Who were "he" and "him" must be inferred. The passage usually has been interpreted to mean Abraham gave the tithe to Melchizedek, perhaps in return for the blessing, bread, and wine.

[50] Historical figures were arrayed in the dress of the time in which they were painted, rather than that of the time in which they lived (should there even have been knowledge of such garb).

[51] See Fred L. Horton, *The Melchizedek Tradition: A Critical Examination of the Sources to the Fifth Century A.D. and the Epistle to the Hebrews* (London: Cambridge University Press, 1976).

[52] The relationship between Melchizedek and Abraham is also grafted onto the *Verus Israel* theme. As Ambrose said, "the mysteries are anterior to those of the Jews. If the Jews go back to Abraham, the figure of our sacraments came before, when the high priest Melchizedek came before Abraham the victor and offered him bread and wine. Who had the bread and wine? It was not Abraham but

Melchizedek. He it is, then, who is the author of the sacraments." Quoted in Jean Danielou, *The Bible and the Liturgy* (Notre Dame IN: University of Notre Dame Press, 1956/1951).

[53] I do not expect the average medieval Christian would have understood even half of this detailed explanation. How then, besides the most enlightened clergy or scholars, might anyone have appreciated it? There were written pilgrims' guides in the Middle Ages, but those that have survived are very sketchy and do not include material this detailed. I have often wondered whether, upon approaching the church, the visitor would be greeted by a guide who offered (for a fee?) to show the beauties of the sanctuary. Perhaps the pilgrim, traversing the byways of Europe, church to church, brought their own guides from home. Many scholars speculate on medieval guided tours. The same idea of the guided tour was put forth by French writer Paul Claudel in 1937. Medieval authorities Louis Grodecky and Catherine Brisac, however, said "this is simply pure fantasy" in *Gothic Stained Glass, 1200-1300* (Ithaca NY: Cornell University Press, 1984) 24. Perhaps, perhaps not.

inal "Righteous Gentile" because he blessed the Jews as represented by Abraham. It is not clear where Salem was, nor what "Salem" means, though general consensus is that it comes from *shalom* ("peace," as in Hebrews 7:2). Melchizedek's offerings of bread and wine can be considered to symbolize both their use in the Jewish Sabbath observance and their central position of the Eucharist (Christian Communion). In addition to these two men, a third, very important figure appears in the upper center of the mosaic. This is the image of Christ (some say the *logos*), His outstretched right hand pointing to Melchizedek.

If this image of the Deity were omitted, the mosaic could be taken for a literal description of the scene without any Christian implications. But since Genesis does not mention the Deity in this scene, His addition must be significant. The outstretched right hand of God (or Christ) signifies divine election, whereas such approval for Melchizedek is not implied in the Hebrew Scriptures. After this brief passage in Genesis, Melchizedek disappears, to be mentioned only once more in Psalm 110. In the NT, the author of Hebrews regardless pays a great deal of attention to Melchizedek and Abraham, to the latter's detriment (Heb 7:1-28).[51] He likens the priest to Jesus, saying he became a priest not through the Law (of Moses), but directly through God, meaning Melchizedek lived under "Natural Law" (see chapter 2). And if there were any doubt about the position of the Jews versus that of the Gentiles, the situation here is made quite clear: as the author of Hebrews says, "It is beyond dispute that the inferior [Abraham] is blessed by the superior [Melchizedek]."[52] Thus this scene of Melchizedek and Abraham is an exquisite example of typological interpretation grafted onto simple description.[53]

Another famous scene in this cycle of mosaics is the story of Abraham and the three men from Genesis (plate 4). This episode has already been discussed in the section on exegesis, but there is more to be said. In this double scene we see Abraham three times, dressed, as in the Melchizedek episode, as a Roman gentleman. At the top, Abraham bows in greeting before his three visitors. Here, the Christian iconographer takes control of the story, depicting the three visitors as holy persons complete with halos, despite the fact that

Abraham had no idea of their divine status. Moreover, the central angel (for so it is) is surrounded by a mandorla, or glory (full body halo), so he must be a prefiguration of Christ. Indeed, the three haloed figures are considered by some to allude to the Trinity. In the lower scene, Abraham turns to Sarah at the left, telling her to hurry and make cakes for their guests. It is interesting that his right hand is raised to Sarah in the blessing position, perhaps alluding to the prophecy made by one of the angels of Isaac's improbable birth.

To the lower right, Abraham presents a platter with the calf, killed and cooked for the meal. There are three cakes on the table and a vase of wine on the ground. These are allusions not only to the bread and wine given to Abraham by Melchizedek, but also to the Eucharist. (A century later, the same scene is depicted with a small

FIG 3-6. Mosaic, Abel and Melchizedek. San Vitale, Ravenna. 547 C.E. On the central table are the wine and two loaves of bread. Abel holds his lamb while Melchizedek has another loaf of bread. These offerings are to God, whose hand points to the table. Moses (in the left corner) feeds his flock and above removes his sandals on Mt. Sinai. Isaiah is to the right.

cross on each cake [mosaic in San Vitale in Ravenna].) There is also a cross above the door of the house behind Sarah. While this obviously gives the scene a Christian flavor, it may have been added during a later restoration.

Not every mosaic panel in Santa Maria Maggiore is so rich in allusions. I have chosen two of the most remarkable to show the interweaving of Old and New Testament typology.

Ravenna. Rome was sacked by Alaric in 410 and again by Gaiseric in 455. It is amazing that during that period architectural masterpieces such as Santa Sabina and Santa Maria Maggiore were built. By the mid-fifth century, the artistic and political centers of the failing Roman Empire shifted to Ravenna. On the Adriatic Sea facing Constantinople, Ravenna was the seat of the last Roman emperor, Romulus Augustus, deposed in 476 C.E. The city, though itself subject to invasion, nonetheless inspired a remarkable series of buildings containing some of the greatest of all Western mosaics.[54]

It is interesting that there are far fewer artistic references to the Jewish versus the Christian Bible here than in Rome. Smalley remarks on this, attributing it to the great influence that Byzantine and Middle Eastern pictorial schemes had on Ravenna's art. In Byzantium, OT allegories were not as popular or as important as they were in the West. (This brings us to the iconoclast controversy, to which we will return in the next chapter.) The choir of San Vitale (dedicated in 547) does, however, contain magnificent figures from the Jewish Bible. We see an image of Moses and Elijah flanking that of the Ascension of Christ, as mentioned in the Gospels of Matthew, Mark, and, Luke. Of particular interest is a complex mosaic (figure 3-6). On the left margin is Moses tending his sheep (below) and taking off his sandals on Mt. Sinai (above). On the right is Isaiah carrying the book of his prophecy. Both men wear haloes. In the semicircle there is an altar with loaves of bread and a vase of wine. To the left of the table is Abel (without a halo), offering a lamb; on the right is not Cain, as might be expected, but a haloed Melchizedek, offering a loaf of bread. Since these two men were hardly contemporaries, the picture must be assumed symbolic rather than descriptive. Both men,

---

[54] See G. Bovini, *Ravenna* (New York: Harry N. Abrams, 1971).

then, are prefigurements of Christ. As in Santa Maria Maggiore, we see the hand of God at top center. This time, however, there is no reason for the hand to point to one or the other of these two equal Christ-figures and, indeed, it points straight down to the Eucharistic symbols on the altar.

There are also a few references to the OT in the Church of Santa Apollonare in Classe, a few miles from Ravenna. But, after a relatively brief eruption, there was a waning of monumental art in Ravenna over the next several centuries as the political and economic forces of the West declined. In fact, aside from a few outstanding manuscripts, such as the so-called Ashburnham Pentateuch (Italian, sixth or seventh century), much of the art produced was influenced by Constantinople. Artistically as well as intellectually, there was a low period in the West until the coming of Charlemagne.

Art and Jewish-Christian Relations, 313-800 C.E.

During the earlier part of this period, Christian public art flourished when the Empire flourished and languished when Rome lost its power and wealth. The audience for Christian art changed as well. The marble sarcophagi were public in the sense that they could be seen by any visitor to the catacombs, yet they were also private in that they belonged to the deceased and his family. (It is not clear when or if they were displayed in churches.) When we arrive at the doors of Santa Sabina and view the mosaics on the walls of the churches of S. M. Maggiore and San Vitale, placed above the entire congregation, we have entered the realm of public art. After this point in art history, much Christian art never left the public arena and never stopped

---

55 "The elder shall serve the younger" is somewhat at variance with *Verus Israel*. In the latter, the patriarchs and their families were the original Christians and were thus were not considered precursor Jews (versus later Christians), as happened in the "elder versus younger" approach.

56 Kurt Weitzmann, *Late Antique and Early Christian Book Illumination* (New York: George Braziller, 1977) figure 28.

57 Wolfgang Stechow, "Jacob Blessing the Sons of Joseph from Early Christian Times to Rembrandt," in Joseph Gutmann, ed., *No Graven Images; Studies in Art and the Hebrew Bible* (New York: KTAV Publishing House, 1971) 261-77.

preaching. One of the recurrent messages seen in such art is the triumph of the younger over the elder, which gave rise to some of the great images of supersessionism.

Elder versus Younger, A Supersessionist Theme. From ancient times and continuing today in certain societies, the advantage given the firstborn son is enormous. Often he receives the entire patrimony. In spite of the this widespread custom, it is noteworthy (yet not always understandable) that in a number of instances in the Bible, particularly in Genesis, it is the younger who receives preferment. Some examples already mentioned include the ascendancy of Isaac over the older Ishmael, Jacob over Esau, Rachel over Leah, and Ephraim over Menasseh. In Genesis 25:23, the Lord said to the pregnant Rebekah that in the case of her unborn twins, "The elder [Esau] shall serve the younger [Jacob]."

Early Christians took that quotation, and indeed the whole concept, to heart. Paul (Rom 9:10-12) repeats the OT phrase "The elder shall serve the younger" in the context of who comprises the True Israel. The phrase seems designed for supersessionist interpretation and indeed Genesis 25:23 is quoted by many writers, including Barnabas, Tertullian, Ambrose, and Augustine, to show that even the very first book of the Pentateuch predicts that Christianity, the younger religion, would rule over the older Judaism.[55] From the standpoint of artistic typology, the theme of the elder serving the younger is best seen in the story of Menasseh and Ephraim.

The image of Jacob's blessing his grandsons Menasseh and Ephraim exemplifies the progress of supersessionist thinking as it translated into art. The scene is described vividly in Genesis 48:12-22. The aging Jacob could not see, so his son Joseph placed the boys in such a way that the older Menasseh would receive the blessing from Jacob's right hand, and the younger Ephraim from his left. Inexplicably, at the last moment Jacob crosses his hands (the Bible is very clear on this point) and, in spite of Joseph's protestation, gives the preferred (right hand) blessing to the younger grandson. Jacob's reasoning is that although both boys will "become a people…yet his younger brother shall be greater than he."

Jacob's blessing is depicted repeatedly, starting as early as in the Via Latina catacombs.[56] As Stechow and others point out, in this image there are *two* supersessionist themes.[57] The first refers to the preference of the younger grandson over the older. The second concerns the crossing of Jacob's hands. Throughout the Middle Ages, this image was invoked as a type or prefigurement of the Cross of the Crucifixion, the central symbol of Christianity. Mâle traces the discussion of this image to the great encyclopedist Isidore of Seville (c. 560-636) and to the *Glossa Ordinaria*. He also notes that the figure of Jacob blessing his grandsons with crossed hands is seen in stained glass windows of Tours, LeMans, and Bourges.[58]

At Bourges, this image assumes great prominence. The New Covenant Window contains many OT types and NT anti-types. For instance, we see Isaac carrying the wood for his own sacrifice on Mt Moriah paired with Christ's carrying the wooden cross for his Crucifixion; Moses and the burning bush versus the Crucifixion; and Jonah's escaping the great fish paired with the Resurrection. But for a single image representing the New Covenant, the artist has chosen Jacob's blessing Ephraim and Menasseh. This scene crowns the very top and center of the window.[59]

Dealing with the Second Commandment

Chapters 1 and 2 briefly discussed the apparently *aniconic* phase of early Christianity. Discussion of this subject has been complicated by the discovery of the frescoes at Dura-Europos, where it seems the Jews abandoned their own Second Commandment in a virtual orgy of painted walls in the sanctuary of the synagogue itself. But, aside from a few figurative mosaics on the floors of Galilean synagogues through

---

[58] E. Mâle, *Gothic Image*, 142.

[59] The New Covenant Window at Bourges is illustrated in Wolfgang Kemp, *The Narratives of Gothic Stained Glass* (Cambridge: Cambridge University Press, 1997). It is curious, however, that even in such a detailed analysis of this window, this culminating

image is not discussed.

[60] Herbert J. Kessler, "Pictures Fertile With Truth. How Christians Managed to Make Images of God Without Violating the Second Commandment," *J.* 49/50 (Walters Art Gallery, 1991-1992): 53-65

the sixth century, it seems Judaism returned to observance of the Second Commandment.

The opposite is true of Christianity. It embraced religious imagery with passion, and it is pertinent to ask how this was justified. The Hebrew Bible contains 613 commandments and, while Christianity comfortably abandoned the majority of these, they did adhere to the Decalogue (otherwise known as the Ten Commandments). But even this statement must be qualified by saying Christianity adhered to only nine of them, seemingly ignoring the part of the Second Commandment that deals with "graven images."

The arguments by which Christian writers justified their use of religious imagery are often subtle. One approach was to claim that in a society such as that of early Judaism, surrounded by tribes of idol-worshippers, it was important that the Hebrew Deity be *invisible*, lest he become just another idol. The God of the Jews was *heard*, not seen. The new dispensation of Christianity, however, arrived via the Incarnation of God in Christ, *the invisible made visible*. So now the Deity could—no, must—be seen.

An even more subtle rationale is well delineated by Herbert Kessler, who argues that the change from the prohibition of images to the glorification of images, from the invisible Deity to God made manifest, is itself a powerful, if not decisive, indication of *supersessionism*. In other words, this abandonment by Christianity of the aniconic requirement of the Second Commandment exemplified the obsolescence of Judaism and symbolized the spiritual ascendancy of Christianity. In the Jewish faith, images were useless anyway because the Jews were blind to the truth—Christianity. But Kessler goes further, getting to the heart of the matter:

> As complicated as were these theological claims, set down in voluminous treatises, images succeeded not because of the theological logic but because of a mystery inherent in art itself. Pictures triumphed in Christian culture because of the magical facility of all art to transform stone and wood and pigments and glass and metal into living things.[60]

Art triumphed over doctrine in Christianity because of the ineffable power of the visible image to suggest and invoke the invisible.

Written and Pictorial Records: Jews versus Christians

To judge from the written word, Christian attitudes toward the Jews during this period had a supersessionist cast. The two scriptures were discussed at great lengths. There was Christian literature of the *Concordia* persuasion, but there may well have been more in the *Adversus Judaeos* stance. To be sure, vitriolic outbursts against the Jews such as the sermons of John Chrysostom were the exception, but the civil and ecclesiastic laws began to reflect a desire to restrict the range of activities permitted for Jewish members of society.

In art, Jewish-Christian relations were less adversarial. Rarely were Old and New Testament scenes directly compared for polemic reasons. The supersessionist position was more subtly expressed, as illustrated in the Santa Maria Maggiore scenes of Abraham and Melchizedek, or Abraham and the three angels. The same is true in the San Vitale mosaic, where Abel and Melchizedek receive equal emphasis. The *Adversus Judaeos* attitude was not yet blatantly displayed on church walls, though later it would be. Peering ahead to images featured in later chapters, it seems there was a "cultural lag" of several centuries between the writings and the images which succeeded them. The full power of supersessionism in art had yet to be seen.

4 | Brilliant Art in Carolingian and Ottonian Epochs (800-1500 C.E.)

Carolingian Times

Charlemagne became sole king of the Franks in 771, and reigned until 814. He inherited from his father, Pepin the Short, a Church-sanctified throne. His conquests led him to control most of Western Europe (except Britain, Ireland and most of Spain). He went to Rome in 800, actually to aid Pope Leo III, who in return crowned him "King of the Romans." Thus he appeared to continue the ancient line of Roman kings and emperors which had ended in 476. Paradoxically, this "coronation" led to enmity between future Popes and Charlemagne's successors, who were called Holy Roman emperors.

Charlemagne established his capital at Aix-la-Chapelle (Aachen) and considered himself to be a spiritual descendant of David—poet, religious leader, and king. He encouraged education among the clergy and wanted to see uniform religious practices throughout his huge domains. When he died in 814 at the age of seventy-two, he was succeeded by his son, known as Louis the Pious. When Louis died in 840, however, the kingdom was divided into three and the Carolingian interlude, brilliant as it had been, collapsed. Western Europe was invaded from three directions: the Muslims came from the south, the Vikings (or Scandinavians or Northmen) from the north, and the Magyars from the east. A time of troubles, indeed!

Little is known about the Jews of Western Europe during the periods before Charlemagne and after Louis the Pious. Within the "Carolingian Renaissance" there is some information, but it is sparse. Charlemagne is considered to have been favorably disposed toward the Jews because he appointed a Jewish ambassador, Isaac, as one of three to visit Harun-al-Rashid, the great Muslim Abbasid caliph, in 797. (Isaac was the only one of the trio to return, and brought with him an elephant!) More importantly, Charlemagne devised a legal oath for Jews which obviated the necessity of swearing in a Christological manner. In general, he protected Jewish rights.[1]

Although Louis the Pious was even more favorable toward the Jews, anti-Jewish sentiment flared during his reign. The apparent provocation was the conversion to Judaism of a heathen slave belonging to a Jewish family. Officially this was not allowed. Agobard, Archbishop of Lyons, wrote letters demanding the slave's release and describing the insolence of the protesting Jews. Agobard tried a number of anti-Jewish approaches, which, in general, failed. The situation got worse when Bodo, "Deacon of the Palace of Louis the Pious," himself converted to Judaism. He was circumcised, married a Jew, and moved to Spain, where he showed himself to be very antagonistic toward Christians.

Amulo, the next Archbishop of Lyons, wrote an outraged letter to King Charles the Bald, called A *Treatise Against the Jews*, (c. 845). It was extremely hostile and warned Christians to avoid the society of Jews. Legislation was then proposed by an anti-Jewish faction, but Charles the Bald refused to enact it. Nonetheless, anti-Jewish sentiments were strong. At about that time, in the area of Lyons, Christian proselytizing increased to the point that there were weekly sermons in the synagogues which were conducted by priests.[2] There appear to have been no public hostilities, however, and our knowledge of the Jews of the Carolingian epoch again fades away.

There was another cultural and political revival in the next century, towards the eastern part of the Holy Roman Empire. It is called the Ottonian Revival after the three emperors named Otto (936-1002) As with the Carolingian period, its art often looked back to the late Roman Empire for cultural inspiration as well as to Byzantium for stylistic direction. This latter factor brings us to a discussion of *iconoclasm*.

---

[1] Bernard S. Bachrach, *Early Jewish Policy in Western Europe* (Minneapolis: University of Minnesota Press, 1977).

[2] S. W. Baron, *History of the Jews*, vol. 4 *Meeting of the East and West*, 53.

[3] For "iconoclasm," see *The New Catholic Encyclopedia*, vol. 7, 327-32; Jaroslav Pelikan,

Imago Dei (Princeton: Princeton University Press, 1990); and Hans Belting, *Likeness and Presence. A History of the Image Before the Era of Art*, trans. Edmond Jephcott (Chicago, University of Chicago Press, 1994.) See also, K Morrison, 1969, 87-89.

The Iconoclast Controversy. Towards the end of the period covered in this chapter, there occurred a memorable epoch in the history of art, and indeed in the story of Europe itself. Although the controversy over the prohibition of religious images (primarily of humans) was centered in the Byzantine Empire, it had significant reverberations in Western European art. As discussed in chapters 1 and 2, the aniconic position of both Judaism and early Christianity was a constant issue. On the one side were those who thought that religious images were an aid to the spiritual experience. On the other were the *iconoclasts,* (the breakers of images) who said that pictures and statues smacked of idolatry.

The controversy became prolonged, complex, and nasty. The prohibition against the portrayal of sacred gods or persons is rooted in the Judaic Second Commandment ("no graven images"), and this injunction itself undoubtedly was a reaction to the practices of the idolatrous neighboring peoples which the growing Israelite nation tried to shun. We have mentioned already that during its first two centuries, even Christian art seemed to have had an *aniconic* bias. But influenced, no doubt, by the Hellenistic environment, burgeoning Christianity soon made the superb representational images we have just seen; yet there could be heard occasional voices of those who were afraid such images would bring worshippers uncomfortably close to idolatry.

Nevertheless, the full outburst of the iconoclastic rage arose in Byzantium and gathered strength in the eighth century. The forces which were involved were not only aesthetic and religious but extremely political as well.[3] Whether the Eastern Empire's proximity to Islam, a new, vigorous, and militantly aniconic religion, was important is difficult to say. The issue first came to a head when the Emperor Leo III published an edict in 726 C.E. which stated that images were idols, that they were forbidden and that they should be smashed. This was the first major assault in a "war" which would have two influential advances and retreats and which would last 116 years. Not only were images broken, but staunch supporters of the use of religious images, called either *iconophiles* (image-lovers) or *iconodules* (image-makers) were subject to excommunication. The monastic orders were particular targets, and monasteries were burned and monks killed.

The iconoclasts accused their adversaries of being idol-worshippers, of being superstitious, and of flouting the Second Commandment. The Christian use of religious pictures was also thought to be a hindrance to the possible conversion of aniconic Jews and Muslims. More subtle arguments have been outlined by Pelikan.[4] The iconoclasts asked how the invisible Deity or the Holy Martyrs could be shown in pictures. The iconophiles responded that, at least with regard to Christ, the Incarnation (God made Man) was one of the foundations of Christianity, and that as Jesus appeared on earth both before and after the Crucifixion, it was proper to portray Him without any impiety.

The issue was critical and the battle—for so it was—remained serious, involving the emperor and the patriarchs of the Eastern Church—always closer to each other than the popes were to Western rulers and the Holy Roman emperors.[5] The first round ended when the Empress Irene, a supporter of the iconophile position, was regent. She arranged the Second Council of Nicaea in 787, which ended iconoclasm as an official policy; the council allowed the use of images, but only under the condition that they be venerated, not adored. (A finely-tuned distinction indeed!)

Twenty-seven years later, in 814, the Iconoclasts were resurgent and a similar scenario ensued. A new patriarch condemned the position of the 787 council and images were smashed once again. Pro-Iconoclastic emperors followed until, in 842, another empress, Theodora, became regent and ruler for her young son. She, like her predecessor Irene, favored the use of images; that same year, yet another synod reversed the decisions of the 814 council, and instead renewed the Second Nicene position. Images have not been officially challenged since then.

---

[4] J. Pelikan, *Imago Dei*.
[5] The attitudes of the various Byzantine rulers are described in *the Catholic Encyclopedia* article on "iconoclasm."

[6] Yves Christe, Tania Velmans, Hanna Losowska and Roland Recht, *Art of the Christian World, A.D. 200-1500* (New York, Rizzoli, 1982).

Artistically, both the Carolingian and Ottonian periods were conservative. Patristic and classical authors were esteemed. These were outstanding times for "art in the miniature," including manuscripts and small ivory carvings, and little in the way of public or monumental creations have come down to us. Much was undoubtedly lost. Still, there was some innovation in Christian iconography. At least three Christian images are first seen with some frequency during these eras—the dead Christ on the Cross, the Resurrection, and the Last Judgment.[6] Nevertheless, there are two outstanding examples of church decoration, one from each period, and a magnificent illustrated manuscript.

Three Masterpieces—Mosaic, Bronze, and Vellum

Germigny-des-Pres. A unique masterpiece lies over the main altar of the tiny church of Germigny-des-Pres on the Loire River. This Greek cross-shaped oratory was built by Theodulf, Bishop of Orleans, about 800. Theodulf, a Visigoth, apparently had a "country estate" about 30 kilometers east of Orleans; this was his private chapel. He was a writer, poet, and theologian, and built himself an exquisite church filled with colored marble, perhaps a reminder of his friend Charlemagne's palace in Aix-la-Chapelle. In fact, the church was dedicated by Charlemagne in 806. Over the centuries, it fell into disrepair. The story of its renaissance is as charming as it is surprising. In 1840, some village children were found playing with small colored stones which had been found in the church. Somebody thought they looked like mosaic *tesserae*, but there were no mosaics to be seen in the church. Perhaps there might be hidden mosaics which had been covered over, maybe by an iconoclastic reformer. Finally, when the stucco over the altar was peeled away, a magnificent mosaic was revealed (plate 5). It shows two large and Byzantine-looking angels poised over a wooden box with two projecting poles at each end. Attached to the corners of the box were two smaller angels. The image was immediately recognized as being from Exodus 25:10-20, where the Ark of the Pact (Covenant) is described in detail. Here, over the altar of Theodulf's private church, is not a Crucifixion nor a

Madonna but the Ark of the Israelites holding the Ten Commandments for the journey across forty years of desert wandering! The mosaic shows the gold rings on the sides with the poles running through them as well as the cherubim above the Ark. Below the mosaic is a most moving inscription:

"Observe the holy oracle and the cherubim;
  Contemplate the splendor of the Ark of the Covenant.
  In this light, think to move by your prayers
  The Master of Sinai, and mention
  I pray you, the name of Theodulf."

The faithful are asked to pray, not to Christ or Mary, but to "the Master of Sinai," which one would take to be Adonai or Yahweh, the God of the Old Testament. Thus, on the face of it, there appears to be nothing specifically Christian about either the mosaic picture or the inscription. One might think that even a Jew would have been comfortable with them (but only in a book, not in a sanctuary).

Why was this picture of the Ark and the cherubim, rather than a crucifixion or a Madonna and child, chosen for the important place over the altar? The answer relates to the echoes of the iconoclast controversy which were clearly heard as far away from Constantinople as the Frankish kingdom in the West. Charlemagne was unhappy. He had not been invited to the Second Nicene Council of 787. Furthermore, he was opposed to the Council's decision to allow the restitution of images which he thought were liable to be worshipped after all. He thought that certain types of pictures were acceptable, indeed desirable, in worship but that the Council had gone too far. For some time afterwards, therefore, Carolingian religious images were restricted to scenes from the Bible and from the lives of the saints.[7]

The mosaic at Germigny-des-Pres (which may have come from Ravenna) clearly follows Charlemagne's and Theodulf's program, and

---

[7] George Zarnecki, *The Art of the Medieval World*. (New York, Harry N. Abrams, 1975) 116. The *Libri Carolini* (Caroline Books) were Charlemagne's and Theodulf's reply to the Second Nicaean Council. See C. Davis-Weyer, 1971, 100-103.

FIG 4-1. Bronze doors. Abbey Church of St. Michael, Hildesheim, c. 1015 C.E. Various Old Testament scenes on the left and New Testament scenes on the right (See text.).

although originally Jewish in meaning, yet it is perfectly acceptable iconography from the supersessionist standpoint. The Ark represents Judaism only as the forerunner of Christianity. In the Catholic liturgy, namely in the Litany of the Blessed Virgin Mary, the faithful recite "Ark of the Covenant, Pray for Us." In this context, the Ark is a type for Mary, the container of wisdom.[8] The cherubim were not objects of worship and were clearly described in the OT. The inscription asks the worshipper only to *contemplate* (not to worship) the Ark. The Master of Sinai is, of course, invisible.

The Bronze Doors of Hildesheim. Moving to the end of the Carolingian-Ottonian period, we see an outstanding achievement in Ottonian monumental art—the pair of bronze doors built for the Abbey Church of St. Michael's, Hildesheim. The church was begun at about the time of the Millennium by Bishop Bernward, a vigorous and scholarly cleric devoted to art. (His interests and approach were similar to those of Abbot Suger in Paris, whom we will meet in the next chapter).

FIG 4-2. Detail of Hildesheim bronze doors. God, Adam, Eve, and the Serpent.

The massive doors are over sixteen feet high. Each was poured as a single piece, a marvel of medieval bronze casting. Bishop Bernward had lived in Rome and perhaps was inspired by the Old and New Testament scenes on the wooden doors of Santa Sabina. At St. Michael's, the scenes are arranged vertically with eight panels on each door (figure 4-1). The left door contains scenes from Genesis, beginning with the creation of Adam and ending with Cain's killing Abel. The right door shows scenes from the life of Christ, from the Annunciation to the Resurrection.[9]

The most famous panel is what Snyder calls the "passing the buck" scene from Genesis (figure 4-2). After the apple has been eaten, God (on the left) points the accusing finger (of his right hand) at Adam; Adam, clutching his fig leaf, points to Eve, and Eve points to the serpent. The hapless serpent, without hands, cannot point at all! Whether the artist meant this scene to be humorous is, of course, unknown, but this detail from the door demonstrates the astonishing technical mastery of the designers and the bronze workers of the eleventh century.

Is it possible that the designer of the Hildesheim doors wished to show parallel typological scenes from the two scriptures? Perhaps. For example, the third panel shows the Fall of Adam and Eve on the left and the Crucifixion on the right. As Christ's martyrdom was to redeem Mankind from Adam's sin, this is a frequent pairing of images. Nevertheless, the supercessionist theme is not heavily emphasized to the extent that it will be later, as in the altar of Klosterneuberg.

These, of course, are among the first of an outstanding group of bronze church doors showing historical and biblical scenes found throughout Italy. Such doors include those at Trani, Ravello, Pisa, Benevento, Monreale (Palermo), and Verona. They represent a tradition which continued into the Renaissance and culminated in the three sets of doors on the Baptistery in Florence.

[8] I am indebted to Father Edward Maginnis of Regis University, Denver, for this reference. Later, Aquinas would consider the Ark as a type for Christ.

[9] J. Snyder, *Medieval Art*.

The Utrecht Psalter. Although I said at the outset of this book that I would consider public (i.e., monumental) art rather than private manuscripts, I must make an exception here to prevent us from ignoring a rare and outstanding example of ninth-century typological art.

The *Utrecht Psalter* was written and illustrated in the early ninth century in Reims, the capital of the Champagne region. It contains the Psalms of David, together with 166 dynamic pictures (figure 4-3).[10] The script is in rather foursquare rustic capitals while the style of the drawing is astonishingly "impressionistic." It is almost a sketchbook, albeit one drawn by a very skilled and experienced hand. It was famous in its day and served as a model for several other Psalters.

There are about 30 pictures of typologies in the Psalter. Figure 4-3 illustrates Psalm number 16, verse 10: "For you will not abandon me to Sheol (the Jewish approximation of Hades) or let Your faithful one see the Pit." The Jewish context of this poetry is quite clear; God will protect the righteous. The illustration accompanying the psalm does not illustrate the Jewish meaning. Rather, the artist clearly casts the interpretation in a Christian mode. In the center we see the three Marys at the empty tomb of Jesus. At the upper right is Christ wearing a crossed halo and six angels. To the lower left Christ (somehow standing on a prone naked woman) pulls two people—presumably Adam and Eve—from the ground. To the right is a group of men (in Limbo?) and below are three haloed Christians, perhaps martyrs, on their biers.

The picture thus involves a major reinterpretation of the original text. The psalm mentions Sheol and the Pit as Jewish symbols of punishment after death, and thus it is one of the few places in the OT to refer to an afterlife. (In general, early Judaism was not very interested in the hereafter, and references to it in the Bible tend to be brief and vague, as in this psalm.) In the hands of the artist, however, Psalm 16:10 has been transmuted into scenes of Christ's resurrection. Indeed, it is transmutations of this kind which enabled medieval

---

10 Koert van der Horst et al, *The Utrecht Psalter in Medieval Art* (Westrenen, Tuurdijk, HES Publishers, 1996).

FIG 4-3. Illustration for Psalm 16. The Utrecht Psalter. Reims. Ninth century. Christ, wearing a tripartite halo, is to the middle right; the three Marys stand at the tomb (bottom center). The story of Christ's pulling Adam and Eve from Hades (bottom left) is usually called "The Harrowing of Hell." It describes Christ's descent into Limbo after the Crucifixion. It is not in the Bible but comes from a medieval work called *The Gospel of Nicodemus (Cath. Encyclop)*.

Christians to believe that the Hebrew scriptures foretell the life, death, and resurrection of Christ. This very verse is quoted in Acts 2:27 with respect to Jesus' Resurrection. The scene at the empty tomb (which we saw at the Christian House in Dura-Europus) comes from Mark and Matthew and came in itself to be a symbol of the resurrection. The descent of Christ into Hell and the rescuing of Adam and Eve (and others), although not in the NT, was a popular theme in the Middle Ages.

In short, certain scenes illustrated in the Utrecht Psalter show a thorough visual Christianization of the Jewish text, supporting the Christian view that the OT was a prophecy of Christian events. The Christological interpretation of the psalms goes back to the works of Barnabas and Trypho which we discussed in the first chapter. Augustine may have been responsible for the most thorough treatment which used this approach. His *Expositions on the Psalms* is a paraphrase of each of the 150 psalms, and *every one* is put into a Christological frame. For instance, the first lines of the familiar 23rd psalm reads (in the Revised Standard Version), "The Lord is my shepherd, I shall not want; he makes me lie down in green pastures, he leads me beside still waters...." For Augustine, however, the speaker is the Church. The psalm begins, "The Lord Jesus Christ is my Shepherd." The "still waters" refer to the rite of baptism.[11] King David, the traditional author of this psalm, might have been surprised at such interpretations!

Art and Jewish-Christian Relations

While it is no longer correct to speak of the "Dark Ages" when discussing these centuries, nevertheless one must realize that social and historical information from this period is not abundant. This is even more true with regard to the Jews of Western Europe. Thus when discussing artistic reflections of Jewish-Christian relations in Carolingian and Ottonian times, both the historian and the student of art history face difficulties. Factual accounts of how Jews and Christians interacted are sparse and tend to reflect only local situations. Whether the animosity of Agobard and Amulo from the Lyons region was representative of other regions is hard to say.

From the artistic standpoint, we are hampered for additional reasons. Monumental and public religious art in Western Europe is not as plentiful as it was in the preceding and following epochs. The *styles* of Carolingian and Ottonian art were suited to manuscript illuminations and many tended to be abstract rather than figurative. There was also the influence of Byzantine iconoclasm as it was perceived in the West. With no less a personage than Charlemagne—not only the Holy Roman Emperor but also a prominent art patron—expressing his opposition to many kinds of imagery, it is no surprise that public figures of typological import are scarce.

Nonetheless, the three masterpieces discussed in this chapter clearly show the supersessionist position. In doing so, however, they show it in three different ways. In Germigny-des-Pres, it is by *implication*, because the Ark of the Covenant refers to Christianity indirectly. In the Hildesheim doors, the parallel OT and NT scenes are more illustrative of the supersessionist theology, but work via *analogy*. In the Utrecht Psalter, where Christ appears in the psalms of David, we see the complete confidence of the Church in its *direct* appropriation of the Jewish scriptures.

Iconoclasm never returned to the Catholic Church. The next era, starting with the Millennium, brought political and economic expansion together with an explosion in what we call Romanesque Art. Also, the art will be beginning to change in tone with regard to its portrayal of the Jew. The three instances described in this chapter do not demonstrate any particular disparaging aspects of Judaism, only that it was obsolete. Some of this will change.

---

[11] Augustine, *Expositions on the Psalms*, (see website {www.newadvent.org/fathers}).

5 | The Millennium: The Crusader Era and the Coming of the Romanesque (1000-1200 C.E.)

Europe Wakes Up and the Romanesque Arrives

This span of two hundred years begins at the Millennium and deliberately overlaps the following chapter. It covers a notable, even momentous change in Western Europe. In brief, "Europe woke up." The Norman expansion, including the astonishing conquest of England, then reaching through the Italian peninsula to Sicily, exemplified the new vigor of the age. The tremendous enlargement of the monastic movement, the renewal of scholarship in those monasteries, and the explosion of Romanesque art and architecture all testify to the awakened Europe. Indeed, Claster calls the period 1050-1100 "The Crucial Half-Century,"—"crucial for internal religious reform, the growth of papal power, and the expansion of the boundaries of the Western church."[1]

The Rise of Scholasticism and the Intensification of *Adversus Judaeos*

What we today call the "scholastics" in the late Middle Ages comprised a diverse series of philosopher-theologians who represented much of the intellectual component of the awakening of Western Europe. Their achievements were easily comparable to those of others in the fields of art, architecture, politics, and economics. The main question they addressed was how to reconcile faith with reason, the latter being represented by the ancient heritage of Plato and especially of Aristotle. Indeed, the motto of St. Anselm of Bec and Canterbury (c. 1033-1109) was *fides quaerens intelligentiam* (faith seeking understanding).

---

[1] Jill Claster, *The Medieval Experience, 300-1400* (New York: New York University Press, 1982) 192.

The activities of the philosopher-theologians also reached into the sphere of Jewish-Christian relations, as the tensions between the two faiths continued to grow. The use of the dialogue form in the tradition of *Adversus Judaeos* continued and intensified. The twelfth century saw a great increase in written accounts of Jewish-Christian disputations. According to Funkenstein, the transition to a more aggressive *Adversus Judaeos* approach was carried forth by pupils and disciples of Anselm.[2] Gilbert Crispin, Bishop of Westminster, dictated his *Disputatio Judaei cum Christiano de Fide Christiana* (before 1098) to Anselm himself and based it on the usual accusations that the Jews did not know that their own scriptures prefigured the story of Christianity.

In other writings, the older arguments were also repeated. The Psalms were really about Christ and the Law of Moses was meant to be temporary. As Jerome had done, the medieval Christians said that the ancient Jewish scholars, when they formed the Septuagint by translating the Hebrew into Greek, suppressed references to the Trinity, even though this translation was made hundreds of years before the birth of Jesus.[3]

A somewhat newer approach—an attack on the Talmud—was mounted by Peter Alfonsi, a Spanish Jew born in 1062. In 1106, he became a Christian, converting his Jewish name, Moses, to Peter.[4] Coming from a Jewish background, and knowing Hebrew, he was able to criticize the rabbis for what he perceived as the absurdity of the midrash (commentaries on the Bible) and the contents of the Talmud.

[2] Amos Funkenstein, *Perceptions of Jewish History*, (Berkeley: University of California Press, 1993) 172-201.

[3] J. Pelikan, *Imago Dei*, 250.

[4] It is probably no accident that the Jew Moses Alfonsi chose to be called Peter after his conversion to Christianity. Moses was considered to be a *type* of Peter. See chap. 2 above, and also T. F. Mathews, 1993.

[5] Jeremy Cohen, *The Friars and the Jews* (Ithaca NY: Cornell University Press, 1982) 20-25.

[6] *Encyclopedia Judaica*, vol. 15, 1208-1209 (Toledot). Also Samuel Kraus, *The Jewish-Christian Controversy From the Earliest Times to 1789*, ed. and revised by William Horbery (Tubingen, J.C.B. Mohr [Paul Siebeck] 1995, originally written in 1948).

[7] Daniel J. Lasker, *Jewish Philosophical Polemics Against Christianity in the Middle Ages* (New York: Ktav Publishing House, 1977). Lasker lists about one dozen works from the twelfth and thirteenth centuries. All were written in Hebrew and so would have been inaccessible to all but a few Christian scholars.

Alfonsi said that Judaism was a primitive religion in which a primitive anthropomorphic God was worshipped. Since the Jews were only capable of a literal comprehension of their own Bible and their Talmud, they could not progress to a more enlightened stage which would allow an understanding of Christianity. Alfonsi further opened the pathway to Christian attacks on the Talmud by maintaining that it contained some important *secret* Jewish doctrines. This attack on postbiblical Jewish sources was new because, in general, Christian apologists did not know Hebrew. This did not hinder their studies of the OT as it was available to them in Greek and Latin translations. The Talmud, on the other hand, was written in Hebrew and Aramaic, and was not translated into more accessible languages. That, and the very abstruseness of its methods of argumentation, made it a subject of curiosity but not of understanding for medieval Christians.

This anti-Talmudic approach was carried further by Peter, Abbot of Cluny (who we will see later in more detail). As he knew little or no Hebrew, he borrowed heavily from Peter Alfonsi. He attacked the Jews because, rather than progressing from the Old Testament to the New, they ignored Christianity and obstinately moved instead to the complexities of Talmudic disputation.[5] The Talmud is, indeed, a complex series of mainly legalistic arguments, difficult to understand if one does not approach it "from within." In the adversarial atmosphere of Jewish-Christian relations as they stood at the time, what one doesn't understand, one tends to ridicule.

Was there, then, any Jewish *riposte* to Christian antipathy? Remarkably little written evidence of Jewish animosity survives (which doesn't mean that such material did not exist). The Hebrew *Toledot Yeshu* (*The Life of Jesus*) was a scurrilous "biography" of Jesus, which appeared in the Middle Ages and which circulated in several versions. It seems to have been written originally in Aramaic sometime between the fifth and ninth centuries. It was seriously anti-Christian, cast doubts on the legitimacy of the birth of Jesus, and tried to explain away some of his miracles.[6]

Toledot Yeshu almost seems an anomaly because in general anti-Christian tracts by Jewish authors were rare before the twelfth century.[7] Nonetheless, there exists the *Nizzahon Vetus*, or *Old Book of*

Polemic. This is an anonymous anthology of anti-Christian arguments written down in the late thirteenth century, probably from much older material. It uses many of the traditional arguments against the Christian supersessionist interpretation of the Hebrew scriptures. Thus, it emphasizes the literal and ignores or downplays the allegorical or symbolic interpretations. For instance, in dealing with the genealogy of Jesus, it states that Christians should not trace the ancestry of Christ to David via Joseph (Mt 1:16 and Lk 3:23) because Joseph, the husband of Mary, was no blood relative of Jesus. Instead, Mary's ancestry should have been considered. As it was not, the text concludes that the Christians did not know Mary's ancestry, and thus she could not have been of royal descent.[8]

Such a document obviously did nothing to improve Jewish-Christian relations. Neither did the next development in this story, the religiously-inspired mass-movements known as the Crusades.

The Crusades

It is difficult to write briefly, or even calmly, about the Crusades. This historical set of phenomena, always capitalized, aimed at the Middle East and actually occupied almost two centuries, from the First Crusade of 1096 to the Ninth Crusade, which occurred in 1271. This era looms large in any recount of Western European history. Each chronicler has a different viewpoint. The Crusader era represents many facets of history: the heights of chivalry, the depths of ochlocracy, the excesses of religious fervor, the geographical bursting of Europe into the East (and vice-versa), and the economic rejuvenation that heralded "the end of the Middle Ages." For the Christians, it meant the end of the "Dark Ages," the triumph of Scholasticism and the flowering of Romanesque and later of Gothic art. For the Jews, on the contrary, the Crusader era demonstrated the crescendo

---

8 David Berger, *The Jewish-Christian Debate in the High Middle Ages.* A Critical Edition of the *Nizzahon Vetus*, with an introduction, translation and commentary (Philadelphia: The Jewish Publication Society of America, 1979)

7. See also M. R. Cohen, *Under Crescent,* 141-43.

9 J. Parkes, *Jew, Medieval* Community (1938).

10 Pope Gregory's letter is quoted by Synan (1965), 65.

in anti-Semitism which would shortly lead to their expulsion from France and England.

Yet the position of the Jews during the Crusades is not easily presented as a single story. We know of the troubles Jews endured, particularly during the First and Second Crusades. We also know that at the same time there was a "Golden Age" of Jewish thought, poetry, and philosophy in Spain, and a similar burgeoning of biblical and talmudic studies by Rashi and his family in Troyes, Champagne. And we know virtually nothing about Jews in other regions the Crusaders did not traverse. This is so often true—the histories of most eras remark on the exceptional. Ordinary lives are left unrecorded.

So while it would be unwarranted to insist that the ills that befell the Rhenish Jews were typical of the treatment of all Jews of that period, it would be incomplete to omit a brief discussion of these facts which have come down to us. The treatment of the Jews in the Rhineland involved important historical principles and concerned some very prominent churchmen and rulers.

Even before the First Crusade was preached in 1095, urging Christians to wrest the Holy Land from the unbelieving Muslims, anti-Muslim violence erupted in Spain. In 1063, a proto-crusade against Muslims included outbreaks against Jewish communities.[9] The attitudes of the ruling clerics were characteristically mixed. The persecutions had the approval (tacit or open) of the Archbishop of Narbonne (which belonged to Spain at the time). However, the Viscount of Narbonne wanted to protect the Jews. A still higher authority, the pope, supported the Archbishop. This situation was a harbinger of things to come. Soon after, the great Pope Gregory VII (1073-1085) wrote to Alfonso VI, King of Leon and Castile, to reiterate the now venerable position of the Church that Jews in Spain must not be permitted to hold power or influence over Christians. To do so would be "to exalt the Synagogue of Satan."[10]

The concept of a crusade to liberate the Holy Land from the Muslims probably originated in the mind of Gregory VII, but it was not until after his death that the First Crusade was called for by Pope Urban II in Clermont, France in 1095. It was quickly organized and set out in 1096, finally leading to the conquest of Jerusalem in 1099.

Culminating as it did in the massacre of the Muslim, Jewish, and Eastern Christian inhabitants of Jerusalem, it was not the glorious episode in Western history that had been hoped for. Still, it stands as a watershed in Western history.

The woes of the Jews during the First Crusade occurred mainly in the Rhineland. They are described in several accounts from reliable sources.[11] The hostilities can be laid at the feet, not of what might be called "the Soldiers of the Cross," that is, the baronial armies of "regulars" on their way to Jerusalem, but rather to unorganized mobs of hangers-on who followed the "regulars." The mobs, not under the control of feudal leaders, survived by pillage and were swayed in their enthusiasms by demagogues such as Peter the Hermit. Peter and the mobs that he inspired carried out what was almost a parallel movement, sometimes called "the Peoples' Crusade."[12]

The major incidents occurred in the Rhine cities of Cologne, Worms, and Mayence (Mainz), with lesser attacks in Trier, Metz, and Speyer. The motives were not economic but religious. The rationale was simple. As the crusaders were embarking upon a many-thousand mile journey to free the city of Jesus (Jerusalem) from the arms of the unbelieving Muslims, right here "at home" were the descendants of the murderers of Christ: "Look you! We set out on a long road in order to reach the Burial Place and to revenge ourselves on the Ishmaelites, and behold! here are Jews, dwelling in our midst, men whose fathers killed Him, all guiltless, and crucified Him. Let us, therefore, take our revenge first on them, and extirpate them from among the nations, so that the name of Israel will no longer be mentioned."[13]

---

[11] Robert Chazen, *European Jewry and the First Crusade* (Berkeley: University of California Press, 1987).

[12] J. Claster, *Medieval Experience*, 199-202.

[13] See Synan, *Popes and Jews*, 71.

[14] Cecil Roth, ed., *The Dark Ages (711-1096)*, vol. 2 of *The World History of the Jewish People*. Medieval Period series. ([New Brunswick] :Rutgers University Press, 1966) 164.

[15] Edward H. Flannery, *The Anguish of the Jews* (New York: The Macmillan Company, 1965).

[16] J. Parkes, *Jew, Medieval Community*.

[17] Solomon Grayzel, *The Church and the Jews in the XIIIth Century*. (Philadelphia: The Dropsie College, 1933) 92-94.

Plate 1. Statue, The Good Shepherd. Fourth century. Pio Christian Museum, Rome. This is modeled on earlier Roman sculptures but refers to Luke 15.

Plate 2. Junius Bassus Sarcophagus, detail. Adam, Eve, the Serpent and the tree.

Plate 3. Mosaic, Melchizedek and Abraham. Santa Maria Maggiore (nave), Rome. Fifth century. Melchizedek (left) offers a basket of bread and a vase of wine after blessing Abraham. Abraham (on a horse) is with his soldiers, who have just rescued Lot (Gen 14). The figure in the sky, perhaps Christ, is an addition to the scene from Genesis.

Plate 4. Mosaic, Abraham, Sarah and the "Three Men." S. M. Maggiore (nave), Rome. Fifth century. A dual scene. At the top, Abraham bows and greets the three "men," shown with haloes (and a mandorla around the central man). Below, Abraham tells Sarah to prepare a meal; Abraham (a third depiction) turns to serve the men with bread and meat. (Gen 18)

Plate 5. Mosaic, The Ark of the Covenant with Cherubim. Germigny-des-Pres (Loire). c. 800 C.E. The Ark of the Covenant, with gold rings and poles through the rings, the cherubim at each end, and cherubim with outspread wings above. (Ex 25:10-16)

Plate 6. The Birds Head Haggadah. Manuscript. Southern Germany, c. 1300 C.E. The Jews are shown with Jews' hats and birds' heads. On the left, Moses receives the two Tablets of the Law from the hand of God. Then Moses (again) passes five tablets (the Pentateuch) to two Jews. On the right, Jews gather manna and quail. (Ex 16)

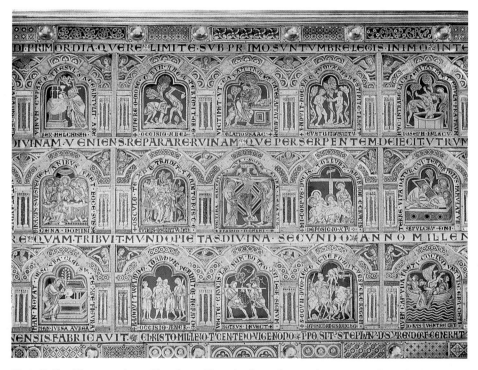

Plate 7. The Klosterneuburg Altar, front. Three horizontal rows show scenes from the history of the Jewish-Christian world. The top row represents the time "Before the Law" (*Ante Legem)*; the middle row "Under Grace," (*Sub Gratia*); and the bottom row "Under the Law" (*Sub Lege*) (See text.).

Plate 8. The Meuse Cross. Third quarter of the twelfth century. At the crossing, Jacob blesses Ephraim and Menasseh with crossed hands. At the top, Moses and Aaron contemplate the Brazen Serpent. To the right, an Israelite paints the sign in lamb's blood so the Angel of Death will "pass over" his house—the sign is a Greek *tau,* interpreted as a cross. To the left, Elijah visits a widow, who collects wood in the form of a cross. At the bottom, two scouts bring a cluster of grapes from the Promised Land.

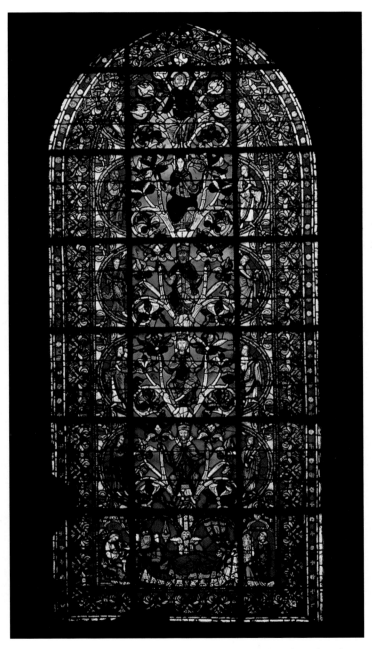

Plate 9. Window, The Jesse Tree. St. Denis. Jesse, barefoot, is asleep. The tree rises from his groin. In the branches are crowned kings of Judea. Above them is Mary; above her are Christ, wearing a halo, and the seven holy virtues mentioned by Isaiah in the form of doves. In the semicircles to the side are Old Testament prophets, each bearing the scroll of his prophecy.

Plate 10. Detail, Jesse Tree window. St. Denis. Nineteenth-century reproduction. The lowest panel shows Jesse asleep in his Jew's hat.

Plate 11. Window detail, Christ between *Ecclesia* (the Church, to his right) and *Sinagoga* (the Synagogue, to his left). Window of the Allegory of St. Paul, St. Denis. Christ again has the symbols of the seven holy virtues on his breast. He may be lifting the veil from Sinagoga.

Plate 12. Window detail, The *Quadrige* (Chariot) of Aminadab. St. Denis (See text.).

Plate 13. Window detail, The Crossing of the Red Sea. Top roundel, St. Denis. At the right, Moses, staff in hand, turns back to tell the Israelites to follow him. Above is God in a red halo. Below are remnants of Pharoah's army. Lower roundel; the Burning Bush. Moses removes his sandals. God appears to him in a circle of fire, representing the Bush. The golden calf is below at the foot of Mt. Sinai.

Plate 14. Window detail, Moses and the Brazen Serpent. St. Denis.

Plate 15. Symbolic window of the Redemption. Chartres (See text.).

Plate 16. Detail, Redemption Window. Chartres. The Crucifixion; the Roman soldier pierces Christ's right side with a lance. To the left of this scene is *Ecclesia*, holding her staff and a church. To the right is a stooped and blindfolded *Sinagoga* with her crown in her hand. A devil-monkey is shooting an arrow into her eyes. Above are two scouts bearing a cluster of grapes that hang from the wooden bar.

The Jews were attacked in their communities. In Speyer, in early May 1096, they were given the classic choice: baptism or death. Some (in spite of earlier strictures against forcible baptism) converted. Others did not, and took the consequences. In Worms, the Jews were accused of poisoning the city's water supply with the body of a murdered Christian. The bishop of Worms was not able to call off the mob, and, rather than submit, about 800 Jews died in a mass suicide. At Mayence, the leading city and Jewish community in the Rhineland, neither the archbishop nor the count could save the Jews and the whole community, perhaps as many as 1,300 people died.[14] Edward Flannery estimates that perhaps as many as a quarter of the Jews of Germany and Northern France were killed.[15]

Distasteful as it is to recount such atrocities, it is a small relief to note that the mob behavior was not always condoned. Some rulers, such as Henry IV, Holy Roman Emperor, and William II (Rufus) of England, allowed those forcibly converted to return to Judaism. The papacy was also unhappy but had no jurisdiction over unruly mobs. Urban II himself was silent on the matter; succeeding popes encouraged the protection of the Jews, but only in regard to rights which were not threatening to Christians. Feudal rulers issued a succession of charters of settlement which, while they might seem on the surface to guarantee the political rights of Jews, were also instruments of control and therefore of possible exploitation.[16] Local clergy were the most unfriendly. Far removed from Rome, they often failed to object to anti-Jewish sentiments and actions.

The anti-Jewish attacks during the First Crusade did lead to some reactions at higher levels in favor of protecting the Jews. A papal bull, *Constitutio Pro Judaeis,* was first issued by Pope Callistus II (1119-1124) and repeated by later popes. It enumerated the privileges granted to the Jews and the hardships they should be spared. In general, it protected their lives and their ability to practice their religion but it did not prevent the abridgment of their civil liberties.[17] In times of stress, however, these principles were not observed, so that when the Second Crusade was preached at Vezelay in 1146, a familiar scenario seemed about to take place. Instead of Peter the Hermit, another preaching monk named Rudolph, again in the Rhineland, stirred up the faithful not only to "take the Cross" but to kill Jews along the way. Thousands of Jews sought protection under the barons.

The family of Rashi (the famous rabbi, scholar, and commentator) was not exempt. His grandson, Rabbi Jacob ben Meir (c. 1100-1171), also called Rabbenu Tam, lived near Troyes in Champagne. An outstanding scholar, he supported his family by lending money. (It was traditional that Jewish scholars not receive money for their teaching and scholarship and so they had to earn their livelihood by some other means.) In 1147, a crusading mob hauled him out to the fields and were about to kill him (as his ancestors had killed Christ) when he was luckily saved by a passing official.[18]

No less a person than Bernard, the Abbot of Clairvaux (later St. Bernard), stepped in. One of the most powerful and famous men of the Church (and sometimes not altogether friendly to Jews), he called for a halt of the persecutions. As usual, he backed his opinion with a scriptural allusion, writing to the clergy and people of eastern France:

> "We have heard, and we are gladdened, that the zeal of God renders you fervent, but it is absolutely necessary that the moderating rule of knowledge be not lacking. The Jews must not be persecuted, they must not be slain, they are not even to be put to flight. Put your queries to those divine pages [the Bible]: I have known what is read in the Psalm as a prophecy concerning the Jews, says the Church: 'As for my enemies, do not kill them, let my people not be forgotten [Ps 58 or 59:11].'"[19]

But the Jews had another adversary, perhaps more formidable than the charismatic monk Rudolph. He was Peter, Abbot of Cluny,

---

[18] J. R. Marcus, *Jews in Medieval World* (1972), chap. 61.

[19] Quoted in Synan, *Popes and Jews*, 75. Bernard wrote a widely-quoted passage objecting to ostentatious art in the monasteries in his *Apologia*, but it did not directly concern problems of iconography. See Conrad

Rudolph, *The "Things of Greater Importance"* (Philadelphia: Pennsylvania University Press, 1990).

[20] Synan, *Popes and Jews*, 76.

[21] *Webster's New Twentieth Century Dictionary, Second Edition*, William Collins, 1979.

called the Venerable after his death. Now the Abbey of Cluny was the controlling center of the largest monastic order in Europe, the church at Cluny was the largest in Christendom (larger even than "Old St. Peter's" in Rome, founded by Constantine), and the Abbot of Cluny ranked second in ecclesiastical power only to the pope himself. Peter, in spite of his many other admirable characteristics was no friend of the Jews. Indeed, his words echo the opinions of the anti-Semites half a century before:

> "What does it profit to track down and to persecute enemies of the Christian hope outside, indeed far beyond, the frontiers, if the evil blaspheming Jews, far worse than the Saracens, not at a distance, but in our midst, so freely and audaciously blaspheme, trample underfoot, deface with impunity Christ and all Christian mysteries?"[20]

Did Peter the Venerable therefore advocate killing the Jews? Certainly not—he opted for a rather more subtle punishment. Since he regarded Jews as society's parasites, he merely wanted their money and material goods expropriated! The money, of course, would fittingly be used to support the conquest of those other infidels in the Holy Land, the Muslims. Indeed, this policy had been foreshadowed earlier by Pope Eugene III who, in 1145, decreed that those willing to take the Cross would be forgiven the payment of interest on loans. Two years later, the king of France ordered the Crusaders to be forgiven all debts to Jews. If these debts were issued on credit rather than on material security, it was a disaster for Jewish money-lenders. They could not recoup their losses.

The Jews and Finance

The subject of finance, including the lending of money, is intimately associated with the Jews of Western Europe. Indeed, the stock caricature of the medieval Jew is that of an avaricious *usurer*. Now any discussion of finance employing the word usury is going to be slanted because current usage of the term includes a pejorative tone. Webster defines usury to mean "the act or performance of lending money at a rate of interest that is excessively or unlawfully high."[21] (The more neutral and simpler definition, "interest paid on a loan," is called *obsolete*.) Rather than discuss what rate of interest might or might not be excessive, I will mainly refer to "money-lending" as a morally neutral term.

As the economy of Western Europe heated up following the Millennium, the expansion required capital in the form of loans. Christians were prohibited from lending at interest (although there were Christians who did so.) The Jews were also prohibited from taking interest *from other Jews*, but they were not enjoined from lending at interest to non-Jews. This principle goes back to Deuteronomy 23:20-21.

However, Jewish involvement in finances antedated this period and probably began as a result of the laws of taxation. Christian landholders were required to pay tithes to the Church. Jews were exempt. Although the Church might enjoy receiving taxes from Jewish landholders, both Christians and Jews saw the contradictions involved in suggesting that the Jews might tithe to the Church. This situation understandably gave rise to envy on the part of tithe-paying Christians. Complications arose when a Jew bought land from a Christian, thereby converting taxable property to a potentially non-taxable status. The Church was unhappy at the prospect of losing the income, so Jews were made to pay tithes on land which they owned but which had previously been owned by Christians. Given the complexity of the laws concerning feudal land rights, it is easy to see how one complication might lead to another. In time, it became harder for Jews to own land at all, and what land they did own was sometimes taken from heirs on the death of the owner.

These policies tended to turn Jews away from agriculture and toward means of earning a living which did not require ownership of large and visible parcels of land. However, it was not necessarily easy

---

[22] See J. Parkes, *Jew, Medieval Community* (1938).

[23] Alfred Rubens, *A History of Jewish Costume* (London: Valentine Mitchell & Co., 1967) 91.

to become a skilled laborer as Jews were often excluded from membership in the guilds which controlled those occupations. Thus, Jews tended to steer toward livelihoods such as medicine, law, commerce (trade), and, inevitably, money-lending.

An extended discussion of the subject of money-lending at interest is beyond our scope,[22] but as the medieval period moved ahead, the Church became more and more intolerant of the practice, equating it with the sin of avarice. The Church tried to discourage and isolate Jewish money-lenders primarily by slowly denying them what we today would call their civil rights. The social marginalization of the Jews is best exemplified by the attitude of the Church toward the *public appearance* of the Jews.

Jewish Dress Codes

The social status of the ordinary medieval Jew is difficult to assess, but a discussion of Jewish dress codes is an important window onto that subject. The requirement of a distinctive identifying device or garment for Jews inevitably reminds us of the yellow star or badge forced upon Jews by Hitler. Unpalatable as this subject may be, the concept itself is of great interest in medieval sociology. Unfortunately, actual pieces of everyday dress for Jews (as well as for non-Jews) have not come down to us. It is ironic that clothing, which defines many of the most important societal characteristics of "who we are and how we ourselves and others see us" rarely has survived the centuries. Both the fragility of the materials themselves and also their very "everydayness" to the wearers and their descendants ensure their non-survival!

The use of distinctive dress to indicate special status is very old. It should be understood and even emphasized at the outset of this discussion that distinctive dress is by no means necessarily to be equated with some invidious purpose or opprobrium. To think so would be to mock the bride in her veil! Jews themselves apparently wanted at times to dress differently from non-Jews. Indeed, the wearing of *tzitzit* (fringes) on certain garments dates from the Pentateuch (Num 15:37-39). In the sixteenth-century codification of Jewish law, the

Shulchan Aruch, it is stated that "we should not...wear a garment which is characteristic of...idolaters."[23] Revel-Neher makes the distinction between items of Jewish dress which are "signs of identity" such as the *tallit* (*prayer shawl*) and the *tzitzit* and those which are "signs of infamy" (see below).[24] But even with these distinctions, it is unfortunate that we do not know as much as we would like about how clothing may have set medieval Jews apart, nor when these adaptations became widespread.

Nevertheless, it is beyond question that the Church wanted the Jews to wear distinctive costumes and thus to be conspicuous. We have regulations from the pope down to lower officials which attest to this policy. Due to our lack of everyday medieval costumes and to the vagueness of the regulations, however, exactly what the dress code involved is not always clear. Thus we need to rely on *pictures* of Jews and their clothing to give us some idea of what they wore. The pictures, although uncommon, are fascinating and the interpretations are of equal interest.[25] Blumenkranz points out that in Carolingian and Ottonian periods, pictures of Jews did not show them to have distinguishing clothes nor personal features.[26] But following the Millennium, pictures of distinctive Jewish dress are frequent. The reasons for the change are conjectural.

The most famous legislation concerning the imposition of a distinctive Jewish dress code occurs rather late in our story. It comes from Canon 68 of the Fourth Lateran Council in 1215:

> "In some provinces, the dress (*habitus*) of Jews and Saracens (i.e. Muslims) distinguishes them from Christians, but in others a degree of confusion has arisen, so that they cannot be recognized by any distinguishing marks. As a result, in error Christians have sexual intercourse with Jewish or Saracen women, and Jews and Saracens have sexual intercourse with Christian women. In order that the crime of such an accursed mingling shall not in future have an excuse and an evasion under the pretext of error, we resolve that [Jews and Saracens] of both sexes in all Christian lands shall distinguish themselves from other people by their dress (*qualitate habitus*)."[27]

Then, in the best clerical tradition, this pronouncement is justified by the appeal to scripture. In this case it is said to be in accord with statements by Moses in Leviticus 19:19 and in Deuteronomy 22:5 and 22:11. (However, although the passages cited deal with clothing, they do not address types of clothing which distinguish certain people from others. Careless usage of scriptural references is not rare.)

Two additional points need attention. First, the decree does not specify what the distinctive mark or garment should be. It mentions neither badge nor device, color of garment, or shape of hat. Presumably these decisions were made at a more local level rather than at the papal level. Second, Jews were not singled out as the only wearers of special garments as the regulations also applied to Muslims, who comprised the other major class of non-Christians.

In fact, a distinctive dress code for minority (and hence marginalized) groups preceded the Fourth Lateran Council by centuries. Perhaps paradoxically, it seems to have originated in Muslim countries in the eighth century, where Jews as well as Christians were to wear identifying garments or a distinctive badge. We do not know when a separate dress code was introduced into the West, but the two distinctive pieces of clothing used to tell Christians from non-Christians were the hat and the badge.

The Jewish hat (*Judenhut* in German) is frequently shown in pictures in which Jews appear. It is pointed, conical, or funnel-shaped, and probably was adapted from the conical cap with the turned-over peak which Phrygians wore (they were a minority in the Persian Empire). We do not know when or where it was first worn, but possibly the earliest picture is in a Bible from Northern France around 1097.[28]

---

[24] Elizabeth Revel-Neher, *The Image of the Jew in Byzantine Art* (Oxford: Pergamon Press, 1992) 97-98.

[25] Ruth Mellinkoff, *Outcasts: Signs of Otherness in Northern European Art of the Late Middle Ages* (Berkeley: University of California Press, 1993).

[26] Bernhard Blumenkranz, *Le Juif Medieval au Miroir de l'Art Chretien* (Paris: Etude Augustiennes, 1966) 15-16.

[27] Heinz Schreckenberg, *The Jews in Christian Art* (New York: Continuum, 1996) 15-16.

[28] Rubens, *A History*.

What the Jew's hat "means" depends upon which scholarly authority you read. Schreckenberg and Revel-Neher believe that the Jewish hat was defamatory.[29] Mellinkoff says that the Jew's hat "usually, if not always, had unpleasant connotations of varying degrees of intensity."[30] The *Encyclopaedia Judaica*, by contrast, claims of the hat, "It would seem, however, that this distinction was instituted by the Jews themselves."[31]

It is true that a pointed hat on a Jew may occur in a Christian picture where the Jew is being ridiculed. I would add, however, that this cannot always be so because there are Christian pictures showing a Jew's hat not only on Joseph, the husband of Mary, but on Christ himself.[32] In this latter instance, it can only be a neutral mark of identity.

In order to discuss in more detail the question of the Jew's hat and its possible derogatory significance, I must digress again and move away from public and monumental art to illuminated manuscripts, and extend our survey to the early fourteenth century.

The most telling argument indicating that a picture of a man in a Jew's hat was not always derogatory would be the existence of a well-regarded *Jewish* book that shows such an image. Just such a book exists.

The Bird's Head Haggadah
—An Anti-Semitic Jewish Book?

One of the most famous illustrated Jewish books of the Middle Ages is in the Israel Museum in Jerusalem. It is a 1300 C.E. German *Haggadah* (the book used for the Passover meal and *seder* service), called "the Bird's Head Haggadah." It is so called because human figures in the illustrations have birds' heads rather than human heads. The usual interpretation of this apparently odd convention is that it provided a way of following the Second Commandment which presumably prohibited only *human* images. Of great interest is that many of the bird-headed figures wear funnel-shaped Judenhuts. In plate 6, even the bird-headed Moses himself receiving the Ten Commandments from the hand of God wears a Jewish hat. It seems inconceivable that a Jewish illustrator of a Haggadah would show

Moses and other Jews wearing such hats if they were symbols of social opprobrium. (It is interesting even to find a picture of Moses in a Haggadah because, although he was the omnipresent leader of the Exodus of the Jews from Egypt, as described in the Bible, he is—somewhat enigmatically—almost absent from the Haggadah itself.)

However, the situation is far more complex. In her recent authoritative (and provocative) text on anti-Jewish images in German manuscripts,[33] Ruth Mellinkoff challenges the idea that the birds' heads were the means of showing human figures without flouting the Second Commandment. She points out that the figures in the Bird's Head Haggadah and in other illustrated Jewish books also show a number of anti-Jewish stereotypical attributes, namely huge hooked and beaked noses (even on human, rather than bird-like, images) and large, ugly mouths. In addition, as a very close observer, she notes what many others have not noticed, that is, that a number of the faces bear ears that are easily recognized as those of a pig. Anathema to any Jew! Furthermore, she points out that these facial features are generally shown in profile, which position she describes as a pejorative view in itself.

Taking all these items together, Mellinkoff concludes that these bird-headed figures with Jews' hats were deliberate anti-Jewish caricatures, and that *they were drawn by Christian artists!* This seems improbable at first, but her opinion is worth considering. If the pictures seem derogatory (as they do according to her well-illustrated book), then how do we account for their presence? She points out that there is evidence for Christian illustrators of Jewish books. Thus, it is possible that a Jewish scribe, having written the text in Hebrew

---

[29] H. Schreckenberg, *Jews in Christian Art*, also E. Revel-Neher, *Image*, 102-103.

[30] R. Mellinkoff, *Outcasts*, 93.

[31] "The Jewish Badge," *Encyclopedia Judaica*, vol. 4 (Jerusalem: Keter Publishing, 1971) 62-70.

[32] Schreckenberg, in *Jews in Christian Art* shows Jesus with a *judenhut* in several pictures, 125, 141-2. Blumenkranz, in *Le Juif*, 133, plate 159, shows a miniature from a psalter belonging to Louis IX in which Jesus and the others, supping at Emmaus, all wear Jews' hats.

[33] Ruth Mellinkoff, *Antisemitic Hate Signs in Hebrew Illuminated Manuscripts from Medieval Germany* (Jerusalem: Center for Jewish Art, The Hebrew University of Jerusalem, 1999).

letters, might have subcontracted the illustrations to a Christian artist, who surreptitiously inserted the unflattering images. What is less easy to believe is that the Jewish scribe (or the patron who commissioned the book) would then permit the caricatures to remain. Couldn't they see how derogatory they were?

These provocative possibilities raise very perplexing issues, and yet there is one further and even more disturbing scenario which Mellinkoff discusses briefly. This is that the Jews—the scribes, the patrons, and the families reading such books around the Passover table—in some paradoxical way may have accepted their degradation at the hands of the Christian majority. Perhaps they began to see themselves as their adversaries claimed they were—caricatures of normal human beings. This would be a dismal example of Sartrean "bad faith." We may never know.

Compared to the information about the Judenhut, much less is known about the infamous Jewish badge. Only rarely do we find pictures of Jews wearing a circular device or *rouelle* (generally yellow or white). In England, the badge was a diptych resembling the two tablets of the Law. Jews in France wore a colored wheel on their outermost garment, but they were exempt from this requirement when traveling outside their living district. If apprehended within their own area without the badge, they were subject to a fine.

Although we do not know how rigorously these rules were enforced, we know that some aspects of distinctive Jewish dress were obnoxious to some Jews because there are on record many requests for exemptions from these regulations.

Romanesque Art

In the previous chapter, we saw that the Carolingian and Ottonian periods produced superb illuminated manuscripts. There seems to have been a relative scarcity of large-scale, that is, "monumental" art, or at least little has survived to today. When the artistic revival occurred about the time of the Millennium, it emphasized large scale production of a public nature, although manuscript and smaller scale art flourished as well.

As Zarnecki points out,[34] the Romanesque style did not begin suddenly nor all in one place. Certainly it was under way by the year 1000, and was dominant in Western Europe in 1050-1150. In some contrast to the art of the preceding eras, it was mainly religious in its themes. The earlier Carolingian epoch catered to small groups surrounding the court, and the Ottonian revival was also centered in the emperor and the nobility. Romanesque art, on the other hand, was more widespread in its provenance and was supported primarily by the Church, which was rapidly growing in size, influence and wealth.

What might be called the "Romanesque Renaissance" coincided with and was an intimate part of both the rapid growth of monasticism and the development of extensive pilgrimage routes. These two movements were interrelated and both required the construction and decoration of churches as well as liturgical objects such as bibles, psalters, reliquaries, vestments, and so forth. Artistry flourished.

Pilgrimages were made to holy places for various reasons, prominent among them being obtaining pardon from sins. The great pilgrimage routes of Western Europe, that is, to Canterbury, Rome, Tours, Toulouse, and especially Santiago de Compostela in northwestern Spain, are examples of a larger phenomenon in history. After all, both Jews and Christians had excellent reasons to make pilgrimages to Jerusalem. In the "window" of Christian occupation of that city, beginning in 1099, European Christians did visit. Jewish pilgrims came as well; they found that the hospitality they received was warmer during the Muslim dominance in the Holy Land before and after the early Crusades than under the occupation of the Christian Crusaders.[35] In any case, for practical reasons most Christian pilgrims chose holy sites in Europe closer than Jerusalem. Many of the routes began in France; at Paris-Chartres, Arles, Vezelay, and Le Puy, each of them important religious sites in their own regard. After moving south across the Pyrenees, these routes coalesced into one great road traveling west through Burgos and Leon to Santiago.

---

[34] George Zarnecki, *Romanesque Art* (New York: Universe Books, 1971) 5-13.

[35] Joshua Prawer, *The History of the Jews in the Latin Kingdom of Jerusalem* (Oxford: Clarendon Press, 1988).

All along these routes, churches were built for pilgrim worshippers and hostels were needed for their accommodation. Monasteries sprang up as well, both in cities and in secluded places in the countryside. All of this required public (as well as private) art for the enrichment of religion.

Emile Mâle, the great French historian of art, dates the reappearance of monumental sculpture in France—and in southern France at that—to the last half of the eleventh century. He uses the word "reappearance" to emphasize the fact that monumental art was a feature in Gaul in the late Roman Empire and then was "eclipsed" for 500 years. He attributes that eclipse to the influence of art of "the East" (meaning Byzantine art) which, while favoring mosaic, neglected sculpture.[36] When monumental sculpture reappeared around 1050, Mâle shows that it was directly influenced by the tradition of illuminated manuscripts, of both Old and New Testaments, a tradition which was not eclipsed but which flourished during those 500 years. Thus, these manuscripts, which are not covered in detail in this book, provided an iconographic bridge between the late Antique and the Romanesque periods.

As an example, Mâle describes the tympanum over the main entrance of the Abbey Church at Moissac (eleventh century) as a translation into sculpture of an apocalypse manuscript from a commentary on Revelation; the manuscript was written in Spain in 784 by Beatus, bishop of Liebana.[37] This was a popular theological work and a frequently used image showing a large Christ in a mandorla, with symbols of the four evangelists, around or beneath which are the twenty-four elders, each with a chalice and a viol (Rev 4:4–5:8).

Symbolism in Romanesque Art. Mâle discusses the rise of symbolism in Christian art. For example, the figure of the evangelist, Mark, shown as a lion (often winged), is a symbol of both the evan-

---

36 Emile Mâle, *Religious Art in France. The Twelfth Century* (Princeton: Princeton University Press, 1978) 3-4.
37 Ibid., 5-10.
38 Wolfgang S. Seiferth, *Synagogue and Church* in the Middle Ages. Two Symbols in Art and Literature (New York: Frederick Ungar, 1970).
39 H. Schreckenberg, *Jews in Christian Art*, 35, from the *Liber Floridus* of Lambert of St. Omer, c.1100-1120.

gelist, and his gospel with its message. The development of public symbolic imagery in medieval Christian art represents a triumph of the human spirit and provides endless fascination for the art historian, the student of religion, and even the humble tourist.

First I will show another example of the translation of manuscript illustrations into public sculpture and then I will discuss some of the conventions and the "rules" of iconography.

Sinagoga and Ecclesia. An extremely interesting pair of artistic images demonstrating the principle of *Adversus Judaeos* began to appear in the ninth century. They involve the personification of two characteristic figures, one identifying Judaism and the other, Christianity. Seiferth, who devotes a volume to this subject,[38] says that the first known instance of such a pair is contained in a manuscript showing two people standing at the sides of the crucified Christ. On Christ's right is a figure who has a banner in one hand and in the other a chalice (the Holy Grail) to catch the blood coming from the wound in Christ's side. This figure, always female, represents *Ecclesia* or the Church. She is an artistic descendant of the figures of *Ecclesia ex Gentibus* and *Ecclesia ex Circumcisione* seen earlier in Santa Sabina and Santa Pudenziana in Rome. On Christ's left side is an old man with white hair; this figure, says Seiferth, "probably" represents Judaism.

In time, these two figures became more defined and their characteristics became more stereotypic. Both came to be depicted as women. Sometimes they have their names written above their heads—*Ecclesia* and *Sinagoga*. Ecclesia is always to Christ's right, Sinagoga to his left. With time, Sinagoga's image evolves. In early works, Sinagoga is seen to turn away from the Crucified Jesus, and indeed to begin to walk out of the scene to our right. Ecclesia, by contrast, stays by the side of Jesus and always looks at her Savior. Ecclesia may have a crown or a halo, or both, but Sinagoga has neither. Seiferth describes a German missal from about 1100 in which Sinagoga wears a Judenhut. More importantly, she carries the instruments of Christ's passion—the jug of vinegar, a sponge, spear, and crown of thorns. This brilliant visual metaphor implicates the Jews as the murderers of Christ. Schreckenberg even describes a manuscript from about 1100 in which Sinagoga is about to enter the open jaws of hell.[39]

There was also a change in the figures, as the Gunhild Cross from either England or Germany shows (figure 5-1). On our left, (Christ's right) is a stern and upright *Ecclesia*, bearing her insignia, banner, and cross. On our right, (Christ's left and sinister side) crouches a partially naked and despondent *Sinagoga* with her insignia broken in two, possibly also representing the tablets of the Law, pulling her hair in despair with her eyes sealed. She cannot see anything, much less the truth of Christian revelation. Finally, by 1170, Sinagoga is shown blindfolded. This image symbolizes not only the blindness of the Jews in failing to see the truth of Christianity but also the veil of Moses (described in the next chapter). There is no more vivid and succinct set of images illustrating what Christians thought of Jews and Judaism than this pair, Ecclesia and Sinagoga. In the next chapter we will see

FIG 5-1. The Gunhild Cross. England or Denmark, c. 1075-1150 C.E. Ivory. To our left is *Ecclesia* with her crown and cross-capped banner, holding the open book of Christian revelation. To our right is *Sinagoga*, old and bowed, pulling her hair, eyes closed. The book of Jewish revelation has fallen to the ground.

that the *Adversus Judaeos* attitude would later become even more pronounced in Gothic versions of these images.

The Romanesque in Burgundy. One of the outstanding features of the period of 1050-1150, a period which began with the "Crucial Half-Century," is the astonishing explosion of monumental sculpture. Any lover of Romanesque art (myself included) is dismayed at having to pick just a small portion of the abundance of artistic riches to illustrate his thesis. There are large volumes solely devoted to Romanesque art and even extensive monographs dealing with a single church. But my task is to be selective, and I will begin by discussing what are probably the outstanding examples of Burgundian art, the Cathedral of St. Lazare (Lazarus) in Autun and the Basilique Ste. Madeleine in Vezelay.

The Cathedral of Autun. Autun became prominent as a Roman city, as did many of the cities of today's France. It was called "Augustodunum" after the emperor Augustus. After the characteristic decline during the Dark Ages it participated in the Romanesque revival, particularly after the relics of Saint Lazarus were brought

there around 1100 and the church was renovated to replace an earlier cathedral dedicated to St. Nazaire.

Of interest is the tympanum over the central door (figure 5-2). It
is a semicircular construction containing an ensemble of many figures
of great sophistication and beauty. Unlike most of the public art of the
Middle Ages, whose creators were anonymous (at least to us), this
tympanum is signed in the stone by its creator, Gislebertus.

The scene is the Last Judgment, a popular set of images depicting
the time when Christ will come again to judge the souls of
humankind, determining who shall go to Paradise and who to Hell. In
the center is a large figure of Christ in a glory or *mandorla*, an oval
halo surrounding his entire body. He is surrounded by four angels, two
of whom are shown upside down. The scene is clearly divided in half;
to our left (but on Christ's right) are the saved and to our right
(Christ's left) are the damned. Below on our left, over the lintel of the

FIG 5-2. Bas-relief, the tympanum over the main portal of the Cathedral of St. Lazare.
Autun (Burgundy), c. 1130 C.E. Christ is shown in a mandorla, between symbols of
the four Evangelists. To Christ's right is Paradise; to his left is Hell.

door are the blessed waiting to ascend into heaven. They do so through a narrow arch on our extreme left where Peter, whom we recognize by the fact that he holds a key, helps a soul. Above Christ's right shoulder is the Virgin Mary and beneath her, on Christ's right, are the apostles. To Christ's left (always the most vivid side) is the weighing of the souls, where one pan of the scale holds the good deeds and the other the evil deeds. A devil sits in the pan of evil deeds to make it heavier and so send the soul to Hell, which is depicted on our extreme right as a devil overseeing bodies in the flames. Over Christ's left shoulder are two figures who may represent Enoch and Elijah.

The "Rules" for Medieval Imagery

This complex picture of the Last Judgment at Autun embodies some of what we may call the "rules" of medieval imagery. Emile Mâle calls them "a kind of sacred mathematics," emphasizing such characteristics as position, grouping, symmetry, and number.[40] They can be listed in part as follows:

1. Larger size suggests greater importance than smaller size. Christ is the most important figure and thus is the largest.
2. Placement to the right is good, to the left is bad. In the case of illustrations of the Last Judgment, such as the one in Autun, this means that the right side of Christ (not the right as we look at the tympanum) is the good side. Heaven and Paradise are always on his right, and Hell is always on his left ("the sinister side"). In the case of Sinagoga and Ecclesia, as mentioned, Ecclesia is always on the right of Christ. Apart from the general "good/bad" orientation seen in many (but by no means all) images, Christ's wound is on his right side; images of Ecclesia began with the personification of the Church, which holds a chalice (the Holy Grail) to catch the blood as it flows from the wound on that side.
3. Higher orientation is better (or holier) than lower. Mary is at the top; on the other side are Enoch and Elijah. These latter two are OT figures who, according to some tenets of *Adversus Judaeos*, might belong on the "bad" Jewish side; but, as they were righteous Jews to

---

40 E. Mâle, *Religious Art*, 5.

the point that they did not die but were translated to Heaven when they were alive, they at least belong at the top of the left side. Below, over the lintel, are the more human souls, again with the elect on Christ's right and the damned on his left.

4. The placement of the images within the church building is usually of great importance. We already saw in chapter 3, when discussing the OT mosaics in S. M. Maggiore, that images were arranged along the side of the nave so that the worshipper, entering by the main door and advancing to the center of the church, had to travel (as it were) through the OT to arrive at the altar for the celebration of the Mass. So too with the placements of illustrations of the Last Judgment. They were often put over the main door of the church for very good reasons, that is, to be seen as one approached the entrance; they were to remind the worshipper that religion, good and bad deeds, and the Savior Himself were of supreme importance, not only in their lives but for eternity. The fanciful and grim figures of the devil and the damned were meant to be sobering influences upon everyone entering the building.

Armed with these few principles, the viewer is already well prepared to uncover some of the iconographic beauties of Christian art. There are many other examples of how the principle of supersessionism is demonstrated merely by the physical placements of the images without regard to their content. For instance, many of the main (usually west-facing) doors of medieval churches contain artistic scenes. While one may think such an important site would be occupied by important NT figures, one often finds instead that they are partly or entirely from the OT. This is true as well with regard to central columns placed between two main side-by-side doors. Such a column, called a *trumeau*, may, as at Souillac in Burgundy, contain an OT scene; in this case it is the binding of Isaac. The placement of such scenes at the entrance of the church again indicates the supersessionist principle that as the Hebrew Bible antedated and prefigured the Christian Revelation, so the worshipper can first experience OT images not simply for themselves, but as prophecies; the worshipper then perforce may move beyond them into the church, the "true" center of Christian worship.

These "rules" and conventions dictated in some ways the constraints laid upon designers of medieval Christian art. The ingenuity which the artisans used, not only to follow conventions but to invent variations on and deviations from them, is just one more facet of the brilliance of this epoch.

The Basilica at Vezelay. A few miles from Autun is the Basilique Sainte Madeleine in Vezelay. It is outstanding for many reasons. The small town of Vezelay (now itself a national monument) occupies a hill in the lush green Burgundy countryside. The main street (in fact, almost the only street) is a single loop which goes up one side of the town and down the other. At the top of the hill stands the abbey church and a small remnant of other abbey buildings. The first structure was dedicated by Pope John VIII in 878. What we see now represents the results of rebuilding after fires, renovation, and enlargement. The church was also extensively restored in the nineteenth century, having been one of the first major projects of Viollet-le-Duc.[41] The church became particularly popular about the time of the Millennium when it was announced that there the body of Mary Magdelene had been found. It is to her that the church is dedicated.

The Basilique then became famous as one of the starting places for the pilgrimage over the Pyrenees to Santiago de Compostela in northwestern Spain. In addition, this church was the place where Bernard of Clairvaux preached the Second Crusade on March 31, 1146. Somewhat down the hill from the church itself is an open field containing a plain wooden cross. Although there is no sign to say so, tradition has it that Bernard addressed the faithful on that spot. It is a moving experience to sit there in the silence.

The church, after its long history of construction and renovation, represents several architectural styles. We enter through the Gothic

---

41 *Eugene Emmanuel Viollet-le-Duc* (London: Architectural Design & Academy Editions) 1980. Kevin D. Murphy, *Memory and Modernity. Viollet-le-Duc at Vézelay* (University Park: Pennsylvania State Press, 2000).

facade and stop in the narthex to admire the central tympanum. It is one of the masterpieces of Romanesque sculpture. A very large Christ presides in a glory (mandorla) over the apostles, the peoples of the earth and even fabulous animals, all symbolizing the universality of the Church's reign.

Important here are the carved capitals on the columns lining the long Romanesque nave. Their images, whether in the original or in restorations, are (as the *Guide Michelin* puts it) "astonishing." The range of the subjects portrayed is large, including secular scenes, allegories, and Old and New Testament stories, all without apparent order. One is amazed by the imagination of the artists who squeezed even complex scenes into the restricted areas available to them at the top of a pillar. There are a number of deliverance scenes, such as Daniel in the lions' den, Isaac's blessing Jacob, Jacob's dream and Peter's deliverance from prison. There is plenty of violence as well—Judith and Holofernes, Moses' killing the Egyptian, and Lamech's killing a man.[42] Jesus is not depicted. There is a capital showing Moses and Aaron and a vivid calf of gold with a spectacular devil springing upwards from its open mouth (figure 5-3).

The most outstanding capital, however, does not portray a scene from either Testament. As figure 5-4 shows, it presents two men curving their bodies around a small hand-turned mill. The upper figure on the left drops coarse grain into the top of the mill and the lower figure on the right collects the finely ground flour into a bag. Who are the men, and what does the image mean? Properly interpreted, this small carving is a supreme symbolization of the doctrine of supersessionism.

The man on the left is Moses; he pours the coarse substance of the Jewish Law into the mill, which represents Christian Revelation. The man on the right is Paul (bald, as is the conventional iconography), who gathers the fine flour of Christianity. This image is called *Le Moulin Mystique* (The Mystic Mill). It is not clear to me where this image originated. It could be taken as an inspired artistic rendering of the concept that the advent of Christ caused the Mosaic Law to be

---

42 Lamech killed a man to avenge Cain. (Gen 4:23-24).

FIG 5-3. Capital, the Golden Calf. Basilica Ste. Madeleine, Vezelay (Burgundy). Moses (to the left) returns from Mt. Sinai bearing the Tablets of the Law and finds the golden calf and a spectacular devil (not mentioned in the Bible) astride. To the right, Aaron crouches (ashamed?).

fulfilled, or superseded by Christian Revelation. We will see in the next chapter that Abbot Suger explained this image which he placed prominently in St. Denis. Whatever the origin, The Mystic Mill has reached the height of allegorical interpretation, on a par with Ecclesia and Sinagoga, yet without any invidious portrayal of Jews. In form as well as in content, it has no superior in Medieval Art.

Figure 5-4. Capital, The Mystic Mill. Basilique Ste. Madeleine. An allegory (see section on Abbot Suger and the stained glass of St. Denis, chapter 6.) Moses (to the left) pours the coarse grain of Judaism into the mill of Christian Revelation. Paul catches the fine flour of Christianity in a sack.

43 Thomas Hoving, *King of the Confessors* (New York: Simon and Schuster, 1981).

44 Elizabeth C. Parker and Charles T. Little, *The Cloisters Cross. Its Art and its Meaning* (New York, Metropolitan Museum of Art, 1994).

The Cloisters Cross

Another major work of art important in this section was most probably made around 1170. It might well be included in the Gothic art of the next chapter. It is not large—just about two feet tall. Neither is it brilliant with color, as it is virtually one color—or rather shades of one color—namely a creamy ivory. Yet it is one of the supreme creations of medieval art and it superbly illustrates the themes of this book in dramatic and complex ways.

The "Cloisters Cross" is an ivory cross which now occupies the central place of honor in the Treasury of the Cloisters, a unique Medieval museum situated in Fort Tryon Park in upper Manhattan. The Cloisters is a branch of The Metropolitan Museum of Art, and the Cloisters Cross is one of its many glories. The history of the cross is almost as fascinating as the cross itself. It is a complex story excitingly told by Thomas Hoving, who obtained the cross for the Metropolitan. In his book, *King of the Confessors,* Hoving describes "the chase and the capture"—the mysterious history (or rather lack of history) of the cross, and the difficulties Hoving had in purchasing it. The book is indeed a true art history "thriller."[43]

The cross is agreed to be English Romanesque, most likely made in the late twelfth century. Exactly where it was made and for whom are just two of its many secrets. It has often been called the "Bury St. Edmunds Cross" after a famous English abbey, but this name reflects primarily stylistic similarities between the cross and the Bury St. Edmunds Bible; it is not based on firm evidence that the cross was made for or found in that abbey. In fact, we are ignorant of almost all of the first seven hundred years of its existence!

My discussion is based partly on my own inspection of the cross during a recent visit to the Cloisters but mostly on the superb text and extravagant illustrations found in the definitive book by Elizabeth C. Parker and Charles T. Little.[44] The cross stands almost 23 inches tall. It is carved elaborately on both sides and so was undoubtedly meant to be viewed from both front and back. It probably stood on an altar and also could have been carried in church processions. The cross once had a statue of the crucified Christ on its front and it is virtually certain that this statue is now in the Oslo Kunstindustrimuseet. Thus the cross that we see today is liturgically incomplete, lacking the figure of Christ. Nonetheless, it is iconographically intact, and has a number of lessons to teach.

Aside from the artistic magnificence of the cross, its iconographic aspect is compelling. Not only are the many images on the cross a veritable encyclopedia of supersessionism but also almost all of them

FIG 5-5. The Cloisters Cross. Ivory. England. Late twelfth century. The front of the cross displays the Moses medallion in the center, the Crucifixion to the right, the women at the tomb to the left, and the Ascension at the top (see text). A figure of the crucified Christ once hung from this side of the cross.

are identified in writing on the ivory itself. Thus there is no ambiguity about who the images represent and what they are doing there. (In this sense, the inscriptions remind one of Abbot Suger's writings in the stained glass windows at St. Denis, made at about the same time as the cross.)

A complete description cannot be made here. After all, Parker and Little devoted 300 pages to various aspects of this masterpiece

FIG 5-6. The Cloisters Cross, back (See text.). The symbols of the four Evangelists are seen: Mark, Luke, John, and (at the bottom) a place for Matthew. The central medallion displays the Lamb; the stem and arms bear Old Testament prophets.

and still did not answer all the questions. Nevertheless, I shall describe briefly the cross itself and indicate some of its iconographic ramifications. (The orientation of the images will be described as to right or left as the viewer faces the cross from either front or back).

The Front of the Cross. On the shaft are small figures of Adam and Eve at the bottom of what is a wooden tree shorn of most of its branches (figure 5-5). This is a "Tree of Life," not a "Jesse Tree" (see chapter 6), so Jesse is absent and Adam is "The First Man." At the end of the right arm is a square plaque—"The Good Friday Plaque"—showing the Crucifixion. At the end of the left arm is "The Easter Plaque," which shows the risen Christ, the Holy Women at the Tomb, and the sleeping Roman soldiers (dressed, not surprisingly, in Crusader armor). At the top of the cross is a plaque showing the Ascension of Christ. In the center, at the crossing, is a large circular plaque showing Moses and the Brazen Serpent (see below).

The Back of the Cross. The largest figures are the symbols of the evangelists on the three ends of the cross—the winged lion of Mark on the left, the winged bull of Luke on the right, and the winged eagle of John at the top (figure 5-6). As there was no other arm available for the fourth evangelist, Matthew is found portrayed in a smaller plaque toward the bottom of the cross. The center of the cross contains a roundel with the lamb of God and several figures. The arms of the back of the cross are covered with portraits of nineteen figures, three on each of the arms and ten on the long stem. These include David (at the top) with Solomon below him; the others are prophets, most (but not all of them) haloed. Among these are Obadiah, Nahum, Haggai, Balaam, Malachi, Amos, Job, Hosea, Isaiah, Micah, Habakkuk, Zephaniah, Joel, Daniel, Ezeckiel, and the evangelist Matthew; at the very bottom was Jonah, whose figure has been lost. Each prophet holds a phylactery scroll with a few words from his prophecy, words believed to foretell the life and death of Christ. We do not know what the words of Jonah might have been in the lost plaque, but it is of interest that right above that lost image is Matthew, whose quotation (Mt 12:40) speaks of Jonah in the belly of the great fish as prefiguring the Harrowing of Hell by Christ.

The Central Medallions. The two central medallions are justly famous, and are of great iconographic interest. The medallion on the front, called the "Moses medallion," shows Moses in front of the Brazen Serpent, which hangs from a forked stick (figure 5-7). The story portrayed comes from Numbers 21:5-9. The Israelites were tired of wandering through the desert. They complained against the Deity, whereupon God sent fiery serpents which bit and killed many people for their sin. When the people repented, God told Moses to erect a bronze serpent; when those who had been bitten looked up at it, they were saved. Thus, the serpent was a sign of salvation.

FIG 5-7. The Cloisters Cross, front (detail). The Moses Medallion. Moses kneels before the Brazen Serpent, which hangs in the fork of a branch. Other figures include Peter, John the Evangelist, Isaiah, and Jeremiah (See text.).

FIG 5-8. The Cloisters Cross, back (detail). The Medallion of the Lamb. The lamb is nearly pierced by the lance of the woman (Sinagoga) turning to the left (See text.).

The Brazen Serpent image appears in various places in medieval art, but its arrangement here is unique. It is also the only complete OT *scene* (as distinguished from a single figure) to appear on the Cloisters Cross. Moses, the largest (and hence the most important) figure, strides across the center of the medallion, unfurling his scroll, which reads, "Your life shall hang in doubt before you; night and day you shall be in dread, and have no assurance of your life" (Deut 28:66). So far, the scene might be considered strictly OT in import, and many of its figures wear Jews' hats. What makes the medallion Christological in meaning are the other figures around Moses. These include John the Evangelist, Peter, Isaiah, and Jeremiah. The first two of these carry scrolls whose inscriptions indicate that the serpent on the forked stick represents Christ on the Cross. Moses, once again, is associated with Christ in the supersessionist mind.

The medallion of the Lamb occupies the center of the back of the cross, analogous to the Moses medallion on the front (figure 5-8). The Lamb, allegorically Christ, stands in the center, looking backward. In front is John the Evangelist, looking toward the Lamb and weeping (Rev 5:4) Beside and below him is Sinagoga. Although she is not blindfolded, her mantle seems to be falling across her face, and she averts her head from the Lamb. Her staff is not broken, but is, in fact, a lance with a pointed fleche at the tip, just touching the breast of the Lamb. This image has provoked much discussion, because in it Sinagoga appears to be ready to slay the Lamb. Her phylactery reads: "Cursed is everyone who hangs on a tree." This phrase appears both in the OT (Deut 21:22) and the NT (Gal 3:13). The OT passage could be (and was) interpreted to refer to crucifixions (which were a Roman, not a Jewish form of punishment). Regardless, Paul's unstated message in Galatians is that for Christianity, the Deuteronomic curse needed to be nullified—in fact, Jesus' Crucifixion did just that. Thus the OT curse is negated and redeemed by the Crucifixion.[45] It is curious that although Sinagoga is shown, Ecclesia is absent, unless its symbol is included in the Lamb.

The roundel also includes, below and behind the Lamb, Jeremiah (haloed) and an angel with a long scroll who says to John, "Weep not"

45 Ibid., 111.

(Rev 5:5). Interestingly, Jeremiah appears twice in this medallion, once below the Lamb and again lying across the top of the roundel as he does in the Moses medallion. The scrolls of the two Jeremiahs on the back refer to the Lamb as victim (Jer 11:19)

Thus, this artistically delicate and sophisticated ivory cross, intended to stand at the center of the worship ceremony, is equally sophisticated in its weaving together the strands of Jewish figures and prophecies with Christian images and reflections.

The Altar at Klosterneuberg

Across Europe, another iconographic masterpiece was being made at the same time as the Cloisters Cross. A master goldsmith, Nicholas of Verdun, created an altarpiece of gold and enamel for the Abbey of Klosterneuburg in Austria in 1181. It presents three horizontal rows of seventeen images each, for a total of fifty-one small medallions. Again, as each is inscribed in Latin, we have no doubt as to what scene is being shown. The inspiration and workmanship are magnificent. Plate 7 depicts the central section, as it is impossible to show all 51 scenes in one picture. Nevertheless, it is in the relations between the images that the iconographic interest lies.

The scenes, reading across (horizontally) fall into three historical eras. The top row contains scenes *Ante Legem* (Before the Law), meaning during the time from the Creation up until the Law (of Moses) was proclaimed at Mt. Sinai. Here we see Adam and Eve and the serpent, Abraham and Melchizedek, Noah and the ark, and so forth. The lowest row contains scenes *Sub Lege* (Under the Law), that is, events happening after the Exodus, such as Moses' receiving the tablets of the Law, several scenes of Samson, Jonah being thrown into the sea, and so forth. The middle row shows scenes *Sub Gratia* (Under Grace), that is, during the new dispensation of Christianity. Here we see the birth of Jesus, the Last Supper, the adoration of the Magi, the entry into Jerusalem, and the Crucifixion, among others. (These hor-

---

46 The parallel between Jonah (in the belly of the great fish for three days) and Christ (in the earth for three days after the Crucifixion) is made explicitly in Matthew 12:40.

izontal divisions are reminiscent of the tiers seen in early Christian sarcophagi, discussed in chapter 3).

At first, the profusion of scenes is almost overwhelming. Yet, as the medieval mind was an orderly one, we expect that the organization of the many scenes on the altar will have its own internal logic. The altar is meant to be "read" from left to right. The first scenes on the left are announcements of the births of the significant figures: Isaac above, Jesus in the middle register, and Samson below. As one moves to the right, it is difficult to find a *chronological* justification of the arrangement of the scenes in the upper and lower rows. At the top, scenes with Melchzedek occur before and after Moses; Noah and the Ark are seen towards the end. In the bottom row, we see Samson before as well as after scenes involving Moses. When the center or explicitly Christian sequence, that is, Sub-Gratia, is examined, everything becomes clear. This middle row is chronologically arranged, beginning with the announcement of the birth of Jesus, proceeding through His life to the Crucifixion and the Resurrection, and ending with the Last Judgment on the right. The scenes on the upper and lower registers are individually keyed to the Christological center row according to the tenets of typology. Thus, the most telling analogies are seen when various sets of three superimposed images are analyzed. It is in this analysis that we see into the heart of supersessionist typology.

For example, on the right side of plate 7 we see the following. On the top (Ante Legem) row, Joseph is thrown into the pit by his brothers (Gen 37:23-4); on the bottom (Sub Lege) row Jonah is pitched into the sea (Jon 1:15); and in the middle row (Sub Gratia) we see the entombment of Christ. What is common to Joseph and Jonah is the theme that the heroes were placed unwillingly into a dark and dangerous hole, while the dead Christ was put into a dark tomb.[46] Without any knowledge of the words around each scene, a Medieval Christian would quickly grasp that Joseph and Jonah are prefigurements of Christ.

The vertical trio of panels on the left of plate 4 show Melchizedek with the bread and the wine on top, the Last Supper symbolizing the Eucharist in the middle, and the collecting of manna at the bottom.

The top and the bottom scenes are clearly meant as prefigurements of the Eucharist.

Perhaps the most intriguing vertical triplet of scenes is, not surprisingly, the central set. In the middle row, and thus in the pivotal and central position of all fifty-one scenes, is the Crucifixion, with the Virgin Mary to Christ's right and Mary Magdalene weeping on his left. Above is a medallion depicting the binding of Isaac. The figure of Abraham (somewhat damaged over the centuries) cowers under the hand of the angel who grasps his right arm. A small Isaac lies on the altar and the ram seems almost to plead to be taken. (We need to remember that not only is Abraham a God-figure but Isaac is a Christ-figure as is, of course, the ram).

The lowest scene of the three is the most impressive, speaking typologically, and we see it for the first time. It is taken from Numbers 13:23-4. Moses had sent from each of the twelve tribes a scout into Canaan to see what kind of country it was and what kind of people lived there, and then to report back to him. A large bunch of grapes was brought back, so big that it had to be carried on "a frame" by two men. Indeed, the panel shows two men who carry a wooden pole from which the cluster of grapes hang. The supersessionist interpretation of this scene, Mâle tells us, is found in the *Glossa Ordinaria* and in the writings of Isidor of Seville.[47] However, I found an earlier reference in another dialogue, *The Discussion Concerning the Law Between Simon, a Jew and Theophilus, a Christian*.[48] This was written about 400 C.E. by Evagrius. Theophilus says to Simon that the cluster of grapes brought by the scouts prefigures Christ hanging on a tree. That is, the grape cluster is the body of Christ (He turned water into wine and turns wine into his blood, symbolized in Holy Communion. He also said "I am the vine" [Jn 15:5].) As the grapes hang from the wooden pole, so the body of Christ hangs from the wooden cross (in the scene above).

Who are the two men, typologically speaking? In the dialogue of Evagrius, Theophilus says that the hindmost man on our right is the

47 E. Mâle, *Religious Art*, 144.
48 A. L. Williams, *Adversos*, 298-305.
49 It may be considered ironical that the quintessential supersessionist image of the two men carrying the pole with the cluster of grapes is also the logo of the Israel National Tourist Office.

Christian, faithfully following the symbol of his Savior. The foremost man, on our left, is the Jew who has literally turned his back on the Messiah, even though (according to the Christians) his own scriptures predicted the Messiah's coming.[49] (In this image, the front "Jew" turns back to look at the grapes. In other renditions of this theme, he looks resolutely ahead.)

The Meuse Cross

The symbol of the Cross, with or without Christ, was (and is still) a compelling image for Christianity. Another outstanding typological example is the copper-gilt and enamel cross in the British Museum (plate 8). It dates from the third quarter of the twelfth century and was probably used in church processions. It holds on one side five distinct OT scenes, each of which was believed to represent the prefigurement of the Crucifixion. In the center panel, Jacob blesses Ephraim and Menasseh with *crossed* hands. At the top are Moses and Aaron and the Brazen Serpent. On the right, an Israelite paints the door of his house with a mark of lamb's blood so the Lord will "pass over" his dwelling during the night of the tenth plague and instead kill the firstborn of the Egyptians (Ex 12:7). What the sign on the door might have been is not described in the Bible, but according to conventional Christian typology it is the Greek letter *tau* ("T"), which represents the Cross. On the left, Elijah visits the widow of Zarephath, who has been gathering wood here shown as sticks in the form of a cross (1 Kings 17:8-12). At the bottom of the cross are two scouts, Caleb and Joshua, carrying a cluster of grapes from Canaan. The grapes, as we have seen in the Klosterneuburg Cross, symbolize Christ's body on the Cross. Here, the man in front—representing Judaism—does not look back but turns away from the grapes.

Art and Jewish-Christian Relations

During the period of the Crusades and after, Jewish-Christian relations became more strained than ever. Legislation restricted the civil liberties of Jews, and neither the civil nor the ecclesiastical authorities were able to protect their lives or their livelihoods.

Romanesque art, more and more sophisticated in its styles and methods, reflects these increasing tensions. The pair of images of Ecclesia and Sinagoga no longer show the naive simplicity of the earlier images. Ecclesia remains young, beautiful, and stately, but Sinagoga is increasingly degraded. She often appears without a halo, is pushed away from the scene of the Crucifixion, and is finally shown blindfolded.

The capitals in the Basilique Ste. Madeleine in Vezelay are, in general, New or Old Testament scenes, primarily of deliverance, without prejudice to the Jews. The image of the Mystic Mill, however, is different. It is neither common nor easily understood, but with proper interpretation by a guide surely shows the worshipper a vivid image of the superiority of Christianity over Judaism.

The Cloisters Cross nearly defies description in its detail and its complexity:

> "No visual precedent exists for such an exhaustive elaboration of the meaning of the Cross for the Christian believer. In essence, the program is a dazzling display of typology, in the belief that the Old Testament directly anticipates the events of the New—as Christ himself expressed to his disciples after the Resurrection: 'all things must needs be fulfilled, which are written in the law of Moses, and in the prophets, and in the psalms, concerning me.' (Luke 24:44)."[50]

What purposes might such a detailed typological commentary serve? Current opinion deems it unlikely that it served as "a polemic against contemporary Jews, reflecting the social opposition that they were beginning to encounter in England at the time the cross was made."[51] It is true that an inscription on the front reads: "Life has been called. Synagogue has collapsed with great foolish effort."[52] Such a statement, however, is to be understood by now as standard, rather old-fashioned supersessionist doctrine. The motives underlying the social pressures, both economic and religious, must have been clear to the Jews. Putting all the typology at hand into one cross would hardly influence Jewish beliefs, opinions, or activities. Jews would unlikely see the cross, and certainly never closely enough to read (or understand) the Latin inscriptions. It was, after all, a unique liturgical object, and a very expensive one at that. Indeed, it is unlikely that ordinary Christians themselves would ever get close enough to read (or understand) the inscriptions. It must have been reserved for and closely guarded by the clergy.

Nevertheless, the pedagogical potential of the Cloisters Cross was tremendous. Would the clergy use the cross as a teaching device, pointing to it during a sermon in order to illustrate various supersessionist doctrines? It is an intriguing idea, although one with no evidence to support it (nor, for that matter, to refute it).

The most likely rationale for this outstanding work of art is that it embodied in visible and palpable form the relation of the Old and New Testament scriptures to the concept of the Cross on which Christ died. The designers of the cross must have put incredible amounts of thought and discipline into planning the design. The concepts behind the carving were of the utmost importance. The force of the symbolism in the final product would necessitate the construction of the Cloisters Cross even if it were kept locked away and invisible.

The individual scenes on the altar of Klosterneuburg are reminiscent of the capitals at Vezelay—mainly Old and New Testament scenes. Nevertheless, the choice of those scenes and their placement relative to one another are instructive. Two choreographic arrangements are important. The three horizontal levels symbolize the three historical eras of Judaism and Christianity. To medieval European societies, who knew virtually nothing about non-European peoples, this meant the history of the world itself. These three eras are described under the principle of *Verus Israel*. The top row—Ante Legem (Before the Law)—shows the True Israel of Adam and Eve, down to Abraham, Melchizedek, and Noah—that is, the original Hebrews living not under Mosaic Law (which had not yet been given at Mount Sinai) but under Natural Law.

---

50 Parker and Little, *Cloisters Cross*, 43.   52 Ibid., 44.
51 Ibid., 175.

Not surprisingly, the lowest level—Sub Lege (Under the Law)—shows the aberrational offshoot of the Jews living under the Law of Moses, which, from the Christian point of view, eventually was abandoned in its literal sense (although it prefigured Christianity). In the central row is Christianity—Sub Gratia (Under Grace)—under the grace brought by Christ. This era is obviously superior to (and thus above) the Mosaic epoch at the bottom.

The vertical sets of triple scenes are equally important. To concentrate on the central set of three, already I have described the binding of Isaac at the top, the cluster of grapes carried by the scouts below, and the Crucifixion in the center. At a simple level which shows analogies between the three scenes, we notice the theme of *wood*. There is wood in each picture. At the top, we see the wood that Isaac carries up Mt. Moriah at his father's bidding. This wood is a prefigurement of the Cross. Indeed, there is a tradition that claims the place Abraham built the altar intended for Isaac's sacrifice would be the setting of Jesus' crucifixion. This concept strengthened the analogy between "Father" Abraham, ready to sacrifice his son, Isaac, and God the Father, willing to sacrifice his Son, Jesus.

Thus, once again the OT prefigured the central event in the Christian drama. The same is true of the lowermost scene in which two men carry the cluster of grapes hanging from a wooden pole. This obvious prefigurement of the Crucifixion places the Jew before and the Christian behind the symbol of the Savior on the Cross; therefore, both upper and lower panels clearly indicate to the believing Christian that his faith and doctrines were prophesied by the OT. The believer also knows that even when the events prophesied occurred and the parallels were pointed out, most Jews were spiritually blindfolded—just like Sinagoga—and failed to see the connections.

The Doors of San Zeno. It is important to note that not all invidious images of Jewry involved supersessionist thinking. One work of art exemplifies the Christian attitude toward Jews without resorting to typology. On the facade of the church of San Zeno Maggiore in Verona is a pair of wooden doors, nailed to which are a series of cast bronze panels. The date usually given for this masterpiece is about 1140, and the craftsmen may have come from as far away as

FIG 5-9. Panel from the bronze doors of San Zeno Maggiore. Verona, c. 1100 C.E. Christ, wearing a tripartite halo signifying the Trinity, holds on to a pillar while a man with a cat-o-nine tails whips him. The man and the onlookers all wear Jews' hats.

Magdeburg. The panels contain both OT and NT scenes portrayed with great simplicity and imagination. Figure 5-9 shows the scene in which Christ, with the tripartite halo of the Trinity, is bound to a pillar. Next to him a man holds a cat-o-nine-tails. The scene is the flagellation of Christ, an essential component of the Passion. The man with the whip and indeed all the other men wear Jews' hats. It must be understood that as the Christian worshippers entering the church would have known the significance of the hats, this graphic display makes perfectly obvious the responsibility of the Jews in the death of Jesus. Since the Jews of the Veronese community may well have worn similar hats, they too were implicated—at least by association—in the crime.

There is another aspect of the Verona flagellation scene, again not typological, which is important as it shows a deliberate anti-Jewish bias in the *interpretation* of the Biblical story itself. Blumenkranz points out that the depiction is extremely misleading because it mistranslates the Gospels. The relevant passages referring to the flagellation of Christ (Mt 27:26; Mk 15:15; Jn 19:1-3) clearly indicate that it was the Roman soldiers, not the Jews, who whipped Christ.[53] The same "mistake" often is seen in manuscript illustrations of the Passion of Christ, in which Jews are seen placing the crown of thorns on Jesus.

The Problem of "the Horned Moses." Nevertheless, it is just as important to ensure that anti-Jewish sentiments are not seen where they were not intended, as in the case of the "Horned Moses." Michelangelo's statue of the seated Moses in Rome is one of the marvels of Renaissance sculpture. Virtually all of its admirers wonder why the figure of Moses has two horns sprouting from his head. The image did not originate with Michelangelo. In fact, it was common to see Moses with horns throughout the middle ages. It is natural for us to want to know whether this was an anti-Semitic symbol.

The history of the Horned Moses is complex. In her monograph devoted to the subject,[54] Ruth Mellinkoff indicates that the verbal image dates to a "mistranslation" by Jerome which occurred when he was deriving the Latin Vulgate Bible from the Hebrew. The passage in question is Exodus 34:29-30, 34. Moses came down from Mt. Sinai the second time, carrying the tablets with the Ten Commandments. Moses "was not aware that the skin of his face was radiant." The Hebrew word which we read as *radiant* is *karan*; this is very similar to *keren*, which refers to horns. Most Hebrew words of any complexity are made out of a root of three consonants; the vowels are usually subscript symbols. In the Torah scrolls of antiquity such as Jerome would have used, and indeed in the scrolls of today, the subscript vowels are not written and must be surmised by the reader according to the context. At times, this leads to ambiguities, as in the case of karan and keren. In English, if you leave out the vowels, the three consonants of karan and keren are identical. So it is in the Hebrew. Thus, while Jerome knew some Hebrew and consulted with Jews while making his translation, it is understandable why he may have thought the word was keren and so translated it as *cornuta*, which means "horned."

It seems that the first graphic image of the horned Moses appeared in England in the eleventh century. It is not clear exactly why this image lay dormant for six hundred years after Jerome's time. Mellinkoff makes the provocative statement that Christians might have taken note of the image by reading Rashi's discussion of the passage from Exodus. Rashi points out that the word "horned" is used because "light radiates from a point and projects like a horn."[55] Another possible source comes from the stage directions for at least one "Prophet Play" (*Ordo Prophetarum*), which indicates that Moses is to be present with horns.[56]

It seems clear, then, that the image of the horned Moses was not an explicit manifestation of anti-Semitism. Indeed, as Kugel points out, horns on headgear were often a sign of authority and distinction.[57] This figure is an example of how careful one must be in interpreting Jewish-Christian relations from the standpoint of art.

[53] B. Blumenkranz, *Le Juif*, 98-104.

[54] Ruth Mellinkoff, *The Horned Moses in Medieval Art and Thought* (Berkeley: University of California Press, 1970).

[55] Ibid., 84.

[56] Ibid., 32.

[57] J. Kugel, *Bible as it Was*, 437.

6 | The Climax of Supersessionism and the Eclipse of Judaism, 1100-1250 C.E.

Triumphs for Some, Setbacks for Others

This chapter deals with two triumphs. The first is the triumph of Christian art, if not of Christianity itself. Art of the period from 1150 to 1250 is called "Early Gothic" in art books. The Gothic period, the successor to the Romanesque era in the West, probably began in structures like the abbey church of St. Denis, near Paris. In architectural terms, the layman knows this transition as the replacement of the Romanesque rounded arch by the Gothic pointed arch. But there was much more—greater flexibility in building styles; an emphasis on light in the cathedrals with the development of large windows of stained glass; and innovation in sculpture and manuscript illumination. During this period we see the completion, or at least the beginning, of some of the churches which remain the pinnacles of medieval art. These include St. Denis; Notre Dame and Sainte Chapelle in Paris; Chartres; Laon; Reims and Amiens not far away; Canterbury and Salisbury in England; and Cologne in Germany. Gardner's *Art through the Ages* says the thirteenth century "represents the summit of achievement for unified Christendom; the triumph of the papacy; a successful and inspiring synthesis of religion, philosophy and art [the scholastic movement] and the first firm foundation of the states that will make modern history."[1]

A western European Jew living during this same period would hardly look at the situation in the same way. The triumph he would see would be that of anti-Semitism. His status in society, never secure, would become even more threatened, and the period would end with

---

1 Horst de la Croix, Richard G. Tansey, and Diane Kirkpatrick, *Gardner's Art Through the Ages* (New York: Harcourt Brace & Co., Ninth Edition, 1991) 381. Nevertheless, one should note that at the time of these triumphs, Western Christendom was responsible for two of history's more brutal accomplishments—the sack of Constantinople in 1204 and the suppression of the Albigensian Heresy from 1208 to 1229.

accusations of ritual murder, the public burning of one of his most sacred books, *The Talmud,* and actual expulsion from several countries. These events are part of a general change in the social and political climate, that is, "a fundamental negative shift in Christian attitudes toward Jews (which) occurred around 1200."[2]

The Papal Positions. During this period, the papacy became stronger with the inclusion of capable men. At the time, many popes died after only a few years in office; yet, there were only six popes in the sixty-three-year span from 1191 to 1254. Such longevity in office provided stability and strength. True, much of the activity was concerned with ongoing disputes with the Holy Roman Emperor; but many papal policies had direct or indirect effects on the Jews.

The Church wished to grow even stronger. "The extension of Christianity to unbelievers was among the chief aims of the Church."[3] The Church still feared the practice of proselytizing by Jews. Jews were forbidden to enter churches, and some local councils forbade them from appearing in public during the last three days of Holy Week. Although these provisions may have been passed off as methods of protecting the Jews against attacks which might occur on emotional days and in religious places, the anti-Semitic aspects of these decisions cannot be ignored.

The Third Lateran Council (1179) condemned usurers, whether Christian or Jewish.[4] Christian usurers were denied communion or Christian burial, but of course the Church had no such power over the Jews (see below). This same council further marginalized the Jews by forbidding Christian midwives or nurses from caring for Jews.[5]

The Fourth Lateran Council (1215) produced a number of decrees which affected the Jews.[6] Concerns about distinctive dress

---

[2] William C. Jordan, *The French Monarchy and the Jews* (Philadelphia: University of Pennsylvania Press, 1989) 46.

[3] S. Grayzel, *Church and Jews,* 13.

[4] J Parkes, *Jew, Medieval Community.*

[5] W. Durant, *Story of Civilization,* vol 3, 387.

[6] Synan, *Popes and Jews* and J. R. Marcus, *Jew, Medieval World.*

[7] E. Synan, *Popes and Jews,* 104.

[8] J. R. Marcus, *Jew, Medieval World,* 137.

[9] The word "ghetto," is Italian, and refers to a section in Venice. The first compulsory ghettos were located in Spain and Portugal in the fourteenth century.

[10] J. Parkes, *Jew, Medieval Community.* Also M. R. Cohen, *Under Crescent.*

and how it might prevent unwanted intermingling between Christians and Jews were discussed in chapter 5. In the realm of finance, Christians were to boycott Jewish money-lenders who charged excess interest, although there was no accepted definition of what was meant by "excess." Jews, once again, were not to hold public office lest they be in positions to control and influence (here read *proselytize*) Christians. Pope Innocent III, as well as previous popes, was concerned about Jews who converted to Christianity and then returned to Judaism. Apparently this backsliding often occurred if the converts continued to observe Jewish practices and perhaps attend Jewish services after their conversion. The Council warned converts not to mix their new-found Christianity with old Jewish practices. Interestingly, this warning was bolstered by a quote from a well-known precept of the Jews themselves: "You shall not put on cloth from a mixture of two kinds of material" (Lev 19:19). The Council also continued policies affecting Christians who took the cross for the Holy Land and who had borrowed from Jewish money-lenders. The interest owed to the Jews was to be forgiven and the payment of principal delayed until the debtors returned. This was often years later—if they returned at all.

In fact, many of these regulations were reissues or restatements of previous rules. Whether the rules were inspired by malice toward the descendants of those who killed Christ or were meant to protect an important minority depends at least partly on one's point of view. Two contemporary historians differ in this respect. Father Synan indicates that these decrees were "inspired by a positive concern with the care of souls,"[7] while Jacob Rader Marcus sees them as further efforts to "segregate the Jew socially even more than he had been in the past."[8] Whatever the intent, the result was that more and more, the Jews were being restricted in their daily living and working centuries before the word "ghetto" was used.[9]

The Jews and the State. The civil status of the Jew was a continual problem which became accentuated after the Millennium.[10] The inability of Jews to defend themselves in a militant Christian society became obvious during the First Crusade. In the peace of 1103 which followed, the Jews were mentioned as being among those who could not protect themselves, similar to the clergy and women. After that, a number of expedients were devised, ostensibly to "protect" the Jews. In the twelfth century, Jews came under the protection of the appropriate ruler, whether king, Holy Roman Emperor, or baron. In 1179 in Germany, Jews were declared to belong to the royal domain. Communities of Jews might receive a charter with rights and obligations. This "protection" was not necessarily a boon. Henry III of England (1207-1272) liked to forgive debts owed to Jewish money-lenders, an act which was surely not considered protective by the Jews. And, of course, there was the perennial unanswered question of whether Jews were to be tried in civil or ecclesiastical courts.

As the twelfth century moved toward its close, anti-Jewish sentiments increased and eventually led to anti-Jewish actions. The reasons behind this crescendo of hate generally are not clear, as those responsible usually backed their opinions by the same "Christ-killing" accusations. Ruether, however, adds a modern and exceedingly subtle rationale for the new levels of animosity.[11] The anti-Jewish riots of the early Crusades had shown several things. First, the Jews were unable to defend themselves. Second, many preferred to die rather than convert to Christianity. If, indeed, Christians had defined Jews as "people of mere legalism and 'carnality,'" it was difficult to justify their steadfastness. If their religion really was as empty as Christians were told, how could it survive under such unfavorable conditions? Was there perhaps some substance to this? Thus, says Ruether, to justify the current anger at the Jews, new kinds of evidence of their perfidy were needed. Whether this attitude was ever prevalent and, even if it was, whether Christians were aware of it, never will be known. Nonetheless, new accusations of Jewish wickedness were made.

Ritual murder was the allegation that Jews killed Christian children to use their blood for ritual purposes, in particular in the Passover meal. The most famous version of this scenario was written in 1173 by a Benedictine monk, Thomas of Monmouth, who

---

11 R. R Ruether, *Faith.*   Marcus, *Jew, Medieval World,* 131-36.

12 J. R. Marcus, *Jew, Medieval World,* 121.   14 Ibid.

13 E. Synan, *Popes and Jews,* 114-15; J. R.

described the event as having taken place in Norwich in 1144. The accepted historical stance emphasizes that there is no evidence for the truth of this story.[12] From a wider perspective in Jewish-Christian relations, it makes little difference whether the story has a basis in fact. "Perception is reality." The readiness with which medieval Christianity accepted such allegations attests to the degree of hostility towards Jews lying beneath the surface of society. In any event, the myth persisted. Of course, most Church officials took no part in such defamation. In 1247, Pope Innocent IV addressed a letter to the prelates of France and Germany; in it he specifically denounced such accusations and asked that Jews be protected from harassment.[13]

In England, the coronation of Richard the Lion-Hearted in 1189 sparked anti-Jewish riots in London which later spread to York. The causation was the usual one—that the Jews first rejected and then killed Jesus.[14]

Expulsion of the Jews from France

Whether Philip Augustus, who became King of France in 1179 at the age of fifteen, actually believed the charges of ritual murder is not clear. His chronicler, Rigord, indicates that he did believe. Soon after gaining the throne, Philip imprisoned French Jews and then released them after ransoms were paid. In 1181 he canceled all loans which Jews had made to Christians. The next year he ordered the Jews out of the territories which he controlled (which were far less extensive than the France of today), but in 1198 he allowed them to return. It is not clear how many Jews were in Philip's royal domain, nor whether the expulsion was aimed at all of them or only at the money-lenders. In any event, in Paris at least, when the Jews returned they were no longer able to live on the Ile de la Cité where most of them previously had lived. Trying to read between the lines of Rigord's biased account, one gets the idea that these maneuvers and counter-maneuvers on the part of the King were motivated financially rather that religiously. After all, the crown regulated money-lending and increasingly exploited Jews in this respect. It is likely that these measures spurred large-scale emigration from France to the Holy Land in 1209 and later.[15]

Louis IX (later Saint Louis) went further by confiscating Jewish property without the pretext of a crusade. This happened repeatedly—in 1234, 1246-1247, and 1268. These financial strictures further marginalized the Jews by taking away their material goods, thus limiting the livelihoods open to them in an increasingly mercantile age.

From the standpoint of the Jews, the restrictions on their livelihoods must have been extremely difficult. Even more demoralizing was the *unpredictability* and apparent *capriciousness* with which their existence was manipulated.

The Burning of the Talmud-The Ultimate Indignity. As pointed out earlier, both the Babylonian and the Jerusalem Talmuds were important books for Jews. They contain what is called the "Oral Law," distinct from the written Law which is the Hebrew Bible. According to Jewish tradition, the Oral Law was conveyed by God to Moses and then was transmitted orally until it was written down in Hebrew and Aramaic during the years 30 B.C.E.-500 C.E. It was (and still is) studied intensively by Jews and Jewish scholars. Conversely, as it was not translated into Latin or Greek, it was not understood by the various popes and prelates. Nonetheless, it was alleged to be full of anti-Christian statements and sentiments. Furthermore, it was supposed to contain *secret* doctrines of the Jews. Thus, it was a symbol of the religious "otherness" of the Jew as well as a subject of suspicion, unease, and even hatred.

These attitudes crystallized just before the middle of the thirteenth century. Nicholas Donin was a Jewish convert to Christianity. He alleged to Pope Gregory IX (1227-1241) that the Talmud was

[15] J. Prawer, *History of the Jews.*

[16] J. R. Marcus, *Jew, Medieval World,* 145-50. Louis' attitude towards the Jews is reviewed differently by various authorities. In the *Encyclopedia Judaica,* one learns of Louis' "implacable enmity" (11:515), while the *New Catholic Encyclopedia* does not mention his anti-Jewish actions at all.

[17] "Talmud, Burning of," *Encyclopedia Judaica,* vol. 15, 768-81.

[18] S. Grayzel, *Church and Jews,* 31. A good description and analysis of this disputation as well as of those in Barcelona (1263) and Tortosa (1413-1414) can be found in Hayam Maccoby, *Judaism on Trial* (East Rutherford NJ: Associated University Presses, 1982).

filled with anti-Christian blasphemies, errors, and wickedness. One of the main objections was that the sense of the Talmud prevented Jews from turning to Christianity. The pope, in 1239, directed the rulers of Western Europe to seize and examine all copies of the Talmud and, if the accusations were true, to burn them. According to Marcus, only Louis IX of France heeded the order. The books in France were confiscated on a Saturday, when Jews would be in the synagogue. [16]

The Jews were directed to send representatives to answer the charges of Donin in public.[17] The trial took place in 1240 in Paris. Donin was the accuser; prominent Jewish scholars were the defendants. The judges at this public event included the archbishops of Paris, Sens, and the King's chaplain. Presiding over the proceedings was none other than Blanche of Castille, the mother of Louis IX and one of the most formidable women of the Middle Ages.

The disputation in fact was not an argument or a debate about the merits or truths of Judaism versus Christianity, but an attack on the Talmud. As Grayzel puts it, "the disputation lasted several days, and while both sides claimed victory, the resultant condemnation of the Talmud and of the works of Rashi, was a foregone conclusion."[18] The logic behind this event is interesting. Christians, although they were exceedingly unlikely to know exactly what was written in the Talmud, knew that the books were important to the Jews who claimed the books contained the words of God. So did the OT, of course, but as the OT legitimized Christianity through the eyes of supersessionism, the Christians could hardly burn it! The Talmud was another matter entirely. It was a set of documents supposedly hostile to Christianity, and, since it postdated Christ, it was invalid testimony. Thus it was not only permissible but desirable to burn it. After some delays, a large number of wagon-loads of Jewish books were burned, also in public, in 1242. The next pope, Innocent IV, urged that another burning take place in 1248. The burning of the Talmud indicates how far the hostility of the Christians had come. The act itself is entirely in consonance with edicts calling for the expulsion of Jews from England and France.

The Culmination of Medieval Art

We approach "the High Middle Ages" and the transition from the Romanesque to the Gothic era in art. During the Gothic era, there was a magnificent efflorescence of activity in all artistic realms. In fact, when people think of "medieval art," it is generally this era that they consider.

The art of the illustrated manuscript was an older form which was raised to new heights in order to express the fervor of religious expression. In these manuscripts, the illustrations became more and more elaborate with time; this contributed greatly to their desirability and to their expense. In illustrated Bibles, typology and allegory flourished as never before.

A Bible for the Poor? Among the most famous of these manuscripts is the so-called *Biblia Pauperum* (Bible of the Poor), a term which must count as a medieval oxymoron; the poor, even if they could read the text, certainly could not afford the book! The dates of its production are uncertain, but an ancestor manuscript existed at least as early as 1250. One version contains forty pages, each composed of three principal scenes.[19] In the center is a NT roundel; on either side is an OT prefiguration. Surrounding the central picture are four prophetic figures. The text is in both German and Latin.

For example, one page depicts the Nativity in the center. The four prophets surrounding this scene are Daniel, Micah, Isaiah, and Habbakuk. The flanking OT figures are of great interest. On the left, God appears to Moses in the Burning Bush, and on the right are the flowering staffs of Aaron and of Joseph, the husband of Mary. Both flanking scenes refer to the Virgin Birth. The fact that the Bush was not consumed is identified with Mary's purity. The miracle of the flowering staff is a symbol of God's approval. Thus, Aaron's staff flow-

---

[19] Avril Henry, *Biblia Pauperum—A Facsimile Edition* (Ithaca NY: Cornell University Press, 1987). Also C. Wetzel, ed., *Biblia Pauperum* (*Armenbibel*) (Stuttgart: Belser Verlag, 1995).
[20] Jacobus de Voragine, *The Golden Legend*, trans. William G. Ryan, (Princeton NJ: Princeton University Press, 1993) 153. This collection of the lives and miracles of a number of saints was written down in the thirteenth century. It was a best-seller for centuries, although its popularity far outweighed its accuracy.

ers with blossoms and almonds, indicating that his tribe of Levi was chosen from among the twelve to be the priestly tribe (Num 17:11). The story of Joseph's staff is to be found not in the Bible but in *The Golden Legend.* The story concerns the choice of a husband for Mary. God said that each suitor should bring a branch to the altar, and the possessor of the one which flowered was to be Mary's husband. The branch that flowered belonged to Joseph.[20] In this connection, Aaron's staff is considered as a prefigurement of Joseph's staff, and hence it points to the marriage of Mary and the Virgin Birth.

There were artistic innovations as well. Included here are two examples: the Jesse Tree motif represents stylistic and typological factors; the medium of stained glass represents a technical advance which was greatly exploited for public typology.

The Tree of Jesse and the Ancestry of Christ. The doctrine of Supersessionism takes an historical approach to the origins of Christianity. The Jewish revelation, described and exemplified in the Hebrew Bible, is *followed by* the Christian revelation, exemplified in the life of Christ and described in the New Testament. We have been dealing with images Christians used to illustrate their supersessionist theology; but images may have their own life and sociology. In the context of medieval art, some images appear earlier and some later. Pictures of Jonah as an OT prefigurement of Christ were present in the earliest catacombs of the third century. Specifically Christian images such as the Virgin and Child as well as the crucified Christ appeared later, as did the pair *Sinagoga et Ecclesia.* Very late in our story—not until close to the time of the Crusades—do we see another extraordinary image: the Tree of Jesse.

No subject was more important to the force of the supersessionist argument than the legitimacy of Jesus as the very Messiah the Christians insisted had been predicted by the Jewish prophets. We have seen that there were six major prophets whose writings and sayings were interpreted to foretell the coming of the Messiah in the person of Jesus Christ. These were Moses, Isaiah, Jeremiah, Daniel, Zechariah, and David.

A related and equally important pillar of this claim exists, however, in the analysis of the genealogy in question. In terms of the genealogy of the Messiah, the most famous and most precise Jewish Bible reference is made by Isaiah:

But a shoot shall grow out of the stump of Jesse,
A twig shall sprout from his stock.
The spirit of the Lord shall alight upon him.
A spirit of wisdom and insight,
A spirit of counsel and valor,
A spirit of devotion and reverence for the Lord. (Is 11:1)

This surely describes characteristics of a Messianic personage. The first line of this section clearly indicates that the Messiah will be a descendant of Jesse. As Jesse was the father of David, the passage implies that anyone who claims to be the Messiah also must be able to trace his ancestry to David. The Messiah must be "of the house of David." Indeed, Jesus said at the very end of the Book of Revelation, "I am the root and the descendent of David" (Rev 22:16).

The ancestry of Christ is so important that the first chapter of Matthew describes the complete lineage from Abraham through Jesse and David to Joseph, the husband of Mary.

Isaiah's wonderful figure of speech that describes the "shoot" growing out of the "stump" of Jesse had not escaped the Fathers of the Church. In the early third century, Tertullian related the prophecy to Jesus, equating the stem (*radix*) with Jesse and the shoot (*virga*) with Mary (*virgo*).[21]

This superb visual metaphor makes one wonder why it took so long for the metaphor to be translated into graphic forms such as illustrations for manuscripts. We are not sure when the first Jesse Tree

[21] Tertullian, *An Answer to the Jews*, chap. 9 (www.newadvent.org/fathers). Also, G. Schiller, *Iconography*, 1:15.

[22] Arthur Watson, *The Early Iconography of the Tree of Jesse* (London: Oxford University Press, 1934).

[23] A. L. Williams, *Adversos*, 321-25. The date and place of origin are unknown.

[24] *The Wisdom of Baruch*, 3:37

[25] See M. F. Vaughan, "The Prophets of the Anglo-Norman 'Adam,'" in R. E. Kaske, et al, *Traditio*, vol. 39 (New York: Fordham University Press, 1983) 81-114.

appeared, but Watson believes it was not seen before the eleventh century.[22]

The Evolution of the Image of the Tree of Jesse. One of the most fascinating enigmas in the study of medieval religious art is the question of how the words of Isaiah, "But a shoot shall grow out of the stump of Jesse," were transmuted into the classic "Tree of Jesse" pictures seen in Bible manuscripts and stained glass. It seems that an intermediate step includes a form of art not yet considered—the drama.

During the Middle Ages, there circulated manuscripts of a work wrongly attributed to Augustine: *Contra Judaeos, Paganos et Arianos: Sermo de Symbolo* (translated by Williams as *Against the Jews, the Heathen and the Arians: A Discourse on the Creed.*)[23] We will refer to it as the *Sermo.* It is unimportant for us that Augustine was not the true author, but his supposed authorship gave the sermon credence and popularity.

In the middle of the *Sermo,* the preacher turns to the Jews, who deny that Christ is the predicted Messiah. Once again, he says that the proofs of the coming of Christ are to be found in the words of the Jews' own prophets. Rhetorically, he exclaims; "Give, O Isaiah, thy testimony to Christ"; then, impersonating Isaiah, he proceeds to read Isaiah 7:14, which speaks of the Virgin's bearing a child. Then he evokes Jeremiah, using the words of Baruch (Isaiah's friend and secretary, as mentioned in the apocryphal book of Baruch). Jeremiah speaks of Wisdom, a female personification of God, who "appeared on earth and lived with humankind."[24] Then the preacher evokes in turn Daniel, Moses, David, and other Jewish prophets, using the typical supersessionist texts from each. The veritable parade of prophets' testimonies was designed to show Christ's prefigurement in the OT.

There is an enormous and somewhat confusing collection of literature concerning what happened next. Many experts believe the *Sermo* was dramatized into what we know as the *prophet play.*

A prophet play (*ordo prophetarum*) was a dramatic enactment presented inside, outside, or alongside the church on special occasions. Manuscripts of the prophet plays are scarce; the best known existing manuscript is Part 3 of *Jeu d'Adam* ("Play of Adam").[25] There also is one dating from the thirteenth century which may well be a later copy of an ancestor drama. It is a Christmas drama from the Cathedral of Laon in Northern France.[26] The Laon manuscript is of great interest for several reasons. First, the predictors of Christ include not only OT but also pagan personages. Thus, supersessionist thinking included both Jews and heathens as precursors of Christianity. Second, the manuscript describes how these prophets are to be dressed. Third, the *Adversos Judaeos* aspect of the play's message is very clear. It is not difficult to see how this scenario, in the hands of a gifted and imaginative artist, could be transformed into a brilliant Tree of Jesse window or sculpture.

In the play, the major OT prophets are listed in the following order: first Isaiah, then Jeremiah, Daniel, Moses, David, and Habakkuk. Then follow Elizabeth ("pregnant") as well as her son John the Baptist, Virgil, Nebuchadnezzar (see below), an unspecified Sibyl ("much like one insane"), Simeon, and finally Balaam ("upon an ass, bearded, holding a palm, plying his spurs").

These thirteen characters form a procession. Although it is not quite clear who the following are, it seems that six Jews (or people dressed as Jews) and six Gentiles (pagans) flank each side of the procession. These provide the audiences to which the messages of the prophet play are directed. Two singers chant the following, presumably to everyone present, including the actors and the Christmas congregation.

Duo Cantores:	The two singers:
Omnes gentes	Let all races,
Congaudentes	Rejoicing together,
Dent cantus letitie!	Sing songs of gladness!
Deus homo	A God-man,
Fit de domo	Sprung from the house of David,
David, natus hodie.	Is born to-day.

---

[26] The text of the Laon *Ordo Prophetarum* is printed in Latin and English in Joseph Quincy Adams, *Chief Pre-Shakespearian Dramas* (Boston: Houghton Mifflin, 1924) 41-48.

The singers then chant the following to the Jews.

Ad Judeos:	To the Jews:
O Judei,	O Jews,
Verbum Dei	Who denied the Word of God
Qui negastis hominem,	Become man,
Vestre legis	Hear in succession
Testes regis	The testimonies of your law
Audite per ordinem.	And of your king.

Then they sing the following to the Gentiles:

Ad Paganos:	To the Gentiles:
Et vos, Gentes,	And you, O Gentiles,
Non credentes	Not believing
Peperisse Virginem,	that the Virgin has given birth,
vestre legis	Banish the darkness
Documentis	On the evidences
Pellite caliginem.	Of your own law.

The two summoners then call upon the prophets to come forth one by one, beginning with Isaiah.

[Duo] Appellatores:	The two summoners:
Isaias, verum qui scis,	Isaiah, thou who knowest the
Veritatem cur non dicis?	truth, Why dost thou not declare truth?

Isaiah answers:

Est necesse	It is necessary
Virgam Jesse	That a scion from the root of Jesse
De radice provehi,	Be exalted;
Flos deinde	A flower, then,
Surget inde,	Will spring thence,
Qui est Filius Dei.	Who is the Son of God.

The two summoners comment:

Iste cetus	Let this gathering
Psallat letus,	Chant in gladness!
Error vetus	Let ancient error
Condempnetur.	Be condemned!

The choir then comments:

Quod Judea	That Judea, the guilty,
Perit rea	Is destroyed,
Hec chorea	This choir
Gratulatur.	Is rejoiced.

This section is then completed.
The summoners then call Jeremiah, who says:

Jeremias:	Jeremiah:
Sic est,	Thus it is:
Hic est	This is
Deus noster.	Our God.

The summoners then repeat:

[Duo] Appellatores:	The two summoners:
Iste cetus, etc.	Let this gathering, etc.

And the whole choir repeats:

Omnis Chorus:	The whole choir:
Quod Judea	That Judea, the guilty,
Perit rea	Is destroyed,
Hec chorea	This choir
Gratulatur.	Is rejoiced.

Thus the body of the play consists of a series of stanzas, each containing the summoning of a prophet, the words of the prophet, the commentary of the summoners, and the moral pointing to Judea, the guilty.

This dramatic presentation concludes swiftly as all the prophets and the clerics sing a verse about the predestination of Christ's coming. Mass is celebrated immediately afterward.

Other plays fit this genre. Although we do not know exactly when or where it was written, the "Anglo-Norman Adam" play may have been written in the twelfth century.[27] It is a melange of three episodes: one of Adam and Eve, one of Cain and Abel, and a prophet play, respectively in Latin, mime, and French. In the prophet play episode, the following appear: Abraham, Moses, Aaron, David, Solomon, Balaam, Daniel, Habakkuk, Jeremiah, Isaiah, and finally Nebuchadnezzar. (Although he is not a Hebrew prophet, great attention was paid to the story of the three Jews—Shadrach, Meshach, and Abednego—who refused to worship the statue of Nebuchadnezzar (Dan 3:1-27). They were saved from the furnace by an angel of God. The deliverance story leads to an apparent conversion of Nebuchadnezzar from paganism to the One True God [Dan 3:28-33].)

These two prophet plays therefore contain OT figures who proclaim the coming of the Messiah in the person of Jesus. Were these plays the direct predecessors of *graphic* illustrations of the Jesse tree? John Colletta suggests the interesting possibility that there was an additional intermediate between the *Sermo* and the manuscript and stained glass illustrations.[28] He believes that the *Sermo* first inspired public sculptural renditions of the parade of prophets, such as is seen on the facade of Notre-Dame-la-Grande in Poitiers. These, in turn,

---

[27] Lynette R. Muir, *Liturgy and Drama in the Anglo-Norman Adam* (Oxford: Blackwell, 1973).

[28] John P. Colletta, "The Influence of the Visual Arts Evident in the *Jeu D'Adam*," in John R. Sommerfeldt and Thomas H. Seiler, *Studies in Medieval Culture*, XIII (Western Medieval Institute: Michigan State University, 1978) 73-83. (I am indebted to Professor Kathleen Maxwell of Santa Clara University for bringing this and reference 18 to my attention.)

inspired the *ordo prophetarum* plays, which would have been enacted directly below the facade. Lastly, the plays led to the Jesse Tree illustrations. In this case, the artistic legacy would be sermon-sculpture-drama-illustration. In any event, the great explosion in the use of Jesse Tree images throughout Western Europe is best exemplified in the medium of stained glass.

Stained Glass

We have arrived at what all must admit to be one of the glories of medieval artistic creation—the great stained glass windows of gothic churches. That they were created when they were must be counted as marvelous. That many of them have survived to today is hardly less marvelous. They have remained objects of aesthetic admiration and religious devotion since their installation. More recently they have become the subjects of intense scholarship, even minute scrutiny.

From the standpoint of this book, stained glass illustrations are great public images which display the riches of medieval Christianity's artistry; they tell of late medieval supersessionist thinking and reflect Jewish-Christian relations. For these purposes, iconographic windows are of great interest.

Some generalizations are necessary. In narrative windows, for instance, such as one that depicts the life of Joseph or Jesus or a saint, a sequence of images illustrates the narrative. Thus, such a window displays a story that has a beginning, middle, and end. In this sense the viewer may be said to "read" the window, often from the bottom to the top. If there are two main images on each level, then the eye usually weaves back and forth as it ascends. Some windows are "read" in the opposite direction. However, in no case should this be thought of as the same as reading a book. There are no pages to turn; the pictures are all present simultaneously. A window is not a substitute for a bible or a psalter, even if the books are illustrated. There are interesting parallels, however, between illustrated manuscripts and subsequent glass windows. In the late twelfth and early thirteenth

---

[29] C. De Hamel, *History of Illuminated Manuscripts*, 115.

centuries, the "Moralized Bible" (*Bible Moralisée*) became popular, particularly in the Paris region. Some of these bibles were richly illustrated and used the typological approach. Some pages contain various scenes that are placed vertically, much like the great windows of the major cathedrals. It is not clear which format inspired the other.[29]

The public nature of these windows also deserves comment. While theoretically the windows were visible to all who entered the church, in practice this was different. Not all parts of the edifice were equally accessible to the populace. Thus, not every window was seen easily by every person. In general, the choir and sometimes the apse were reserved for the clergy and royalty. Ordinary people stayed in the nave and transepts. In the pilgrimage churches, on the other hand, particularly those with ambulatories, the populace had access to virtually the entire building.

Finally, we must discuss the iconography. It is inevitable that we view and study these windows with attitudes vastly different from those of twelfth-century viewers. We have at our fingertips the scholarship and artistic perspective of centuries before and after the twelfth century. Thus we can (and do) bring to these images a degree of historical and artistic understanding which would be unknown to the medieval viewer. On the other hand, the attitude of the medieval viewer would have been different from ours. If he were royal, noble, or a cleric, these attitudes may have involved closer familiarity with religious knowledge and texts which subsequently have been lost. And virtually all medieval Christians would enter a religious structure such as a cathedral for purposes which would be foreign to most scholars and tourists in our secular age.

Astonishing as it may be that so much fragile glass has survived the centuries, nevertheless much of the original creations have been lost. Where there is knowledge of the originals, reproductions have been made. However, it has also been discovered by diligent research that during several waves of dismantling and reconstructing the glass, some windows have been *rearranged*. That is, the original or reproduced panels have changed place within a window, or even have moved to another window. These situations create severe challenges for the iconographer.

The Jesse Tree at St. Denis. It is likely that the first public display of a Jesse Tree window occurred during the dedication of the apse of the Abbey Church of St. Denis in 1144. The church is Abbot Suger's masterpiece, and the ceremony was attended by Louis VII and his queen Eleanor of Aquitaine. Today, this outstanding church lies in the busy suburb of St. Denis, a few miles north of Paris, and is shorn of nearly all of its abbey buildings. In the twelfth century, of course, it was situated in open country. Most of its details were designed by Suger, who seems to have been something of an organizational genius with a strong artistic and mystical sense. He was particularly interested in opportunities to teach in his church and therefore used the images, particularly the stained glass windows, to make clear his messages of faith.

Placement is a key feature in cathedral art, and Suger's Jesse Tree window is no exception. There are seven (the mystic number) radiating chapels in the apse of St. Denis. The central and most important chapel is dedicated to Mary (often this was called The Lady Chapel in England). Each chapel has two windows. In Mary's chapel, one window contains scenes from the life of Christ—the Annunciation, the Nativity, the Magi, the flight into Egypt, the dispute with the Doctors of the Church, and the dormition of Mary. The other window contains the Jesse Tree. Thus, the most important chapel in the cathedral devotes one window to the "Old Dispensation" or Jewish Bible and one to the Gospels.

---

30 This panel of glass is a nineteenth century reproduction. Probably it is very close to the original, as it was modeled after the Jesse Tree window in the western facade of Chartres Cathedral (which we will soon discuss); that window in turn was closely modelled after the lost original of this scene in St. Denis.

31 The ancestry of Jesus is given in both Matthew and Luke, but the two accounts differ somewhat. Mary and Joseph were said to be related, but that relationship was not clearly stated in the NT. According to Jacobus da Voragine, who wrote *The Golden Legend* in about 1250 (see ref. 20), Joseph and Mary had a common ancestor, Nathan (or Matthan); this ancestor, in turn, was a descendant of King David. The genealogy of Jacobus indicates that Mary and Joseph were half-cousins, three times removed. (I am indebted to my wife, Janet Stewart, M.D. for this genetic analysis.)

32 W. Durant, *Story of Civilization,* 3:745-47.

The Jesse Tree window (plate 9) is a tower of five vertical sections surmounted by a semicircle. Each of the lower sections contains a central figure flanked by two men in horizontal lunettes. The top central panel and the semicircle contain a larger figure.

At the bottom in the center, a man sleeps (plate 10). He wears a Jew's hat, and represents Jesse. This is a wonderful night-scene.[30] Jesse is asleep; the oil lamp hangs from the ceiling. He is barefoot, as befits a prophet. The window of his bedroom is undoubtedly open as the curtains on the right are blowing in the night breeze.

Out of Jesse's pelvic area grows a large (obviously phallic) tree stump. As the tree rises into the four central panels above Jesse, it sprouts branches and twigs, leaves and flowers. Placed within the branches in each of the first three panels above Jesse, a man who wears a crown holds on to the branches as he peers out at us. Each figure obviously is a royal descendant of Jesse, beginning with David and then rising to Solomon. It is not always clear which king is represented above Solomon. In some Jesse Trees, the name of the king is given. However, the precise identity of the figure is not as important as the symbol of the crown on his head. The crown indicates kingship and clearly means that Jesus was of the royal house of David.

Above David is a woman, also wearing a crown; she must be Mary (crowned as Queen of Heaven). She is the immediate ancestor of Jesus who is the highest (and therefore most important) figure on the window. Indeed, Jesus is the end, the acme and the *raison d'etre* of this pedigree.

The placement of Mary in the section below Christ deserves comment. Although Mary is considered to have been related to Joseph, the lineage presented at least in the first chapter of Matthew is patrilineal.[31] That is, the ancestry of Jesus runs through the male line from Abraham via David to Joseph, who is the husband of Mary. Joseph has always been a less prominent and less popular figure than Mary. This was particularly true in the Middle Ages, when the popularity of Mary grew to great intensity.[32] Her placement in the genealogy of Jesus therefore is understandable.

The figure of Christ in majesty occupies the top semicircle of the window. He wears a halo (Mary does not) and behind him is the top of the tree with seven branches. Each branch ends in a circle containing a dove, and together they symbolize the seven holy virtues mentioned by Isaiah.

The pairs of men in the lunettes at each side of the central figures are prophets. Although they are not named in this window, they are named in other windows. They personify such Hebrew Bible figures as Daniel, Isaiah, Jeremiah, and others who are considered to have foretold the coming of the Messiah. This vertical procession of prophets is reminiscent in a sense of the processions in the prophet plays. These prophets, as usual, carry scrolls which represent (and often are inscribed with) their prophetic words. Camille refers to the thirteenth-century bishop Guglielmus Durantis (or Durandus), who said that the antique scrolls symbolize the ancient (and imperfect) message of the OT prophets in contrast to the complete books (open or closed) often shown with the Evangelists and Apostles.[33]

At the bottom right, a place usually reserved for the donor of the window, we see Abbot Suger himself. Remarkably, he holds up a miniature window illustrated with the Tree of Jesse. (This is a modern panel—it is not certain whether it accurately reflects the original design.)

This image of the Tree of Jesse, the first large-scale display of the theme in medieval art, immediately became a model. It was widely copied and adapted throughout Western Europe. (As Eleanor of Aquitaine, wife of Louis VII of France, was present at the dedication

---

[33] Michael Camille, "Visual signs of the sacred page: books in the Bible Moralisée," in *Word and Image*, 5 (1): 111-30, 1989. See also J. M. Neele and B. Webb, *The Symbolism of Church and Church Ornaments, of William Durandus* (Leeds: T. W. Green, 1843). The distinction is not absolute, as we see NT figures' carrying scrolls in the Moses medallion of *The Cloisters Cross*.

[34] St. Peregrinus was the first Bishop of Auxerre. He was martyred (c. 304) during the persecutions of Diocletian. his relics later were transferred to St. Denis. See F. G. Holweck, A *Biographical Dictionary of the Saints* (St. Louis: B. Herder Book Co., 1924).

[35] See Branislav Brankovic, *Les Vitraux de la Cathedrale de Saint-Denis* (Castelet: Villefranche-de-Rouergue, 1992); and Louis Grodecki, *Les Vitraux de Saint-Denis* (Paris: Centre National de la Recherche Scientifique, 1976). Also Herbert Kessler, "The Function of *Vitrum Vestitum* and the use of *Materia Saphiroram* in Suger's St.-Denis," in *L'Image* (Paris: Cahiers du Leopard d'Or, 1996) 5:179-203.

of St. Denis, her subsequent career as the wife of Henry II of England may have had something to do with the appearance of a very large Jesse Tree window in Canterbury Cathedral soon afterward.)

We do not know whether Notre Dame de Paris had an early window of this sort. The Western Rose window is, in part, a Tree of Jesse, but it is of a much later date. Chartres and Sainte Chapelle include Jesse Tree windows, as we will see shortly.

Windows of Allegory. As pointed out during the discussion of Jesse Trees, the mind of Suger and the artistic productions he sponsored at St. Denis are a treasury of typological imagery. In the chapel of St. Peregrinus are two fascinating allegorical and typological windows.[34]

Today the windows are called "The Allegories of St. Paul" and "The Life of Moses." They have been the subjects of extraordinarily detailed analysis by Grodecki, Kessler and others.[35] These analyses conclusively have shown that the windows we see today comprise original as well as nineteenth-century glass. More importantly, much of the glass has been lost and the remaining panels have been rearranged so that what we see is not quite what Suger intended. The details of these renovations and reconstructions are available for the scholar, but I shall discuss the windows as they are today. They remain astonishing productions.

The Allegories of St. Paul. This window is on our right. Two of the five panels contain original twelfth-century glass. The bottom roundel places Christ between the Church and the Synagogue (plate 11). The large figure of Christ, haloed and crowned, occupies the center. On his chest seven circles, each containing a dove, symbolize the seven holy virtues mentioned by Isaiah as characteristics of the Messiah. Christ's right hand rests on the head of the lady named Ecclesia. His gesture symbolizes the *election* of the Church. It is with his *left* hand that he lifts the veil from the face of Sinagoga. The symbolism comes from 2 Corinthians 3:14: "For to this day, when they [the Jews] read the old covenant, that same veil remains unlifted, because only through Christ is it taken away." Thus the blindfold which had been on Sinagoga represents the blindness of all Jews to the *real* meaning of their Law.

The Concealed and the Revealed—The Symbol of the Veil. This concept of sight versus blindness is a central theme of medieval Christianity. We must make a digression at this point to discuss the "veil of Moses." The question of which biblical meanings were hidden and which were obvious was of great concern to the Church. The supersessionist thesis was that the tenets and the history of Christianity were hidden in the Jewish Scriptures but were brought to light with the coming of Jesus and the teachings of the early Christians. The most famous and most succinct formulation of this position was made by Augustine, who wrote: "In the Old Testament the New is concealed; and in the New Testament, the Old is clarified."[36]

This opposition between the hidden and the revealed was ripe for artistic development. The original proof-text for one of the images is Exodus 34:29-35. Moses returns from Mount Sinai the second time, bearing tablets. We discussed the image of Moses with "horns" at the end of chapter 5. Here we are concerned with the consequences of the fact that, because he had spoken with God, Moses' face "was radiant"; or, as Kugel translates the LXX passage, "became glorious."[37] The next passages are difficult to interpret. It seems that the change in Moses' appearance frightened Aaron and the Israelites, so Moses put a veil over his face (but only *after* he had spoken with them). Then the text says that Moses wore the veil "until he went in to speak with Him [God]." Thus, Moses was without the veil when he was teaching, but he must have put it on at some point because he needed to remove it when he returned to the Deity. Ruether accuses Paul of "misreading" this passage (2 Cor 3:7-18);[38] whether he did misread the passage, certainly he reinterpreted it in true supersessionist fashion. He claims that though the written code brought down by Moses was the "dispensation of death," nevertheless it came with splendor.

---

36 W. Seiferth, *Synagogue and Church*, 15.

37 J. Kugel, *Bible as it Was*, 435.

38 R. R. Ruether, *Faith*, 99.

39 Erwin Panofsky, *Abbot Suger on the Abbey*

Church of St.-Denis and its Art Treasures (Princeton NJ: Princeton University Press, 1979) 75.

40 Ibid.

In Paul's understanding, Moses put the veil over his face so that the Israelites could not see that the splendor in his face *was fading*. Allegorically, Paul believed that the splendor which was fading was Judaism, and it was the veil which hid this fact. Paul then generalized this concept to all Jews, including the ones of his day, to indicate that their minds were metaphorically veiled and could become unveiled only if they turned to Christ.

To return to the window of the Allegories of St. Paul, the roundel above the picture of Sinagoga and Ecclesia continues the theme of the veil. Although the original panel is lost, we know from Suger what it showed. In this scene, the veil is taken from the face of Moses, and Suger comments, "What Moses veils, the doctrine of Christ unveils."[39] The image closely follows the passage in Corinthians.

Above this panel is one entitled "The Mill of St. Paul." The original is lost, but it showed Paul turning a mill while Jewish prophets brought sacs of grain. (The modern panel is artistically weak). Suger's verse on the scene is:

By working the mill, thou, Paul, take the flour out of the bran. Thou makest known the inmost meaning of the Law of Moses. From so many grains is made the true bread without bran.[40]

This is the same theme we saw in the sculpted capital of *Le Moulin Mystique* at Vezelay. The Jewish Scriptures were the coarse wheat; Paul showed how the new dispensation of Christian revelation (the mill) was able to separate the old chaff (Judaism) from the fine flour of Christianity. Where the quotation originated and which image was the first are irrelevant to the power of the symbolism.

Above a roundel with a scene from the Apocalypse is the final panel, a unique representation called "The Ark of The Covenant or the Quadrige (Chariot) of Aminadab" (plate 12). In the center is a small figure of Christ on the Cross, which is held in the hands of a large figure of God. The symbols of the four Evangelists are at the edges. The Cross stands on a gold box on four wheels. The box apparently contained images of the tablets of Moses and the rod of Aaron before the renovations[41]; thus it is an OT symbol. Suger's text in the window says that the altar of the Cross (Christianity) is based on but is superior to (and thus placed above) the Ark of the Covenant (Judaism). The image comes from chapter 9 of Hebrews (previously thought to have been written by Paul) in which the golden altar of the Tabernacle is described. Later portions of Hebrews describe the supersession of the sacrifice of Christ over the bloody rituals of the Jewish Temple sacrifices. The inscription below the wheeled altar refers to an obscure passage in the Song of Songs, 6:12, which mentions (in some Hebrew versions) the chariots of Aminadab. We are not sure what Suger had in mind. Crosby thinks the chariot was meant to symbolize the Church, supported by four wheels (the Evangelists).[42] Nonetheless, this window is a stunning example of the translation of Suger's rather intellectual theology to glorious visual imagery.

The Life of Moses. The other window in the St. Peregrinus chapel contains scenes from the life of Moses. In contrast to the St. Paul window it is more narrative than symbolic, but the inscriptions make clear that Suger—ever the teacher—wanted to point out the supersessionist aspects in five episodes in the life of the Jewish leader. The lowest panel shows Moses' salvation from the Nile by Pharoah's daughter. Suger's inscription indicates that she is the Church and that Moses, a Christ figure, is saved by the vivifying waters of the Nile.

The next panel represents Exodus 3:2, where Moses encounters God in the Burning Bush (plate 13, lower roundel). To Suger, the bush which burns but is not consumed represents the fire of faith which warms but does not destroy. As we have seen previously, it also refers to the perpetual virginity of Mary.

In the middle panel (plate 13, upper roundel) Moses leads the Israelites across the Red Sea. As the waters of the Red Sea saved the Israelites, so Christians are saved from sin by the waters of Baptism.

---

41 S. M. Crosby, J. Hayward, C. T. Little, and W. D. Wixom, *The Royal Abbey of Saint-Denis in the Time of Abbot Suger* (New York: Harry N. Abrams, 1998).

42 Ibid.

43 Allen Temko, *Notre-Dame of Paris* (New York: Viking Press, 1952); Alain Erlande-Brandenburg, *Notre-dame de Paris* (New York: Harry N. Abrams, 1998).

In the fourth roundel Moses receives the Law on Mt Sinai (Ex 24:12), a motif we have seen since the early sarcophagi (see chapter 3) Aaron stands on the left; the Jews with the golden calf are at the right and below. To Suger and to medieval Christians, the Law Moses receives is *dead* (that is, stone). The inscription is based on 2 Corinthians 3:6: "for the written code kills, but the Spirit gives life."

The top panel depicts the passage in Numbers where God tells Moses to make a fiery (or bronze or copper) serpent and mount it on a staff so that any of the Israelites (depicted in their conical hats) who had been bitten by snakes could look at the serpent and be saved (plate 14). Clearly this is a deliverance image. To Suger, the saving serpent on the pedestal represented the saving Christ on the Cross (Jn 3:14-15); above the serpent is an image of the Crucified Christ.

Taken together, these five scenes are all of a deliverance type. They clearly illustrate both the themes of *Concordia* and of *Adversus Judaeos*: the Hebrew Scriptures, properly interpreted, predict Christianity.

Notre Dame de Paris

This cathedral perhaps is the best known and best loved of the churches of France. Located in the heart of the French capital, it has been a great religious magnet and the subject of voluminous scholarship.[43] Expense was not spared in its construction and decoration.

At Notre Dame, we see an outstanding rendition of the images of *Sinagoga* and *Ecclesia* at the center of the main facade, where two large statues flank the central western doorway. So characteristic and illustrative are they that I chose them for the frontispiece (q. v.). What we see today are nineteenth-century reproductions, but, as with the figure of Jesse in the St. Denis window, there is no reason to doubt the authenticity of their symbolism. (It is curious that these figures are not mentioned in some of today's guidebooks for Paris. Why not? Would they be considered politically incorrect? To the contrary, I believe that understanding them is crucial for a real appreciation of medieval Christian art.)

The figure to our left is an attractive young woman, wearing a crown and standing straight. She holds a chalice (the Holy Grail) in her right hand and a staff with a banner in her left. She faces the central doorway. The images of *Ecclesia et Sinagoga* almost always flank a crucifixion scene, and here there is no crucifixion. But, if one projects the positions of these two figures back into the cathedral, they flank the altar, which does have a central crucifixion. This woman looks authoritative—indeed she is The Church. To our right is another woman. She is much older and has poor posture. What looks like a blindfold is actually the body of a serpent which covers her eyes. Her left hand holds a staff which is broken in several places. This is not the result of vandalism but is the artist's way of depicting that her authority is broken. In her right hand are the two Tablets of the Law, pointing *downward* and about to slip out of her grasp and fall to the ground. Her head is turned *away* from the central doorway frame. Her crown has fallen to her feet. She is, of course, *Sinagoga.* In fact, she echoes the words of Lamentations 5:16-17, which describe the unhappiness of the Jews in Biblical times: "The crown has fallen from our head; woe to us that we have sinned...because of these (things) our eyes are dimmed." Later sister statues at Bamberg and Strasbourg are blindfolded.

A similar scene was well described by Albertus Magnus around 1250 (Magnus presumably was speaking in pictorial terms but did not describe an actual scene):

> To the right of the Crucified, a maiden is portrayed with a joyful expression and beautiful face and crown; it is Ecclesia, who reverently receives the blood of Christ in the chalice...whereas on the left stands a figure with eyes blindfolded, a sad expression and bowed head from which the crown falls; it is Sinagoga, who has spilled this same blood and still despises it.[44]

The disgrace, replacement, and powerlessness of the Medieval Jew and his doctrines hardly could be more publicly and vividly displayed.

Chartres Cathedral

The culminating art section in this book deals with Notre Dame de Chartres, a cathedral in the city of Chartres 60 miles west of Paris. Without question, it is the supreme embodiment of supersessionist imagery of the late Romanesque and early Gothic periods. Both in quality and in quantity, in stained glass and in sculpture, it has no equal in medieval times. The imagery is so abundant that entire books have been written about single aspects of its art. The classic meditation, of course, is Henry Adams' *Mont St. Michel and Chartres*.[45] Almost intoxicated by Mary and her cult, this Boston Brahmin weaves an enthusiastic encomium to medieval Christianity. The book is fascinating in its romantic approach and baroque style, but definitely it is not for everyone. The tourist who visits Chartres today may be lucky enough to arrive in time to take one of Malcolm Miller's guided tours of the cathedral. If one misses the tour (and even if one takes it) Miller's book, *Chartres Cathedral* is invaluable both for text and for pictures.[46] Katzenellenbogen's comprehensive book *The Sculptural Programs of Chartres Cathedral* tells almost everything anyone may want to know about the sculpture.[47] My discussion relies heavily on these authoritative works.

Somewhat paradoxically, many of the artistic glories of Chartres owe their existence to a major disaster. The fire of 1194 destroyed most of the existing Romanesque church, but fortunately it did not harm the crypt and the western facade containing the entrance ("the Royal Portal") and much stained glass. All of this section is Romanesque in style. In the best tradition of turning defeat into opportunity, the citizens realized that the holiest relic of the church, the tunic of the Virgin Mary, had been spared. This meant that the fire must have been a signal to build a new and even more sumptious sanctuary for the Queen of Heaven. A vigorous fund-raising campaign followed the fire; the revenues allowed the rapid reconstruction

---

[44] W. Seiferth, *Synagogue and Church*, 102.

[45] Henry Adams, *Mont-Saint-Michel and Chartres*, first published in 1904.

[46] Malcolm Miller, *Chartres Cathedral*, second edition (Pitkin Guides, Ltd., 1996).

[47] Adolf Katzenellenbogen, *The Sculptural Programs of Chartres Cathedral* (Baltimore: Johns Hopkins Press, 1959).

of the nave, transepts, choir, and apse, most of which were completed between 1200 and 1250 in the Gothic style. Thus the student of medieval art has two excellent opportunities at Chartres:to compare and contrast the pre-fire Romanesque with the later Gothic style and to appreciate the enormous variety of artistic creations of the Gothic period which were made in a relatively consistent manner.

Because of time and space limitations and because we already have appreciated much of the iconographic and typological imagery in earlier sections, my discussion here will be selective.

The Plan of Chartres. The plan of the cathedral as a whole shows iconographic strategies. The western Royal Portal has three doors, each displaying scenes of Christ on the tympanums. Over the central and largest door is a haloed Christ in a mandorla, his right hand raised in blessing. Around him are the four winged symbols of the Evangelists. In the jambs on the three doorways were twenty-four columnar statues; most have survived. They probably represent kings, queens, and prophets of the OT, all ancestors or predictors or prefigurements of Christ, and all on the *outside* of the actual entrance. Above these are three vertical windows which, almost miraculously, still hold their twelfth-century glass. Seen from the inside, they progress in an historical procession. A Jesse Tree showing Christ's ancestry is to the right, the Incarnation is in the center, and the Passion and Resurrection are on the left. Above is the west rose window, a Gothic (c. 1215) rendering of the Last Judgment. So the west facade, where most of the worshippers probably entered, is Christological in import.

The cathedral as a whole may be divided into lateral halves, north and south, with the sculptures of the two exterior porches of the transepts carrying a large portion of the iconography. It is not by accident that the north porch at Chartres (and in other churches) is devoted mainly to the OT. At the latitude of Chartres (48 degrees north, about the same as Seattle and Quebec City in the western hemisphere), this is the "dark" or shaded (or "Jewish"?) side of the

---

48 M. Miller, *Chartres Cathedral,* 50.

cathedral. By contrast, the south side is sunny most of the year and is dedicated to the triumphant Christ. The north rose window displays Mary in the center encircled by OT figures. The south rose window shows the Apocalypse with Christ in the center. In fact, the cathedral as a whole may be considered as an earthly reflection of the celestial city, that is, *The New Jerusalem* (Rev 21:10-21).

The Stained Glass. For Henry Adams, the stained glass was "the crowning glory of Chartres." He is enthusiastic—in fact, grandiloquent—in his praise. Rightly so, as it is the most outstanding collection of medieval stained glass in the world. Unfortunately, it is not possible here to analyze more than a fraction of these panels rich in iconographic imagery. I have chosen a few large windows with OT components. Not surprisingly, most of them are on the "dark" left side of the cathedral.

The Redemption window is in the nave, just to the west of the north transept (plate 15). Henry Adams called it the window of the New Alliance and paid no more attention to it. To be fair, he was not at all enthralled by typology. More pertinent with regard to this particular window is that when he saw it, a number of important panels, including the carrying of the grapes, were missing.[48] Now that the reproductions are in place, it shows a superb set of scenes.

Schematically, the window has four ensembles. Each ensemble has five panels—a central square and four adjacent lunettes, one for each side of the square. Three pairs of lateral lunettes are set between the ensembles and there are two demi-lunettes on the sides at the bottom. The window is meant to be read from top to bottom. The highest lunette shows the enthroned Christ; the rest of the window below shows events leading up to the enthronement. The four large squares depict the following: Christ's carrying the Cross, the Crucifixion, the Deposition, and the Entombment.

There are dozens of figures; we must limit our discussion to a few of the most interesting. Plate 16 shows some details of the scenes. At the sides of the Crucifixion are Ecclesia and Sinagoga. Sinagoga has the traditional symbols of the broken staff and falling crown. She also has a serpent around her head, covering her eyes and emphasizing her blindness. And, a unique motif, there is a small devil in front of her preparing to shoot an arrow into those eyes.

Above the Crucifixion, and appropriately so, is the now familiar pair of scouts who return from Canaan bearing a cluster of grapes which hang from a wooden pole. In this case, the symbolic Jew in front has both his head and his back turned away from the symbol of Christ on the Cross.

Between the Crucifixion and the Deposition to our left, a horned Moses holds up the staff with the brass serpent (Num 21:6-9). Other figures in this window—all prefigurements of Christ and Christianity—are Abraham and Isaac; Elisha and Elijah; David; Samson; Jacob crossing his hands to bless his grandsons, Ephraim and Menasseh.

Next to the Redemption window are two other typological narrative windows, those of Joseph and of Noah, each a prefigurement of Christ.

In the upper story of the nave, at the back of the choir, are five windows of interest. As they are high up, each is occupied by one or two large figures, since smaller and more detailed panels would not be clearly discernable at such a distance. In the center—the place of honor—is the Virgin and Child; the cathedral is dedicated to the Virgin. Flanking her are Aaron and Isaiah; each holds a flowering staff, symbolic of the Virgin birth, as in the *Biblia Pauperum* (see above, reference19). On these figures' sides are the other major OT prophets of Christianity: Daniel and Jeremiah, Ezekiel and David.

"On The Shoulders of Giants"—The Essence of Supersessionism. Chartres also boasts a complete set of one of the simplest yet most telling supersessionist images. The south transept (on the side that receives the most light and the most Christological symbolism) has a

---

49 It is unfortunate that these large lancet windows are not in good condition. M. Miller, *Chartres Cathedral*, 90-91 shows how they appear today.

50 Robert K. Merton, *On the Shoulders of Giants (A Shandean Postscript)* (New York: Harcourt, Brace Jovanovich, 1965). This is one of the most brilliant (and amusing) historical detective stories, tracing the origin of the statement usually attributed to Newton. It is a gem of academic legerdemain, and is known to the cognoscenti by the acronym of its title, OTSOG.

51 M. Miller, *Chartres Cathedral*, 44-47.

huge rose window with Christ in the center, surrounded by the twenty-four Elders of the Apocalypse. Beneath it are five vertical lancet windows. The central window depicts the Virgin Mary, who holds the Christ Child. On each side of Mary is a pair of vertical windows. Each window displays a large standing man (not wearing a halo); on the shoulders of that man sits another man wearing a halo. The large standing figures are Jeremiah, Isaiah, Ezekiel, and Daniel. The haloed figures on their shoulders are, respectively, Luke, Matthew, John and Mark.[49]

These four double portraits allude to an epigram later attributed to Isaac Newton: "If I have seen further it is by standing on the shoulders of giants." In fact, this aphorism has been credited to a number of writers in addition to Newton. Because of the exhaustive researches of Professor Robert K. Merton, we know that the originator (hardly Newton, who came centuries after these windows were made) was one Bernard, appropriately enough, of Chartres, who in 1126 put forward the epigram.[50]

The implication is clear. Because the NT is based on the OT, the seers of the Christian revelation see further because they sit on the shoulders of the Hebrew prophets. Indeed, this is the ideal allegorical or typological image for the doctrine of supersessionism as regards its true etymological meaning, that is, "sitting upon."

The Sculpture of the North Porch. The sculptures of the north porch include another encyclopedic compilation of carefully choreographed supersessionist imagery. Each of its three doorways contains a tympanum with archivolts as well as elaborate extended piers containing large statues. The theme is that of Mary. While this choice at first may not seem appropriate for an "Old Testament" side of the cathedral, we should remember that Mary was considered as "the instrument by which the prophecies were fulfilled."[51]

The central portal shows the triumph of the Virgin in the tympanum, where she sits next to Christ. She is crowned (as Queen of Heaven). The coronation of the Virgin is not in the Bible, but the image arose in the Middle Ages and was frequently portrayed. Her triumph over death and her resurrection are shown over the lintels. Katzenellenbogen writes about the resonances of the themes of Mary, the Church, and the Song of Songs. The Middle Ages saw a perfect parallel between Mary and the Church. The Church was considered a virgin and the bride mentioned in the Song of Songs. Thus the bride is both Mary and the Church.

The left portal shows the Magi in the tympanum and, on the lintels, the Nativity and the annunciation to the shepherds. On the right tympanum is Job, whose suffering is a prefiguration of the affliction (Passion) of Christ. On the lintel is the judgment of Solomon. The iconography of this scene is of great interest. The wise King Solomon is a prefiguration of Christ, and his bride the Queen of Sheba is a prototype of the Church. In the judgment theme, the false and wicked mother represents the Synagogue and the Jews, while the true moth-

FIG 6-1. Sculpture showing Old Testament prefigurements and predictors of Christ and Peter. North porch, Chartres. Read from left to right. The small figure is Elisha, followed by Melchizedek, Abraham (sheltering Isaac), Moses, Aaron or Samuel, and David.

er, who is willing to give up her baby so that it may live, again represents the Church and Christianity.[52]

On the lateral piers of the central bay is a row of twelve superb standing figures, six on each side. The outermost figures are slightly smaller than the other five and are without haloes. To the left is Elisha, who symbolizes the Incarnation of Christ because he revived the dead son of the Shunamite (2 Kings 4:17-37). To the right is Elijah, who symbolizes the Ascension of Christ. The five larger figures on each side are among the masterpieces of Chartres. They are from both the Old and New Testaments, all wearing haloes, and they are arranged in chronological order from left to right.

Figures 6-1 and 6-2. First we see Melchizedek with his bread and wine, *preceding* Abraham, who shelters a small figure representing Isaac; the ram lies beneath Abraham's feet. Next we see an "unhorned" Moses, holding a decalogue tablet and pointing to the brass serpent; Aaron (or Samuel) exemplifies the priests with a sacrificial lamb; and closest to the door is a crowned King David complete with staff and cup. Then, crossing the door to the right we see Isaiah carry his prophetic scroll and flowering rod; Jesse is asleep under his feet. Next is Jeremiah, who bears a cross as a symbol of his prophecy of Christ's Passion; Simeon carries the infant Jesus; and a tired John the Baptist wears his hair cloak and points to the lamb (*Agnus Dei*) he carries. Finally, Peter holds the keys given him by Jesus; there is a twelve-stone pectoral on his chest. Together these symbols indicate that Peter is the founder of the true Church which is the legitimate inheritor of the priesthood of the Twelve Tribes. On Peter's head is a mitered hat which mirrors the cap of Melchizedek, who, not surprisingly, is placed directly across from Peter. Thus, the prototype of Peter and the Church is not the Jewish priest Aaron (or Samuel); rather, in the *Verus Israel* tradition, it is the "Ante Lege" priest of Salem, Melchizedek, who faces him.

---

[52] A. Katzenellenbogen, *Sculptural Programs*, 59.

Sainte Chapelle

Sainte Chapelle, on the Ile de la Cité in the center of Paris, is the last monument to be described in this book. Perhaps it should not be considered as *public* art as it was the private royal chapel of King Louis IX (later Saint Louis) and his family. Nevertheless, not only is it an astonishing work of art, but the entire building and its contents should be considered as a set of supersessionist messages, designed to bring Jewish history into thirteenth-century Paris.[53] King Louis built this royal chapel to house a collection of unique and preeminent relics. Most of these were related to the Passion of Christ and included the crown of thorns, the holy lance and sponge, a piece of stone from the sepulchre in Jerusalem, and fragments of the True Cross. These relics were taken from Constantinople when the city was sacked during the Fourth Crusade (during which thousands of Christians—in addition to Muslims and others—were slaughtered.) The relics then were sold to Venice and in 1238-1241 were bought by Louis and carried to Paris with much pomp and ceremony. The chapel was built quickly, between 1244 and 1248, and thus it shows a unity of style rarely seen in medieval art. While the lower story is dark and was made for the servants of the royal household, the upper chapel proper is truly astonishing—a large single room with soaring stained glass windows for walls on all sides.

Because of the holiness of the relics and because of the king's piety and historical consciousness, the chapel was designed from the start with OT symbolism in mind. As Weiss puts it, the entire building was conceived "as a Christian equivalent of Solomon's building complex in Jerusalem."[54] Of course, no one in the Middle Ages had any reasonable idea of the appearance of Solomon's Temple aside from what is mentioned in the OT (nor do we know much more today). As to the physical layout of Sainte Chapelle, it was in fact directly modeled on the chapel in the Boukoleon Palace in

---

[53] Daniel H. Weiss, *Art and Crusade in the Age of Saint Louis* (Cambridge: Cambridge University Press, 1998). I am indebted to this recent, splendid volume on Sainte Chapelle by Daniel H. Weiss for much of the following material.

[54] Weiss, 5.

FIG 6-2. Figures opposite the previous doorway. Chartres. From the left are Isaiah, Jeremiah, Simeon and the Christ Child, John the Baptist, and Peter. The small figure to the right is Elijah.

Constantinople, where the relics had previously been kept. In shape it is a large aisle-less structure, rounded at the east end (figure 6-3). As the walls are made almost entirely of stained glass, it becomes apparent that Louis IX designed the building housing the relics of the Passion to be a giant jeweled reliquary itself! The building as reliquary—a new concept.

At the east end, the relics were displayed in a complex structure (destroyed during the French Revolution) which, according to Weiss, was based on and meant to symbolize the throne of Solomon described in 1 Kings 10:18-20. Following the supersessionist symbolism here, it would seem that Louis IX considered himself the legitimate heir of Solomon, combining again in one person the attributes of power and national as well as spiritual leadership. If Louis were "the new Solomon," then surely the French people were the new

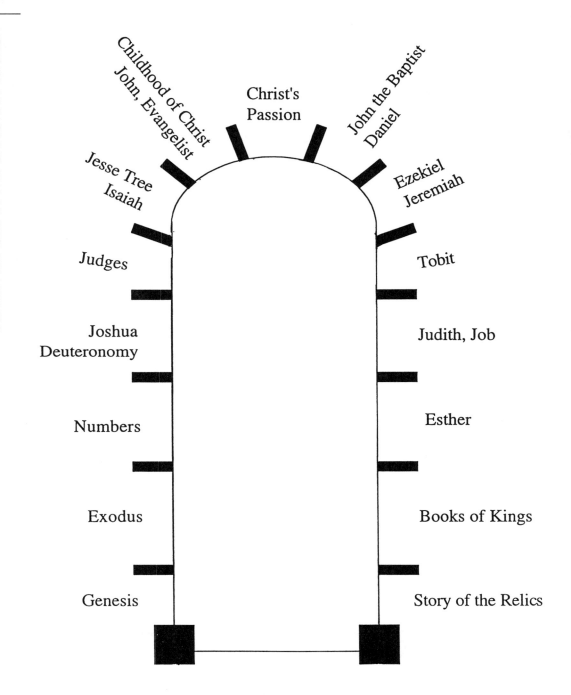

Figure 6-3. Windows of Sainte-Chapelle, schema.

Chosen People. Pushing the analogy further, Sainte Chapelle held the relics of the Passion and symbolized the New Dispensation; thus it could be considered to replace the Israelites' Ark of the Covenant which, according to Hebrews 9, contained as its relics a jar of manna, Aaron's rod, and the Tablets of the Law.

As the relics and the *grande chasse* which contained them no longer remain, Sainte Chapelle's glory today lies in its walls of colored glass, through which Louis' supersessionist ideas are carried forward. The windows of Sainte Chapelle honestly may be called a bible in color and light. These enormous panels of stained glass present a dazzling synopsis of key parts of both the Christian and the Hebrew bibles. It is of some interest that the great majority of the stories are from the Hebrew Bible.

The very ordering of the subjects is noteworthy. The chapel is "U"-shaped. If one faces the altar from the entrance at the open end of the "U", 15 windows extend along the side walls and curve around the chancel. Figure 6-3 shows the arrangement of the windows and the biblical subjects of each window.[55] There are four large windows to the left and four more to the right, each with four lights (vertical strips of panels). There are seven (the mystic number) narrower two-light windows around the curve of the chancel. The central, or axial, window is directly behind the altar.

The subjects of the windows are carefully arranged. Once again, we may consider the drama the worshipper experiences in entering this chapel and proceeding through the hall to the altar. The congregant encounters most of the Pentateuch to the left. On the right are seen many of the typological heroes of Judaism, as portrayed in the books of Esther, Kings, Judith, and Job.

As one approaches the altar, the tension of the drama increases as the seven narrower windows deal directly with the OT foretellers of Christ, the Hebrew Prophets and John the Baptist; John the Evangelist; and, finally, in the center, the life, death, and, resurrection of Christ.

---

[55] Michel Dillange, *The Sainte Chapelle* (Rennes: Editions Ouest-France, 1994).

The details of the various windows can be described only in a lengthy monograph. For instance, the Exodus window contains 121 scenes, some of which describe little-known incidents. They must have been, however, of sufficient significance to warrant inclusion in the entire scheme. An additional (but perhaps irrelevant) point is that—due to the extreme height of the windows—the topmost images are difficult to appreciate and decipher, even for the modern-day admirer equipped with binoculars. In spite of this, it is likely that the medieval architect and glasier believed that having a certain biblical image in a window, even if it were difficult to see, validated the concepts behind the imagery and its typological significance.

This idea gains support from recent scholarly analysis. Weiss points out that in the OT imagery there seems to be a disproportionate number of scenes showing kings on thrones. These he interprets in the context of the throne-of-Solomon imagery and Louis' self-image as Solomon's heir.

The only window that does not deal directly with biblical texts is the first one to the right, concerning the history—both ancient and contemporary (thirteenth century)—of the relics themselves. Here we see Jesus wear the crown of thorns, and Helena, mother of Constantine, dig up the True Cross in Jerusalem. There are scenes of the building of Sainte Chapelle and indeed of Louis carrying the relics into Paris. The window is a completely logical *terminus* for the study of Christian supersessionist imagery as symbolized by the arrival of the symbols of Christianity in France in 1248 when the chapel was dedicated.

Louis would soon leave Paris on the next Crusade, which hoped, once again, to deliver Jerusalem from the Muslims. It failed, however, even to the extent of Louis' capture and release by ransom. Dauntless, Louis nevertheless later embarked on the Eighth Crusade but died in Tunis in 1270, having failed to liberate the Holy Land.

Art and Jewish-Christian Relations, 1100-1250

We have seen that during this final period of our survey, the Jews in Western Europe came under increasing civil and social pressure.

The pressure ranged from the accusation of ritual murder and the imposition of a dress code to the banishment from France and England as well as the public burning of the Talmud. At the same time, supersessionist images in public art became more numerous, vivid, and explicit.

It is pertinent to ask whether there is a link between the growing social and political marginalization of the Jews and the increase in explicit supersessionist images (often containing derogatory anti-Jewish implications). Such a link may not be easy to find, but it is instructive to survey the artistic achievements of this period with that question in mind.

The Tree of Jesse concept—that the Messiah would be "of the house of David"—and its Christological interpretation by Tertullian and others long antedated the illuminated manuscript depictions of the tree itself. If the image became public via the prophet plays, then the critical point is that the play itself was a far more impressive demonstration of anti-Judaism than was a picture hidden in a book. In the public play, the "choir"—assembled to hear the OT prophecy of Isaiah as applied to Christ—says (or sings) that they rejoice that "Judea the guilty" is destroyed for rejecting the words of its own prophets. Thus the plays are perfect examples of the *Adversus Judaeos* attitude. Christians, publicly assembled on a holiday, saw the prophets and heard the condemnation of Judaism. Such a dramatization was more forceful and *audacious* than a mere private picture in a bible. (One wonders whether some Jews were compelled to attend the prophet plays.) That Christianity felt free enough to engage in this very public ritualized form of anti-Jewish sentiment is an index of how comfortable the majority was in its supersessionist ideas.

The Jesse Tree motif was translated into magnificent, brilliantly colored stained glass. The pedigree of Christ, as shown in the windows, is more evident in the *Concordia* than in the *Adversus Judaeos* mode, and less forceful, perhaps, than a prophet play. Nonetheless, the fact that Jesse Tree windows were not experienced only on certain holidays but were seen on every visit to the church gave strength to the image and its religious implications.

The pair of images *Ecclesia and Sinagoga* may be the most succinct summary statement of how the medieval majority viewed Judaism by comparison with Christianity—the Old Testament and the New. The Church is portrayed as an upright, attractive young woman complete with halo, crown, chalice, staff, and banner. The Synagogue is, of course, older and stooped. She wears no halo, her crown has toppled, her staff broken, and she holds the Ten Commandment tablets pointing downwards. Most importantly, she is blindfolded, symbolizing her inability to see the truth of Christianity. As such, the image of Sinagoga is the image of the shame and ignorance of the Jews. To put these two symbols, larger than life, on the sides of the main portal of the central church of the capital of France—Notre Dame de Paris— is to trumpet the historical disgrace of the Jews.

These images are also linked to the concept of "the veiled and the revealed," seen so well in the windows of St. Denis. The interpretation is that Sinagoga (representing the Jews) was blindfolded just as Moses was veiled; the doctrines of Christianity were *hidden* in Jewish Scripture and were *revealed* by Christ and the clear-sighted Church.

Again, the same supersessionist approach is exemplified in Chartres perhaps more literally where the Four Evangelists sit on the shoulders of Jeremiah, Isaiah, Ezekiel, and Daniel, thus seeing further than their Jewish antecedents.

It would be difficult to prove that the increase in anti-Jewish legislation and social pressure was either the cause or the effect of the growing number and incisiveness of anti-Jewish public images. Indeed, it is not necessary to do so. Rather, the two phenomena may be considered to march together step by step toward the political ostracism of the Jews in Western Europe.

Summary

The 1050-year period discussed in this book (200-1250 C.E.) witnessed a complete transformation of Western Europe. As the period starts, the Roman Empire has just passed its zenith, although it was still mighty in the third century and would remain so for many years. Religiously, state-sponsored polytheism dominated but, in general, tolerated new cults as long as they did not challenge the established pantheon. By the end of this period, Roman culture was but a dim memory. The empire had been replaced by a number of political entities, including governments on the Italian and Spanish peninsulas, as well as in Gaul, Britain, and Germany. Secular leaders, however, were overshadowed by an omnipresent Christian Church that influenced all aspects of Western European life. The change was astonishing.

In the year 200, Judaism and Christianity both were minority religions in trouble precisely because they refused to honor the Roman pantheon. The Jews had just lost two disastrous wars to Roman soldiery. Christians, less organized than the Jews, had not even considered playing a political role. Instead, they concentrated on consolidating their theology, liturgy, and church organization—when they were not occupied with surviving the sporadic official persecutions.

Once Christian leaders realized not all Jews were going to convert to their nascent religion, the Church put its proselytizing energy elsewhere. It first struggled to differentiate itself from Judaism, then turned to the much larger constituency of pagan Roman subjects.

Contentious aspects of the Jewish-Christian relationship at first centered on the Bible. Jews and Christians fought over the meanings of, and the resultant connections between, their respective scriptures (the Jewish Old Testament and the Christian New Testament). The conflict was complex. Christianity rejected Judaism, particularly its Sabbath, its dietary laws, and circumcision. Christians claimed it was the Jews who rejected Christianity by denying that Jesus was the very

Messiah predicted in the Jewish scriptures. So, interestingly, while Christianity rejected many aspects of Judaism, it did not reject the Jewish Bible. Instead, Christianity appropriated and—more importantly—reinterpreted the Hebrew scriptures. The Christian stance was that the Old Testament, when properly interpreted, predicted (and therefore validated) the tenets of the Christian faith and unequivocally pointed to the messiahship of Jesus.

This Christian attitude that Christianity replaced Judaism as God's chosen revelation has been termed "supersessionism." Judaism, though, still provided the basis for Christianity in the latter's interpretations of Hebrew scripture. It is in this sense that Christianity "sat upon" the shoulders of its Jewish ancestors; hence, the literal meaning of supersessionism.

The Jews, not surprisingly, refused to accept the supersessionist reinterpretation of their Bible. To make matters worse for the Jews, Christians in *their* Bible emphasized the responsibility of the Jews for the death of Christ. The animosity of the Christians towards the Jews became more pronounced after Constantine's reign, which ended in 337. Soon after that time Christianity replaced paganism as the official religion of the Roman Empire and its successor states in western and eastern Europe. Thus, political power was now largely centered in the Church, and Jews found their civil opportunities increasingly restricted. Gradually, they were marginalized as decrees and laws began to separate them from their neighbors, especially during the "Dark Ages" between 500 and 1000.

These changes were reflected in the art of the Church. Previously, as seen in the frescoes of the Christian Catacombs, pictures were chosen more from the Jewish scriptures than the Christian. Salvation was a common theme: the deliverance of Daniel from the lions' den, of the Israelites from Pharaoh's armies, of Lazarus from the dead, and of Jonah from the great fish are all widespread images. These themes were perfectly appropriate for a necropolis in view of the Christian preoccupation with resurrection after death. The freedom with which Old and New Testament images were mixed indicates how comfortable Christians were using Jewish stories to illustrate their theology.

A number of supersessionist images begin to appear, such as the elevation of Melchizedek over Abraham. Similarly, the three men who encounter Abraham under the oak of Mamre are pictured in a Christological way, and it is common to see Jewish prophets pointing ahead to Jesus.

The pace of history, as well as our knowledge of it, accelerates after the millennium. This period brought great economic prosperity, growth of the monastic movement, and the strengthening of the Church. It also brought the Crusades, a potent mix of religious fervor, economic and geographic expansion and, toward the Jews, of bigotry and antagonism. In their determination to free Jerusalem from the far-away Muslims, militant crusaders did not hesitate to physically abuse, or even murder, Jews nearer home. Anti-Jewish literature abounded and Jews were forced to turn from the well-respected occupations of agriculture and crafts to money-lending. Decrees required Jews to dress distinctively so they could be easily recognized.

It was in this setting that Romanesque art arose, incorporating ever more prominent and explicit supersessionist imagery. Symbolic figures of *Ecclesia* (Church) and *Sinagoga* (Synagogue) started flanking the Crucifixion. While *Ecclesia* remained crowned, erect, and honorable, gradually *Sinagoga* became. old, haggard, and eventually blindfolded, graphically depicting the Jewish refusal to see the truth of Christianity.

As Romanesque public art developed, it became more sophisticated. Artists followed rules which regulated the presentation of images from the Jewish Bible. These rules determined not only the kind of image used, but also its placement among neighboring pictures, its relative size, and its location in the church. For example, events and persons believed to be "types" or precursors of Christian events or of Jesus tend to be located at the entrance or in the nave of the church. The worshipper, entering the edifice and moving toward the altar with its crucifix and New Testament images in the apse, very literally progresses through Judaism to the Christian Revelation which replaced it. Supersessionism is acted out as the worshipper walks to where mass is celebrated.

Other symbolic representations of the relationship between Judaism and Christianity include the imaginative Mystic Mill. Here, Moses pours the course grain of Jewish scriptures through the mill of Revelation (turned by Paul) to produce the valuable flour of Christian faith. Intense supersessionist programs often stimulated very special artistic creations, where themes of the Old and New Testaments are interwoven in new and imaginative ways. For example, on the Cloisters Cross, the Meuse Cross, and on the Klosterneuburg Altar, the image of the Numbers tale of two scouts carrying a cluster of grapes to Moses clearly refers to Christ Crucified, with the two men representing the Jew (in front) and the Christian (behind). At Klosterneuburg, additional force for this reinterpretation comes from its placement directly below the central Crucifixion, which itself is below the Binding of Isaac, another type scene of the Crucifixion. These three images carry a single message: the ascendancy of Christianity over Judaism.

Adversus Judaeos literature was further publicized and ritualized in the "prophet plays" acted out in or near churches on holidays. Jewish Biblical characters, such as Moses, Isaiah, and Jeremiah, speak those lines from their writings which were interpreted by Christian theologians to foretell the life and death of Jesus. The general Jewish populace, however, was denigrated for not believing in these presumed prophecies of their own leaders.

These performances may well have inspired a new supersessionist set of images, namely, the Jesse Tree. This image embodied the pedigree of Christ, insofar as he was the Messiah predicted in the OT, who would be a descendant of Jesse and David. The Jesse Tree was a potent supersessionist symbol. It showed Judaism as the *root* but Christianity as the *flower*.

Public demonstrations of supersessionist thinking became prominent and often were richly made. Processional crosses carried by the clergy through the church proclaimed the triumph of Christianity. The Cloisters Cross is crowded with Jewish prophets holding their prophetic scrolls, but they are there not to illustrate Judaism but to show it as pointing to the Crucifixion, Resurrection, and Ascension of Christ.

The Meuse enamel should be thought of as "a cross of crosses" because it illustrates five Old Testament scenes in which Christians thought were hidden references to the Cross of the Crucifixion. These range from Jacob crossing his hands to bless Ephraim and Menasseh to the scouts bringing the cluster of grapes to Moses from the promised land.

The teminus of a procession in which such a typological cross was carried was the main altar. In Klosterneuburg we see the entire range of human religious history (which was, to the medieval mind, the entire history of the world, as no other society was considered to be of importance). The Jews from Adam to Moses (*ante legem*) and from Moses to Jesus (*sub lege*) are the precursors of the drama of Christianity (*sub gratia*).

The climax of this book and the events that it covers comes from the years around 1200. At that time and after, toleration of Jews diminished in Western Europe to the point that it was demanded (but not always enforced) that they wear distinctive clothing to identify them to perhaps unsuspecting Christians. Jews became "the other" and their civil liberties suffered further encroachment. When they were often forced from agriculture and trade to money-lending, their new occupation was doubly galling to Christians. They provided a necessary service in an increasingly capitalistic society but, when successful, became rich and hence the target of envy. Eventually, the Jews were told to leave England and (repeatedly) France. The symbol of their rejection by Christian society was the public burning of the Talmud.

In art, the supersessionist images were repeated and intensified. Sinagoga is now blindfolded or even has a devil shooting an arrow into her eye, as at Chartres. Christ is flagellated by men wearing the *judenhut* which clearly identifies them as Jews, although the Gospels say it was the Romans who whipped Jesus. The veil on Moses or Sinagoga symbolizes the blindness of Judaism.

Finally, in a brilliant, although less adversarial set of windows, again at Chartres, we see the Evangelists sitting upon the shoulders of the Old Testament prophets. While the latter are large and imposing, they cannot see as far as their Christian "descendants" on their shoulders.

A Paradox Resolved?

Drawing together the various themes of this book, let me point out what many people consider to be a true paradox: How does one reconcile depictions of Abraham and Moses wearing haloes with the social and political oppression of the Jews in Western Europe? How does one reconcile the Church's handsome and authoritative figures of David, Isaiah, and Jeremiah with banishment of the Jews from France and England and the public burning of the Talmud? Is it not inconsistent to venerate the Jewish Ark of the Covenant and yet discriminate against one's Jewish neighbors down the street?

By no means (as Paul would say) were these actions considered contradictory. According to the principle of *Concordia*, the Jews of the Hebrew Bible were "good Jews." Their religion was the necessary predictor of Christianity, though they knew it not. Their own Jewish scripture, laws, and practices were interpreted by Christians to contain the kernel of the Christian Revelation. But the Jews of Christ's time were completely different. They refused to recognize his messiahship and were assumed guilty of killing Him. If we accept the Christian view that the Jews of medieval Europe were descendants of the guilty "bad Jews," while the Jews of the Old Testament were the legitimate ancestors of Christianity, or "good Jews," there was no inconsistency at all. It was perfectly consistent to show the "good Jews"—the necessary precursors of Christianity—with haloes, while at the same time persecuting the "bad Jews" of the current times as they refused to recognize Christ as the Messiah and were in fact descended from those who killed Him.

Supersessionism Today

This is a history book about Jewish-Christian relations in Europe and the magnificent art that mirrors those relations. But it is not just a book of stories of yesterday. If the events of the last hundred years—which include more genocides around the world than one would like to remember —have anything to teach us, it is that history is extremely relevant. Without belaboring the obvious, we need to learn from the past. The main principle of supersessionism, that is, that Christianity replaced Judaism as God's chosen revelation, seems to many people, at least at first, quite unexceptional. But the world changes, and the world and its peoples have grown and diversified, and many think differently. That no Jew or Muslim believes in that principle should give us pause.

Furthermore, the principle of supersession is an essentially elitist tenet. That is, supersessionism says that Christianity is not only different but it is better. In this sense, a supersessionist stance can be used to justify unfavorable attitudes towards, and even actions against, non-Christians.

As we move into and then beyond the twenty-first century, we should all be cognizant of this danger and hence avoid it.

References

Adams, Joseph Quincy *Chief Pre-Shakespearian Dramas*, (Boston, Houghton Mifflin, 1924)

Augustine, *Expositions on the Psalms*, (see website www.newadvent.org/fathers)

Bachrach, Bernard S. *Early Jewish Policy in Western Europe*. (Minneapolis, U. of Minnesota Press, 1977)

Baron, Salo W. *Social and Political History of the Jews*, vol. 3, *Christian Era: The First Five Centuries*, Vol. 4, *Meeting of the East and West*, 2d ed. (Philadelphia: Jewish Publication Society of America, 1952)

Beckwith, John *Early Christian and Byzantine Art* (Harmondsworth/Middlesex: Penguin Books, Ltd., 1970)

Belting, Hans *Likeness and Presence. A History of the Image Before the Era of Art*, (transl. Edmond Jephcott). (Chicago, University of Chicago Press, 1994.)

Berger, David *The Jewish-Christian Debate in the High Middle Ages. A Critical Edition of the Nizzahon Vetus* (Philadelphia, The Jewish Publication Society of America, 1979)

Blumenkranz, Bernhard *Le Juif Medieval au Miroir de l'Art Chretien*. (Paris, Etude Augustiennes, 1966)

Bovini, G. *Ravenna* (New York: Harry N. Abrams, 1971)

Brankovic, Branislav *Les Vitraux de la Cathedrale de Saint-Denis*. (Castelet, Villefranche-de-Rouergue, 1992)

Camille, Michael "Visual signs of the sacred page: books in the Bible Moralisée. (*Word and Image*, 1989)

Cassidy, Brendan ed. *Iconography at the Crossroads* (Princeton: Princeton University Press, 1993)

Chazen, Robert *European Jewry and the First Crusade*, (Berkeley, University of California Press., 1987)

Christe, Yves, Tania Velmans, Hanna Losowska and Roland Recht, *Art of the Christian World, A.D. 200-1500*. (New York, Rizzoli, 1982)

Claster, Jill *The Medieval Experience*, (New York, New York University Press, 1982)

Cohen, Jeremy *The Friars and the Jews*. (Ithaca, N.Y., Cornell Univ. Press, 1982)

Cohen, Mark R. *Under Crescent and Cross*, (Princeton University Press, 1994

Crosby, S.M. J. Hayward, C. T. Little, W. D. Wixom, *The Royal Abbey of Saint-Denis in the Time of Abbot Suger*. (New York, Harry. N. Abrams, 1998)

Danielou, Jean *The Bible and the Liturgy*, (Notre Dame, IN: University of Notre Dame Press, 1956/1951)

Danielou, Jean *The Theology of Jewish Christianity* (London: Darton, Longman and Todd, 1964.

Davis-Weyer, Caecilia *Early Medieval Art, 300-1150, Sources and Documents* (Englewood Cliffs, NJ: Prentice Hall, 1971)

De Hamel, Christopher *A History of Illuminated Manuscripts* (Boston: David R. Godine, 1986)

De la Croix, Horst, Richard G. Tansey, Diane Kirkpatrick; *Gardner's Art Throught the Ages*. Ninth edition, 1991. (New York, Harcourt Brace & Co.)

de Voragine, Jacobus *The Golden Legend*, transl. William G. Ryan, (Princeton, NJ Princeton University Press, 1993, 2vols.)

Dillange, Michel *The Sainte Chapelle,* (Editions Ouest-France, 1994)

Duchet-Suchaux, Gaston and Michel Pastoreau, *The Bible and the Saints* (Paris: Flammarion, 1994)

Durant, Will *The Story of Civilization*, vol. 3, *Caesar and Christ* (New York: Simon and Schuster, 1944)

Eisenbaum, Pamela M. *The Jewish Heroes of Christian History: Hebrews 11 in Literary Context* (Atlanta: Scholars Press, 1997)

Encyclopedia Judaica, (Jerusalem, Keter Publishing, 1972)

Erlande-Brandenburg, Alain *Notre-dame de Paris.* (New York, Harry N. Abrams, 1998.)

Evans, G.R. *The Language and Logic of the Bible: The Earlier Middle Ages* (Cambridge: Cambridge University Press, 1984)

Ferrua, Antonio *Catacombe Sconosciute* (*The Unknown Catacomb*) (New Lanark, Scotland: Geddes and Grosset, 1991)

Finney, Paul C. *The Invisible God: The Earliest Christians on Art* (New York: Oxford University Press, 1994).

Flannery, Edward H. *The Anguish of the Jews,* (New York, The Macmillan Company, 1965)

Funkenstein, Amos *Perceptions of Jewish History,* (Berkeley, Univ. of California Press, 1993)

Gager, John G. *The Origins of Anti-Semitism* (New York: Oxford University Press, 1983)

Gameson, Richard ed., *The Early Medieval Bible: Its Production, Decoration and Use* (Cambridge: Cambridge University Press, 1994)

Gibson, Margaret T. "The Twelfth Century Glossed Bible," *Studia Patristica,* vol 23, (Leeuven, Peeters Press, 1989)

Goodenough, Edwin R. *Jewish Symbols in the Greco-Roman Period* (New York: Bollingen Foundation/Pantheon Books, 1953)

Grabar, Andre *Christian Iconography. A Study of Its Origins* (Princeton: Princeton University Press, 1968)

Grabar, Andre *Early Christian Art,* (New York, Odyssey Press, 1969)

Grayzel, Solomon *The Church and the Jews in the XIIIth Century.* (Philadelphia, The Dropsie College, 1933)

Greenspahn, Frederick E. ed., *Scripture in the Jewish and Christian Traditions,* (Denver: University of Denver, 1982)

Grodecki, Louis and Catherine Brisac *Gothic Stained Glass, 1200-1300* (Ithaca, NY: Cornell University Press, 1984)

Grodecki, Louis *Les Vitraux de Saint-Denis.* (Paris, Centre National de la Recherche Scientifique, 1976.)

Gutmann, Joseph *No Graven Images: Studies in Art and the Hebrew Bible* (New York: KTAV Publishing House, 1981)

Gutmann, Joseph *The Dura-Europos Synagogue. A Reevaluation (1932-1992)* (Atlanta: Scholars Press, 1992)

Hall, James *A History of Ideas and Images in Italian Art* (New York: Harper & Row, 1983)

Hall, James *Dictionary of Subjects and Symbols in Art* (New York: Harper and Row, 1932)

Hanson, R.P.C. "Biblical Exegesis in the Early Church, 412-453 in *Cambridge History of the Bible* , ed. Peter R. Ackroyd and C. F. Evans, vol 1(Cambridge: Cambridge University Press, 1970)

Henry, Avril *Biblia Pauperum - A Facsimile Edition.* (Ithaca, N.Y. Cornell University Press, 1987)

Holtz, Barry W. ed. *Back to the Sources,* (New York, Summit Books, 1984)

Holweck, F.G. *A Biographical Dictionary of the Saints,* (St. Louis, B. Herder Book Co., 1924)

Hopkins, Clark *The Discovery of Dura-Europos* (New Haven: Yale University Press, 1979)

Horton, Fred L. *The Melchizedek Tradition: A critical Examination of the Sources to the Fifth Century A.D. and the Epistle to the Hebrews* (London: Cambridge University Press, 1976)

Hoving, Thomas *King of the Confessors,* (New York, Simon and Schuster, 1981)

Jordan, William C. *The French Monarchy and the Jews.* (Philadelphia, University of Pennsylvania Press, 1989)

Justin Martyr *Dialogue of Justin, Philosopher and Martyr, with Trypho, A Jew,* see Roberts, A. and J. Donaldson

Kaske, R.E. et al, *Traditio,* vol 39, (New York, Fordham University Press, 1983)

Katzenellenbogen, Adolf *The Sculptural Programs of Chartres Cathedral.* (Baltimore, Johns Hopkins Press, 1959.)

Kemp, Wolfgang *The Narratives of Gothic Stained Glass* (Cambridge: Cambridge University Press, 1997)

Kessler, Herbert "The Function of *Vitrum Vestitum* and the use of *Materia Saphiroram* in Suger's St.-Denis. *L'Image,* (Paris, Cahiers du Leopard d'Or, vol 5, 1996)

Kessler, Herbert J. "Pictures Fertile With Truth. How Christians Managed to Make Images of God Without Violating the Second Commandment," (J. 49/50 Walters Art Gallery, 1991-2)

Kitzinger, Ernst *The Art of Byzantium and the Medieval West: Selected Studies* (Bloomington IN: Indiana University Press, 1976)

Kraeling, Karl "The Christian Building," *The Excavations at Dura-Europos* (New Haven: Dura-Europos Publications, 1967)

Kraus, Samuel *The Jewish-Christian Controversy From the Earliest Times to 1789,* ed. and revised by William Horbery. (Tubingen, J.C.B. Mohr [Paul Siebeck] 1995, originally written in 1948

Krautheimer, Richard *Rome: Portrait of a City, 313-1308* (Princeton: Princeton University Press, 1980)

Kugel, James *The Bible as it Was* (Cambridge MA: Harvard University Press)

Langmuir, Gavin I. *History, Religion, and Antisemitism* (Berkeley, CA: University of California Press, 1990)

Lasker, Daniel J. *Jewish Philosophical Polemics Against Christianity in the Middle Ages.* (New York, Ktav Publishing House, 1977)

Levine, Lee I. ed., *Ancient Synagogues Revealed* (Jerusalem: The Israel Exploration Society, 1981)

Lieu, Judith, John North and Tessa Rajak, *The Jew Among Pagans and Christians* (London: Routledge, 1992)

Lowden, J. *The Octateuchs - A Study in Byzantine Manuscript Illustration* (University Park, PA: Pennsylvania State University Press, 1992)

Maccoby, Hayam *Judaism on Trial.* (East Rutherford, NJ, Associated University Presses, 1982)

Malbon, Elizabeth S. *The Iconography of the Sarcophagus of Junius Bassus* (Princeton University Press, 1990

Mâle, Emile *Religious Art in France. The Twelfth Century.* (Princeton, Princeton University Press, 1978 (1st edition 1922, revised 1953)

Mâle, Emile *The Gothic Image, Religious Art in France of the Thirteenth Century* (New York: Harper and Row, 1958)

Marcus, Jacob Rader *The Jew in the Medieval World* (New York: Athanaeum, 1972)

Mathews, Thomas F. *The Clash of Gods: A Reinterpretation of Early Christian Art* (Princeton, NJ: Princeton University Press, 1993)

McCall, Andrew *The Medieval Underworld* (London: Hamish Hamilton, 1979)

Meeks, A. Wayne ed. *The Harper Collins Study Bible* (London: Harper Collins Publishers, 1993)

Mellinkoff, Ruth *Antisemitic Hate Signs in Hebrew Illuminated Manuscripts from Medieval Germany.* (Jerusalem, Center for Jewish Art-The Hebrew University of Jerusalem, 1999)

Mellinkoff, Ruth *Outcasts: Signs of Otherness in Northern European Art of the Late Middle Ages.* (Berkeley, University of California Press, 1993)

Mellinkoff, Ruth *The Horned Moses in Medieval Art and Thought.* (Berkeley, Univ. of California Press, 1970)

Merton, Robert K. *On the Shoulders of Giants (A Shandean Postscript)* (New York, Harcourt, Brace Jovanovich, 1965)

Miles, Margaret "Santa Maria Maggiore's Fifth-Century Mosaics: Triumphal Christianity and the Jews," *Harvard Theological Review* (1993)

Miles, Margaret R. *Image As Insight* (Boston: Beacon Press, 1985)

Miller, Malcolm *Chartres Cathedral,* second edition, copyright Pitkin Guides, Ltd., 1996)

Morey, Charles R. *Medieval Art* (New York: W.W. Norton, 1942)

Morrison, Karl F.*Tradition and Authority in the Western Church, 300-1140* (Princeton: Princeton University Press, 1969)

Muir, Lynette R. *Liturgy and Drama in the Anglo-Norman Adam.* (Oxford, Blackwell, 1973)

Murphy, Kevin D. *Memory and Modernity; Viollet-le-Duc at Vézelay* (University Park, PA Pennsylvania State University Press, 2000)

Neele, J.M. and B. Webb, *The Symbolism of Church and Church Ornaments, of William Durandus.* (Leeds, T.W. Green, 1843)

Neusner, Jacob *Judaism and Christianity in the Age of Constantine* (Chicago: University of Chicago Press, 1987)

New Catholic Encyclopedia (New York: McGraw-Hill, 1967)

Panofsky, Erwin *Abbot Suger on the Abbey Church of St.-Denis and its Art Treasures,* (Princeton, N.J. : Princeton University Press, 1979)

Parker, Elizabeth C. and Charles T. Little, *The Cloisters Cross. Its Art and its Meaning.* (New York, Metropolitan Museum of Art., 1994)

Parkes, James *The Conflict of the Church and the Synagogue* (New York: Soncino, 1934/New York: Atheneum, 1974)

Parkes, James *The Jew in the Medieval Community* (London: Soncino Press, 1938)

Pearl, Chaim *Rashi* (New York: Grove Press, 1988)

Pelikan, Jaroslav *Imago Dei,* (Princeton, N. J. Princeton U. Press, 1990)

Pelikan, Jeroslav *The Christian Tradition,* vol. 3, *The Growth of Medieval Theology (600-1300)* (Chicago: University of Chicago Press, 1978)

Piccirillo, Michele *The Mosaics of Jordan* (Amman, Jordan: American Center of Oriental Research, 1993)

Prawer, Joshua *The History of the Jews in the Latin Kingdom of Jerusalem.* (Oxford, Clarendon Press, 1988)

Revel-Neher. Elizabeth *The Image of the Jew in Byzantine Art* (Oxford, Pergamon Press, 1992)

Richter, Jean Paul and A. Cameron Taylor, *The Golden Age of Classic Christian Art* (London: Duckworth & Co., 1904)

Roberts, Alexander and James Donaldson, eds. *The Ante-Nicene Fathers*, (New York: Charles Scribner's Sons, 1905)

Roth, Cecil ed. *The World History of the Jewish People. Second series: Medieval Period. Vol 2 The Dark Ages* (711-1096) (Rutgers Univ. Press, 1966)

Rubens, Alfred *A History of Jewish Costume.* (London, Valentine Mitchell & Co. 1967)

Rudolph, Conrad *The "Things of Greater Importance",* (Philadelphia, Pennsylvania University Press, 1990.)

Ruether, Rosemary Radford *Faith and Fratricide* (New York: Seabury Press, 1974)

Rutgers, Leonard V. *The Jews in Ancient Rome* (Leiden/New York: E.J. Brill, 1995)

Sandmel, Samuel *Judaism and Christian Beginnings* (New York: Oxford University Press, 1978)

Schiller, Gertrude *Iconography of Christian Art*, vol. 2, *The Passion of Jesus Christ* (London: Lund Humphries Ltd., 1971)

Schreckenberg, Heinz and Karl Schubert *Jewish Historiography and Iconography in Early and Medieval Christianity* (Minneapolis: Fortress Press, 1992)

Schreckenberg, Heinz. *The Jews in Christian Art. An Illustrated History*, (N.Y. Continuum, 1996)

Seiferth, Wolfgang S. *Synagogue and Church in the Middle Ages. Two Symbols in Art and Literature.* (New York, Frederick Ungar, 1970)

Shanks, Hershel ed. *Christianity and Rabbinic Judaism* (Washington, D.C.: Biblical Archeological Review, 1992)

Shanks, Hershel *Jerusalem, An Archaeological Biography* (New York: Random House, 1995)

Siker, Jeffrey *Disinheriting the Jews: Abraham in Early Christian Controversy* (Louisville: Westminster/John Knox Press, 1991)

Simon, Marcel *Verus Israel*, 2d ed., rev., trans. H. McKeating (New York: Oxford University Press, 1986)

Smalley, Beryl *The Study of the Bible in the Middle Ages* (Notre Dame, IN: University of Notre Dame Press, 1964)

Snyder, James *Medieval Art* (N.Y. Harry N. Abrams, 1989)

Sommerfeldt, John R. and Thomas H. Seiler, *Studies in Medieval Culture, XIII,* (Western Medieval Institute, Michigan State Univ., 1978)

Steinzaltz, Adam *The Talmud, A Reference Guide* (New York: Random House, 1989)

Stevenson, James *The Catacombs: Life and Death in Early Christianity* (Nashville, Thomas Nelson, Inc. 1985/Thames and Hudson, 1978)

Synan, Edward A. *The Popes and the Jews in the Middle Ages* (New York: Macmillan Company, 1965)

Szarmach, Paul E. ed. *Aspects of Jewish Culture in the Middle Ages* (Albany: State University of New York Press, 1979)

Temko, Allen *Notre-Dame of Paris.* (New York, Viking Press, 1952)

Terrien, Samuel *The Iconography of Job Through the Centuries* (University Park, PA: Pennsylvania State University Press, 1996)

Tertullian, *An Answer to the Jews,* Chap. IX Catholic Encyclopedia

Thoumieu, Marc *Dictionnaire d'Iconographie Romane* (Zodiaque, 1996)

Trebolle Barrera, Julio *The Jewish Bible and the Christian Bible* (Leiden: Koninklijke Brill, NV, 1998)

Trigg, Joseph W. *Origen, the Bible and Philosophy in the Third-century Church* (Atlanta: John Knox Press, 1983)

Tronzo, William *The Via Latina Catacomb. Imitation and Discontinuity in Fourth-Century Roman Painting* (University Park, PA: Pennsylvania State University Press, 1986)

van der Horst, Koert, et al, *The Utrecht Psalter in Medieval Art.* (Westrenen, Tuurdijk, HES Publishers, 1996)

Vermes, Geza "Bible and Midrash - Early Old Testament Exegesis," *The Cambridge History of the Bible*, Peter R. Ackroyd and C.F. Evans, ed. (Cambridge: Cambridge University Press)

Viollet-le-Duc, Emmanuel (London, Architectural Design and Academy Editions, 1980)

von Campenhausen, Hans *The Formation of the Christian Bible* (Philadelphia: Fortress Press, 1972)

Wallis, Faith *Bede:The Reckoning of Time.* (Liverpool University Press, 1999)

Watson, Arthur *The Early Iconography of the Tree of Jesse.* (London, Oxford Univ. Press 1934)

Weiss, Daniel H. *Art and Crusade in the Age of Saint Louis.* Cambridge University Press, 1998

Weitzmann, K. ed. *The Place of Book Illumination in Byzantine Art* (Princeton: Princeton University Press, 1975)

Weitzmann, Kurt and Herbert Kessler, *The Frescoes of the Dura Synagogue and Christian Art* (Washington, D.C.: Dumbarton Oaks, 1990)

Weitzmann, Kurt *Illustrations in Roll and Codex* (Princeton: Princeton University Press, 1947)

Weitzmann, Kurt *Late Antique and Early Christian Book Illumination* (New York: George Braziller, 1977)

Wetzel, C. ed., *Biblia Pauperum (Armenbibel),* (Stuttgart, Belser Verlag, 1995)

Wilken, Robert L. *Judaism and the Early Christian Mind* (New Haven: Yale University Press, 1971)

Williams, John *Imaging the Early Medieval Bible* (University Park, PA Pennsylvania State University Press, 1999)

Williams A. Lukyn *Adversus Judaeos, A Bird's-eye View of Christian Apologiae Until The Renaissance* (Cambridge: Cambridge University Press, 1935)

Wilson, Stephen G. *Related Strangers; Jews and Christians, 70-170 C.E.* (Minneapolis, MI: Fortress Press, 1995)

Zarnecki, George *Romanesque Art,* (New York, Universe Books, 1971)

Zarnecki, George *The Art of the Medieval World.* (New York, Harry N. Abrams, 1975)

Index